A history (~80% of diagnosis) and assessment should always be completed to give you the opportunity to **build a connection, show your expertise, and create a baseline of function**. Examining a patient uses the senses of sight (observation & inspection), touch (palpation), hearing, smell & most importantly of all - thought (**critical thinking**).

It will **give you an insight** to what contributing factors might make it better or worse (sleep, stressors, nutrition, exercise, social connection, ADLs, job, prior treatment, goals etc.). **This will help significantly in creating treatment goals.**

Listen

Most people listen with the intent to reply. We need to **listen with the intent to understand.**

People will tell you what they need.

Realize that **in most cases no one sign is of absolute significance in isolation**, & each individual finding should be evaluated only in the context of other findings & the patient as a whole. **You should have a minimum of 3 history and exam findings that support your differential diagnosis (DDx).**

The order of assessment can be remembered with the **acronym oHIPMNRS.** It is important to **test from least invasive to most invasive** to ensure accurate results and better patient tolerance.

During the history and examination here are some basic items to keep in mind:

- Be professional, prepared & competent. Your voice should be clearly audible and **use language appropriate to patient's level**.
- **Attend to patient comfort** (always ask if they are comfortable or doing well)
- **Rule out other systemic pathologies and in adjacent regions (compensations)** or other areas that may refer symptoms

Informed Consent = PAR-Q

- **Procedures** (where, what, when, why)
- **Alternatives** (other treatment options)
- **Risk/Benefit** (+/- common outcomes)
- **QUESTIONS** (from patient)

Continually check-in with patient to ensure consent is maintained through entire visit.

informed consent of assessment process

↓

Case History
(goals & outcome markers ~80% DDx)

↓

Inspection

Palpation ⇄ **Motion**

Neurovascular & Referral

↓

Special Tests

outcome markers & functional tests

↓

Clinical Impression DDx

informed consent of treatment process

↓

Treatment
and
Self Management Strategies

Exercise is the most underutilized antidepressant.

PMID: 38602313, 30007951, 2883885, 37832814

Pathology forms the cornerstone of effective clinical decision-making, enabling practitioners to differentially diagnose and treat a wide range of conditions with precision. Understanding the interplay between structural, functional, and systemic factors is essential for identifying the root cause of patient concerns. This **RAPID REVIEW content** aims to provide a concise, practical guide to the most common pathologies encountered in clinical practice, highlighting their diagnostic features and management strategies. By integrating **evidence-informed approaches,** this section empowers clinicians to apply best practices for assessment and treatment.

The content is structured to serve as a quick reference, simplifying the complexity of differential diagnosis. Special emphasis is placed on manual therapies, including massage techniques, to align with holistic and person-centered care models.

Grouped Sections by Body Region

This chapter is organized by anatomical regions, allowing for streamlined navigation and application. Each section includes condition-specific tables summarizing the following:

History: Key patient-reported elements aiding in diagnosis

Signs & Symptoms (SSx): Observable or measurable clinical findings

Treatment (Tx): Recommended therapeutic interventions

Why Patient History Matters - A detailed patient history is one of the most valuable diagnostic tools, identifying the reason for care and how the issue affects daily life. **Studies show that a subjective history identifies 74–90%** of diagnoses. Information gathering should continue throughout treatment using active listening, empathy, and open-ended questions like, "How can we help you today?" Accurate information shapes clinical decisions and builds rapport.[1,2,3,4]

Key Factors for Lasting Change

1. **Positive Past Experiences:**
   - Highlight previous successes to build self-efficacy.
   - Reinforce strengths and **celebrate small wins**.
2. **Practical Learning (Modeling):**
   - **Show, don't just tell.** Demonstrate exercises or skills.
   - Provide **visual aids/handouts** and feedback for home practice.
3. **Positive Persuasion:**
   - Boost confidence by showing belief in their ability to succeed.
   - Use encouragement like, **"You're stronger than you think."**
4. **Psychological States:**
   - Foster **optimism and confidence.**
   - Address fear and hesitation with relaxation techniques and cognitive behavioral strategies (CBT).

MOTIVATIONAL INTERVIEW

Motivational Interview Keys

1. Open-Ended Questions

- Ask: "What's going on?" Focus on beliefs vs. actions.
- Listen, then summarize their interpretation to ensure understanding.

2. Provide Information

- Offer information only if patient requests it.
- Use **positive, simple language - Words count!**

Words to avoid	Alternatives
Chief Complaint	**Core Concern**
Disease	Condition
Wear and tear	Reparable injury
Degeneration	Normal age changes
Instability	Needs better strength
Effusion	Swelling

3. Explore Concerns

- Ask: "What makes this change difficult?"
- Support autonomy & look for inconsistencies between thoughts and actions.

4. Use Scaling Questions

- **Importance:** "How important is change to you 0–10?"
- **Confidence:** "How confident are you 0–10?"
- **Goal Setting:** "What would help you get closer to 10?"
  - High importance, low confidence → Provide encouragement.
  - Low importance, high confidence → Explain why change matters.

5. Shared Decision-Making

- Discuss options and ask questions (e.g., PAR-Q for exercise readiness).
- Emphasize patient autonomy: **"You are the best judge of what works for you, and I'm here to help."**

Stop Teaching **Dependence, start Instilling Resilience** in those with **Chronic Pain**. It MAY **improve** long term **experience**.

PMID: 20425199 33981934 30184082

PMID: 15826439, 17716083, 30335780, 35344379

History Considerations

A detailed patient history is a crucial diagnostic tool, revealing the reason for care and its impact on daily life. Studies show **history identifies 74-90% of differential diagnoses.** People will literally tell you what is wrong and what they think will work best to help.

Red Flags* for More Serious Pathology	
History of...	**Signs & symptoms**
• Violent trauma, significant fever	• Temperature > 100° F / 37.8° C
• Carcinoma, unexplained weight loss	• Blood pressure > 160/95 mm Hg
• Systemic steroid use	• Resting pulse > 100 bpm
• Drug abuse, HIV, Hepatitis	• Resting respiration > 25 bpm
• Recent unexplained weight loss	• Auscultation of bruits - carotid, abdominal
• Constant, progressive non-mechanical pain	• Widespread neurological deficits
• Bowel and/or bladder dysfunction	• Saddle anesthesia, writhing in pain

***Red flag** = pathognomonic sign or symptom that is very suggestive & almost always associated with a given condition (e.g. shooting or electrical pain radiating down the back of the leg into the heel is a "red flag" for lumbar radiculopathy). PMID 32438853, 29959102

Effective Communication in Health-care

Effective Communication in Healthcare

Stating Facts, Avoiding Interpretations
- Patient exaggerates pain" vs "Patient reports severe pain
- Patient claims 10/10 pain" vs "Patient reports pain at 10/10

Critical Thinking About Identifiers
- The 45-year-old Hispanic male" vs "A 45-year-old male
- Low-income patient" vs "Patient experiencing chronic pain

Avoiding Stereotypes & Generalizations
- Non-compliant patient" vs "The patient has challenges
- Poor historian" vs "The patient has difficulty recalling

Person-First Language
- Diabetic patient" vs "A person with diabetes
- Epileptic" vs "A person with epilepsy

Assigning Blame to the System
- Patient refuses medication" vs "Patient declined medication after discussion
- Missed appointments" vs "Faces transportation or scheduling challenges

Eliminating Pejorative Terms
- Convict" vs "Incarcerated person
- Prostitute" vs "Sex worker

Using Active Voice
- Medication was not taken" vs "The patient did not take the medication
- Antibiotics were prescribed" vs "I prescribed antibiotics

Condition	AROM	PROM	RROM	Comments
Muscle Injury (strain or tendinopathy)	↓ AROM (painful)	WNL (pain at end ROM)	Pain	• Dull ache - sharp pain when challenged • **Pain with palpation, stretching or contraction of damaged muscle** (possible weakness) • *Unidirectional* pain with motion in muscle fiber direction
Fascial Strain (adhesion or scaring)	↓ AROM (painful)	↓ PROM (painful)	WNL (painless)	• May have palpatory subcutaneous adhesions, limited ROM or non-dermatomal pain & posture changes
Ligament Injury (sprain)	↓ AROM (painful)	↓ PROM (painful)	WNL (painless)	• Injured at full end ROM with tearing • **Pain with palpation or stretching** of ligament (passive over pressure) • **Instability** due to full ligament rupture may show an empty end feel, ↑ PROM or repeatable 'clunk' with motion
Capsulitis	↓ AROM (painful)	↓ PROM (painful)	WNL (painless)	• Pain with direct capsule palpation or ***multidirectional* pain with motion** - pain in a single direction indicates muscle or tendon damage
Joint Injury (arthropathy)	↓ AROM (painful)	↓ PROM (painful)	WNL (painless)	• Mild loss of ROM or pain • **Crepitus with scour tests** • AROM may show repeatable 'snapping' & 'popping' • Pain may change with weather
Joint Dysfunction (subluxation)	WNL or limited segmental ROM	Limited in specific ROM	WNL or weak	• Pain or point tenderness • Asymmetry/misalignment • **PROM abnormality or restriction** - joint "feels stuck"
Bone Injury (fracture)	↓ AROM (painful)	↓ PROM (painful)	↓ RROM (painful)	• Hx of trauma - **perform fracture screen** • Pin point tenderness, dull ache but very sharp when challenged
Nerve Injury	↓ or WNL	WNL	Weak	• **Numbness, tingling or muscle weakness** & shooting electrical pain with stretch or compression of nerve
Visceral Injury	• **Writhing or cramping pain** secondary to internal organ capsule distension or vascular compromise, deep achy, often **poorly localized** & may be immobilizing in more severe cases (eg. intestinal cramps, PMS, appendicitis) - pain is often **NOT relieved by change in body position**			

↑ = increase, ↓ = decrease, WNL = within normal limits, Hx = history, **World Health Organization 'Subluxation' definition** - "A lesion or dysfunction in a joint or motion segment in which alignment, movement integrity and/or physiological function are altered, although contact between joint surfaces remains intact. It is essentially a functional entity, which may influence biomechanical and neural integrity." Vascular injuries often present with bruising, throbbing pain, changes in local body temperature and altered capillary refill times (> ~2 sec). Cutaneous (skin) injuries are easy to locate and visualize. The table above is for common general presentations. Patients often have ranges of presentation depending on the specific scope of their injury or condition.

The goal of History and Assessment is to find outcome markers to monitor patient progression. Any parameter that has the ability to be proven valid & reliable & can be objectively measured has the potential to become a clinical outcome marker. Below are some commonly accepted markers:

Outcome Markers

Activities of Daily Living (ADLs)

- Walking, sitting, chewing, range of motion (ROM)
- Balancing on one foot, hobbies, sports
- Sleep quality and duration
- Missed workdays over time

Pain (Subjective)

- Visual Analogue Scale (VAS) or 0–10 verbal pain scale
- Medication/botanical use and dosage
- Symptom patterns—centralization, duration, frequency

Flexibility (ROM)

- Global ROM: AROM, PROM, sit-and-reach, Beighton score
- Reach behind back (distance to C7)
- Tools: Goniometer, inclinometer, posture chart

Neurological

- Reflexes, sensory deficits, muscle strength
- Centralization, decrease in nerve pain

Strength & Endurance

- Muscle grading (0–5), weightlifting (kg/lbs, reps)
- Movement quality—'Does it feel different? How?' Tools: Dynamometer, grip strength
- Endurance: Walk/run distances, plank time, push-ups

Quality of Life

- Assess overall satisfaction: Excellent to very bad
- Questions: "Why is that?", "What could help?", "What supports do you need?"

Special Tests & Motion

- Assess active/passive ROM with goniometer, inclinometer
- Tests: 10-meter walk, Borg Scale for exertion

Outcome Questionnaires

- Reliable but may feel lengthy for patients
- Examples: Oswestry, Roland-Morris, McGill Pain index, Roland/Morris Disability
- More available at prohealthsys.com

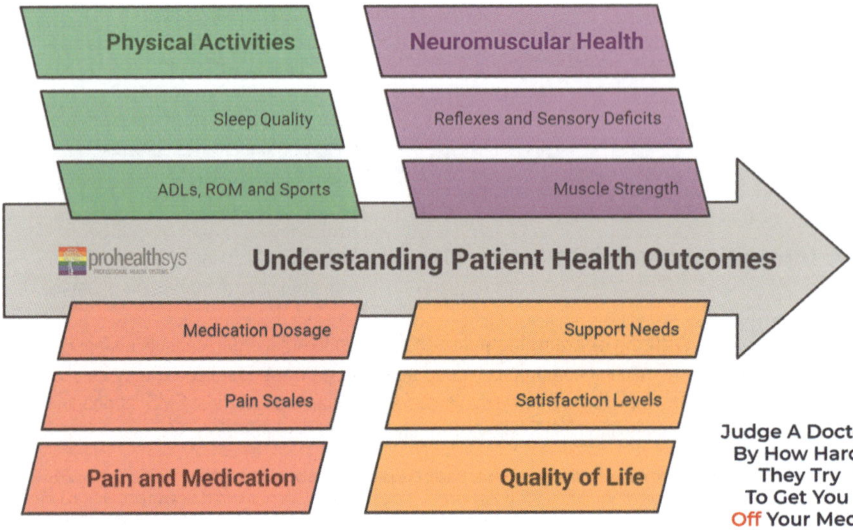

Judge A Doctor By How Hard They Try To Get You Off Your Meds

Measuring Pain

The proper use pain assessment can show both statistically and clinically significant treatment effects. The **most evidence supported measures are functional capacity evaluations (FCE)** and self reported measures (questionnaires).

Functional Capacity Evals (FCE) Examples

- Range of motion (ROM)
- Loaded forward-reach test for back pain
- Timed "Up & Go" test for osteoarthritis
- Grip strength for rheumatoid arthritis
- Ability to perform specific tasks (ADLs)
- Playing sports, hobbies, intercourse
- Days of missed work in a set time frame
- Medication intake for pain management

Three main methods are used to measure pain intensity, that have been proven valid and reliable include: **visual analogue scale (VAS), verbal rating scale (VRS)**, and **0-10 numerical rating scale (NRS)**. [21621130, 30099210] The faces pain scale is recommended for use with younger children & elderly in parallel with numerical self-rating scales.

Application: ask the patient to "**rate current pain on a scale from 0-10, 0 being no pain, 10 being totally incapacitated.**" Patient states a number or points to corresponding pain level. Separate body regions should be rated individually; for example, in a patient with LBP & leg pain (which may or may not be related).

Other Considerations

1. **Ask separate questions**
   - What is your current pain?
   - What is the pain at its worst? (triggers?)
   - **What is the pain at its least?** (associate activities with least pain & do more of this)
2. **Chronic pain cases -** Consider recording the "least pain" the patient has been experiencing (research suggests patients recall "least pain" more accurately than "usual or worst")
3. **Measuring symptoms other than pain -** 0-10 scale can be applied to different symptoms (discomfort, fatigue, stress, etc.)

Numeric & Faces Pain Scale (as used on ProHealth Goniometer & Posture wall chart)

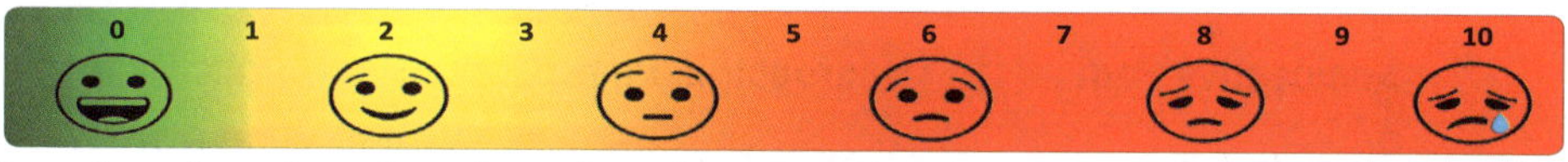

0	2	4	6	8	10
Alert smiling	Serious face CAN BE IGNORED	Furrowed brow INTERFERES WITH TASKS	Raised upper lip INTERFERES WITH CONCENTRATION	Slow blink INTERFERES WITH BASIC NEEDS	Moaning - crying BEDREST - REQUIRED
NO PAIN					Totally Incapacitated

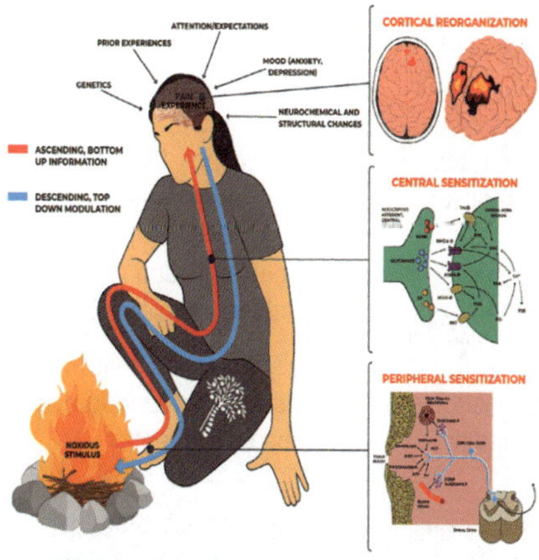

Pain perception **can be influenced by** a number of factors including **prior experience, mood (anxiety/depression), genetics, sensitization, attention and even expectations**

PIECES OF THE PAIN PUZZLE

PMID 21614795, 19074744, 17620877, 37372912, 36983849

Nociceptive Pain

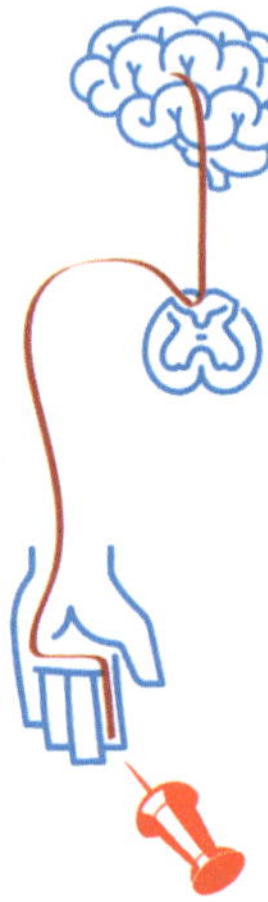

Arises from activation of nociceptors

Neuropathic Pain

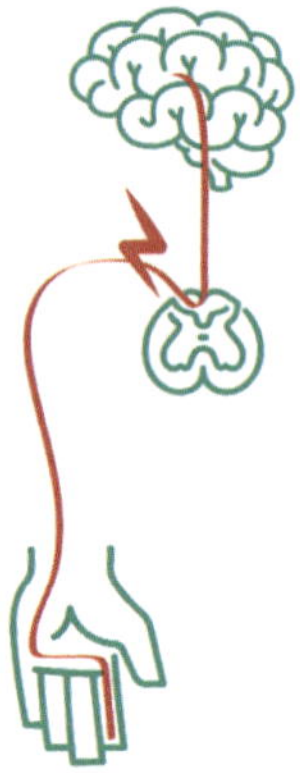

Caused by a lesion or disease of the nervous system

Nociplastic Pain

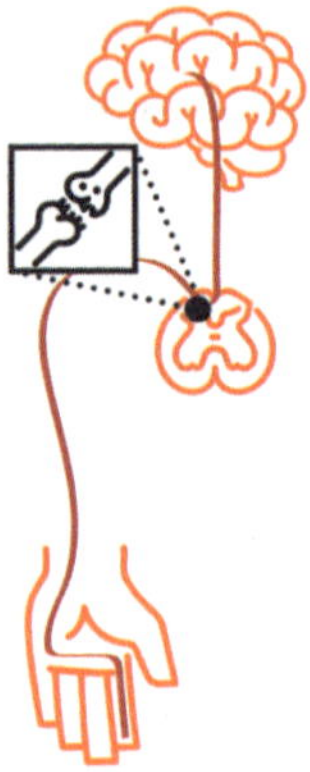

Arises from altered nociceptive/pain processing (central sensitisation)

	Nociceptive Pain	Neuropathic Pain	Nociplastic Pain
Define	Pain from **actual or potential harm to body tissues**, usually linked to an obvious cause like injury or inflammation	Pain caused by injury or malfunction of the nervous system (burning or shooting, electric shocks)	Pain perceived as arising from **altered sensory processing** in the central nervous system without clear evidence of damage (central sensitization)
Features	Very common - changes with movement/body position, predictable pattern, consistent with extent of injury, usually confined to specific area	Follows a **nerve pathway** or a "band-like" distribution, **numbness, tingling** or "pins and needles", **(+) nerve tension tests** (eg. Straight leg raise)	Pain is inconsistent and less predictable; intensity is out of proportion to any apparent physical findings. Widespread or shifting pain areas
Sensory Assess	Normal pain sensitivity or localized increased sensitivity Generally shows minimal psychosocial factors	History of nerve injury or conditions affecting the nervous system Possible increased sensitivity to pressure or temperature	Disconnect between reported pain and identifiable pathology Possible increased sensitivity to pressure or temperature in local and remote areas
Example	**Arthritis, muscle strains, pain after surgery, bruises, fractures, inflammation from injury**	**Sciatica**, diabetic neuropathy, **post-herpetic neuralgia, carpal tunnel synd., nerve root compression, stroke**	**Fibromyalgia, chronic low back pain without a clear cause, IBS, some TMJ disorders**

PMID: 21614795, 19074744, 17620877, 30831273, 32805127

FEAR AVOIDANCE MODEL

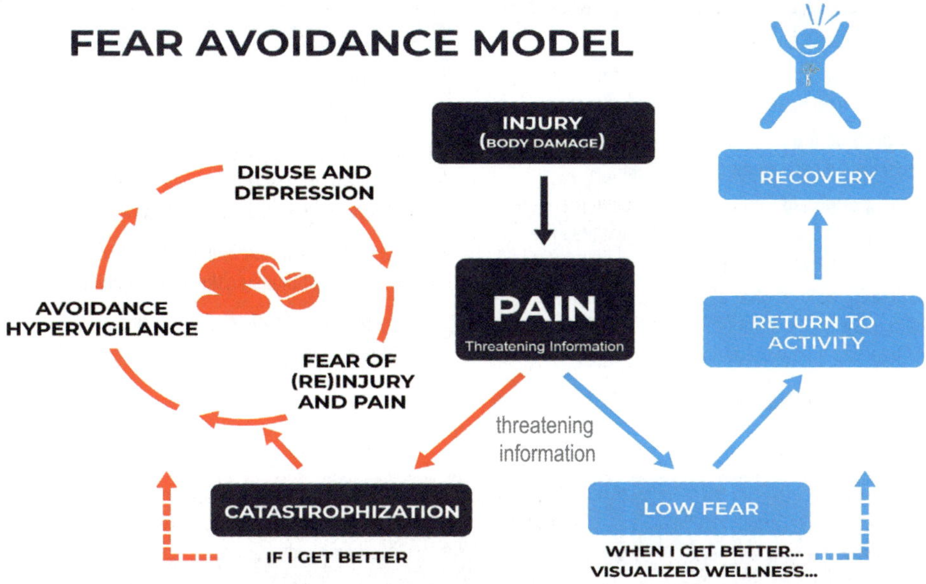

Catastrophization, avoidance & fear of future injury creates a cycle for the development of chronic pain
Research & personal experience show that the best chance for recovery is a return to normal ADLs
It is important to have this conversation with patients for their own understanding & healing

Visceral Pain Referral

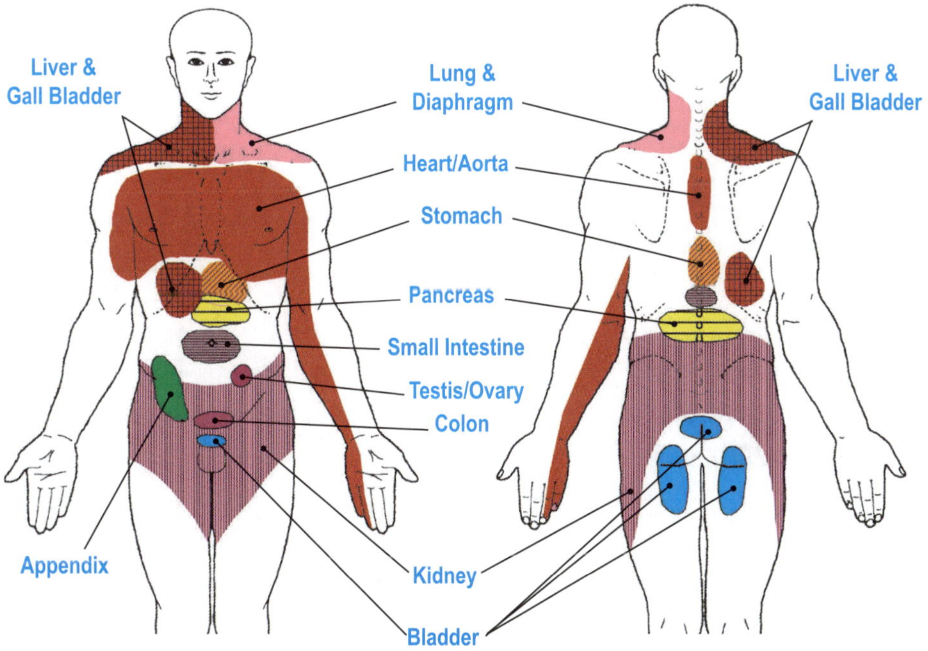

PMID 30109720, 24412032, 33302214, 28655562, 35939664, 32212745, 35345623

An accurate & objective measurement of muscle strength is useful for many reasons:

- **Neurologic screen** - assessment of muscle strength also assesses motor nerve function
- **Diagnostic aid** - helps clinician identify specific muscles that are weak or damaged
- **Therapeutic aid** - creates an objective measure of progress & allows the patient to witness the effect & necessity of treatment
- **Mortality risk** - higher strength is associated with a lower risk of mortality in adults, regardless of age and follow-up period [29425700]

Common Muscle Testing Findings

- Strong **painless resistance** indicates **normal tissue integrity**
- Weak & painless resistance indicates a loss of motor nerve supply or complete rupture of musculotendinous structure
- **Painful resistance** indicates **partial tear** or rupture of musculoskeletal structure
- 'There is no muscle strength without nerve strength and motivation'

Muscle Strength Grading

Grade		%	Definition [31939642, 32430807, 22189568]
5	Normal	100%	Patient can maintain position against *full* examiner-applied resistance (4+ if shaking with resistance may indicate stabilizer weakness or proprioceptive issue)
4	Good*	~75%	Patient can maintain position against gravity & against *moderate* examiner-applied resistance (3+ resist *minimal* force)
3	Fair*	~50%	Movement against gravity but *not* against examiner's resistance
2	Poor*	~25%	Movement possible, not against gravity
1	Trace	~5%	Evidence of slight contractility; *little* or *no joint motion (twitch)*
0	Zero	0%	No palpable or perceivable evidence of contractility (*flaccid*)

% = % normal strength, ROM = range of motion, *Pain, muscle spasm or contracture may limit strength or ROM
Chart as a rating out of 5; e.g.; 5/5, 4/5, 3/5, 2/5, 1/5, 0/5

Muscle Strength vs Length

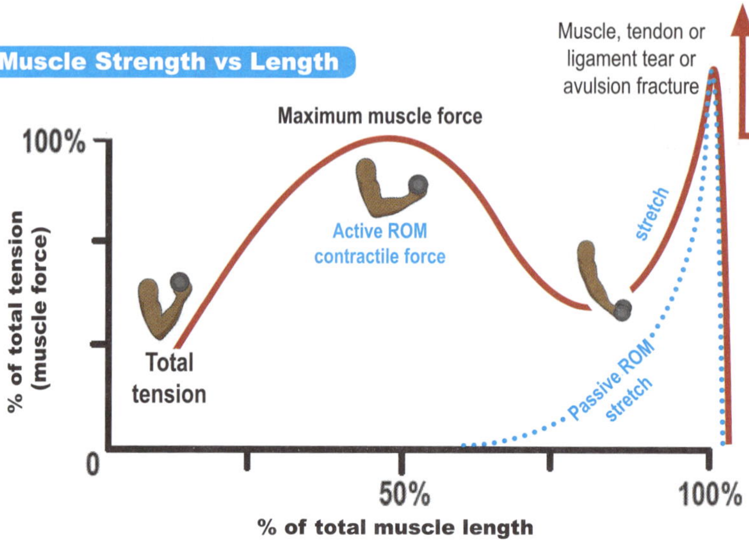

Video demos of muscle tests with variations and common errors available prohealthsys

PMID: 31939642, 37928783, 33255648, 32430807, 22189568

ABCs of Manual Muscle Testing (MMT)

- **Active Range of Motion (AROM):** Tests full joint motion, establishes function baseline, (activates muscles and neurovascular structures).
- **Break Test:** Measures muscle strength with isometric contraction; examiner gradually applies force along muscle fiber direction (origin to insertion).
- **Concentric Contraction:** Patient performs AROM against resistance; examiner resists but allows patient to succeed.
- **Stretch Test:** Determines muscle flexibility and length by passively moving origin away from insertion (PROM).

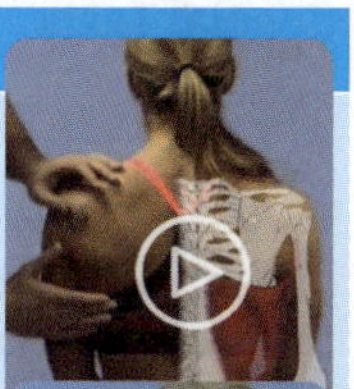

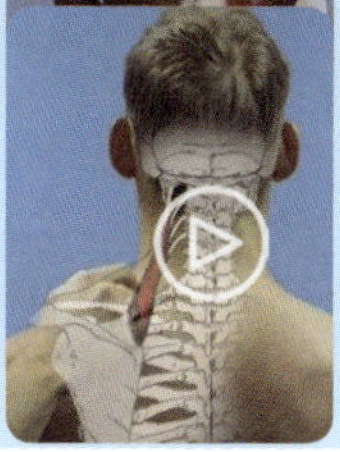

Position & Stabilize: Optimize posture, stabilize proximally, isolate target muscle

Palpation: Confirm activation, detect abnormalities

Instruct: Say: "Don't let me move you" or "Resist my force." Hold ~5 sec, repeat if needed

Resistance: Gradually oppose muscle action; test strong muscles functionally (e.g., standing plantar flexion)

- Functional - 5 sec hold, 5-6 reps
- Fair - 3-4 sec hold, 2-4 reps
- Poor - 1-2 sec hold, 1-2 reps
- Non Functional - 0 sec, 0 reps

Variations: Hold 5–10 sec, test up to 10 reps, use multiple angles (eccentric/concentric/isometric). Avoid excessive joint strain

Bilateral Comparison: Assess dominant vs. non-dominant strength

Muscle Length Testing:

- **Excessive Length** = Weak/lax
- Short Length = Contracture
- Stretch via passive/active-assisted movements

Consistency: Follow standardized protocols for reliability. Structured practice improves accuracy

Muscle Testing

Video

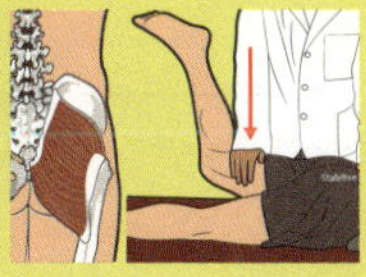

Muscle Testing Procedure

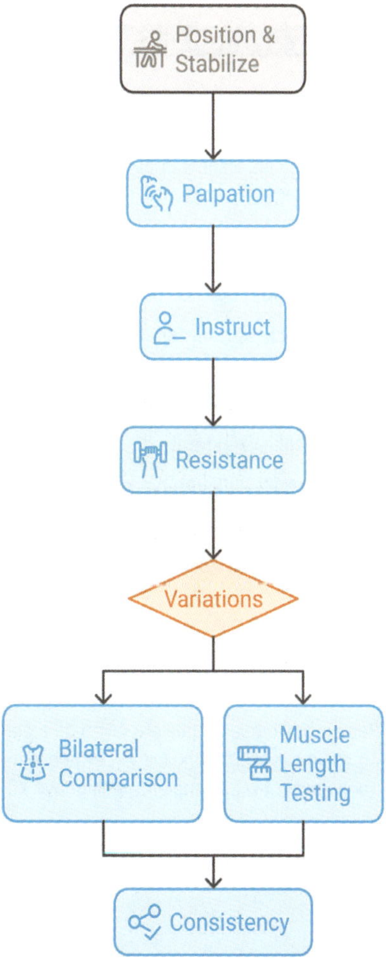

PMID: 21505416, 556816, 20391500, 16180603, 36721348

Special Tests

Special tests are indicated if they have good diagnostic value, if there is still uncertainty on the differential diagnosis or they are going to change treatment options. Special tests can also be used as our outcome markers (better blood test results, slower respiration, less pain with provocative tests). Special tests include:

- ☐ **Vital Signs**
- ☐ **Orthopedic (provocative) tests or injection of local anesthesia in specific tissue (pain reduction shows damaged tissue)**
- ☐ **Diagnostic imaging / Scans: X-rays, U/S, CT, MRI, thermography**
- ☐ **Lab tests: blood, urinalysis, biopsy etc.**

learn more

Special Tests

Straight Leg Raise (SLR) ★★★★★

Procedure

Patient supine; examiner places one hand under patient's ankle & other hand over patient's knee (to ensure knee stays extended during action). Examiner then proceeds to passively elevate the straight leg.

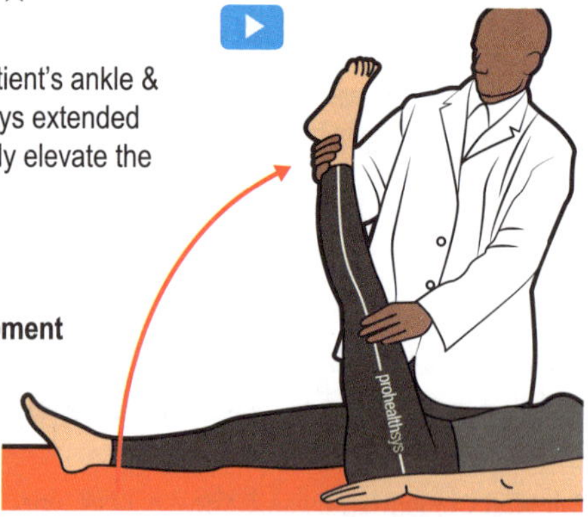

Interpretation

(+) Radicular pain past the knee → Nerve root compression, disc herniation, piriformis entrapment

(+) Low back pain → SI/lumbar sprain/strain

Degrees of flexion → tissue involved*

0° to 40°→ hip joint

40° to 80°→ disc/nerve root involvement

> 80°→ SI/lumbar joint pain

* Exact ROM can vary based on patient underlying flexibility

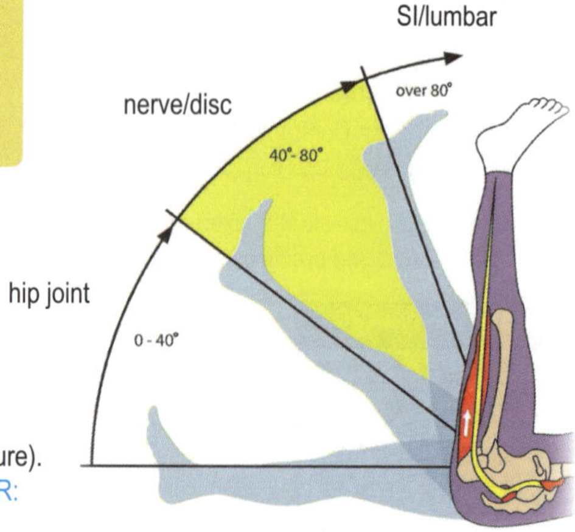

Clinical notes

First ask patient to perform an active straight leg raise as a measure of functional capability.

Remember, these ranges are given as a general guideline; patients who are hypermobile may only present with symptoms well above 70°.

SLR also assesses hamstring tightness (contracture). (R: 0.92 SN: 78-98 SP: 11-64 +LR: 1.03-2.2 -LR: 0.05-0.86)[30969539, 23220802, 35245880, 29190853, 18391677]

Orthopedic tests must be evaluated with other findings and the patient's overall condition. Avoid relying on isolated results, especially "soft" signs with subjective bias. Record detailed findings (e.g., symptoms, pain, numbness) for accurate assessment.

Diagnostic imaging is indicated only if it may change the diagnosis or treatment. Most patients don't need imaging, and few require advanced scans (MRI, CT). Focus on treating the person, not their images. Consider risks, benefits, and liability, and base imaging decisions on history, exams, and diagnostic value.

Vital Signs

- **Blood Pressure (< 120 / 80 mmHg)**
- **Temperature (37° C / 98.6° F)**
- **Pulse (60-100 bpm)**
- **Respiration (12-20 bpm)**
- **Observe skin throughout exam**
- **Diet, Sleep & Exercise = vital signs**

youtube: Vizniak fracture screen

VOMIT PMC1126156 (victims of modern imaging technology)

BARF (brainless application of radiologic findings)

Abnormalities found on scans in asymptomatic 'NORMAL' people

Findings DO NOT = pain

Treat the person, NOT their pictures.

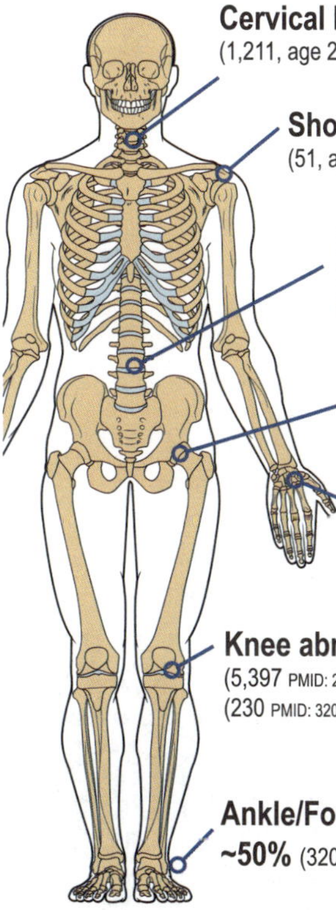

Cervical Disc Bulging ~87% (1,211, age 20-70 - PMID: 25584950)

Shoulder abnormalities ~96% (51, age 40-70 - PMID: 21940544)

Disc Degeneration ~37-96% (3,110, PMID: 26359154 Systematic Review) Frequency increases with age

Hip abnormalities ~68% (2,114 PMID: 25636988 Systematic Review)

Scaphoid fracture missed ~21% (2,507 PMID: 32025360)

Knee abnormalities ~40-97% (5,397 PMID: 29886437 Systematic Review) (230 PMID: 32060622)

Ankle/Foot abnormalities ~50% (320 PMID: 22835390, 21111975,)

What the scan shows

What the report says

PMID: 29886437, 26359154, 25584950, 25636988

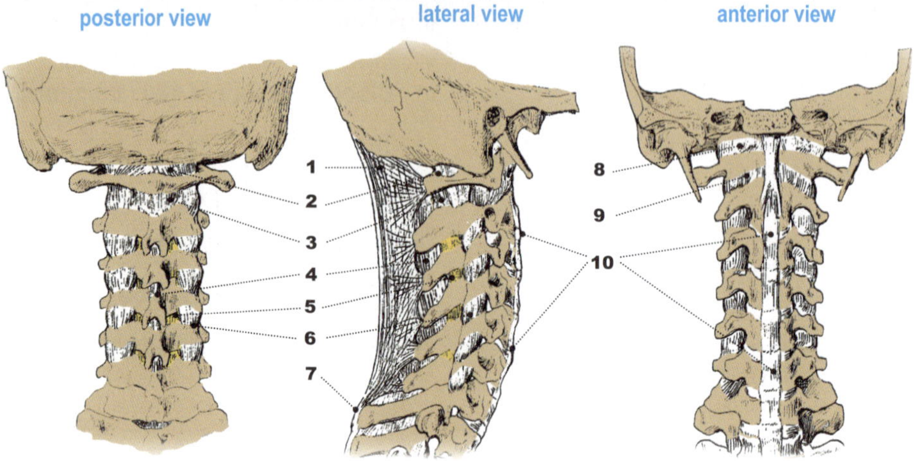

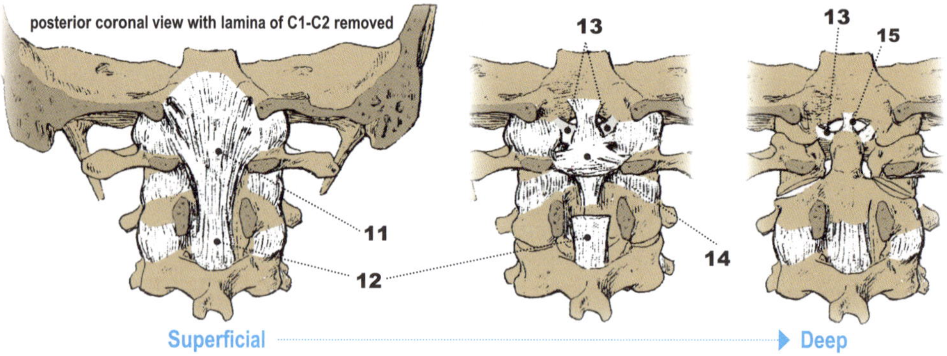

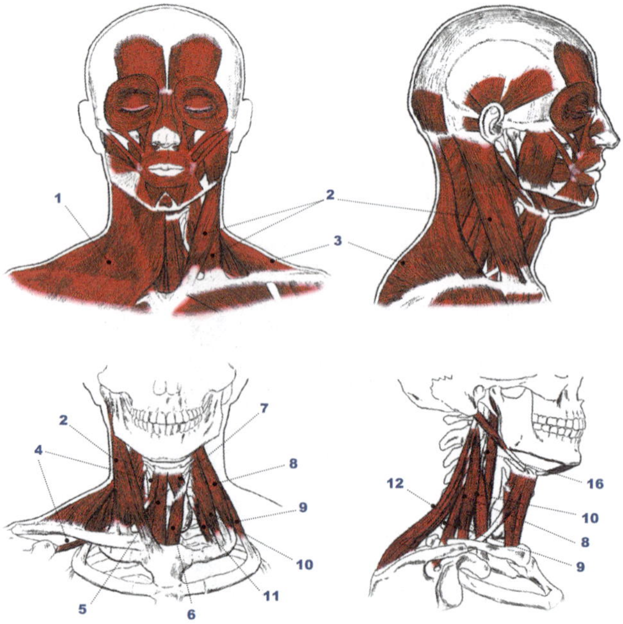

1. Platysma
2. Sternocleidomastoid
3. Trapezius
4. Omohyoid
5. Sternohyoid
6. Sternothyroid
7. Thyrohyoid
8. Middle scalene
9. Posterior scalene
10. Anterior scalene
11. Scalenus minimus
12. Levator scapulae

Head & Neck

Cervicothoracic Regional Exam

☑ Check normal, circle & describe abnormal

Patient: ______________________ date: ______

Insurance: ______________________

Chief complaint & significant history: ______________________

____

Vital Signs: Height: ________, Weight: ________, Blood Pressure: L ______/______, R ______/______, Resp: ________/min, VBI: L ______ R ______

Inspection: □ WNL

Development: □ good, □ fair, □ poor

□ Posture: ______________________

□ Skin (bruising, scars): ______________________

□ Antalgia: ______________________

□ Asymmetry: ______________________

Observation		L	R
Cervical	Head tilt		
	Head rotation		
	Head carriage (ant. / post.)		
	Lordosis (hyper / hypo)		
Thoracic	High shoulder		
	Scoliosis		
	Kyphosis (hyper / hypo)		
	Adam's sign		

Palpation: □ WNL

Palpation	L	R
Skin (masses, temp)		
Lymph nodes		
Temporalis		
Masseter		
TMJ		
Scalenes		
SCM		
Levator scapulae		
Trapezius/rhomboids		
Suboccipitals		
Posterior c-spine muscles		
Trachea mobility		
Thyroid gland		
Clavicle / thoracic outlet		
Rotator cuff		

Mark on drawing □ pain (circle), □ spasm (s), □ edema (e), □ fibrotic (f), □ MFTP (x), □ ache (a), □ burning (b), □ tingling (t)

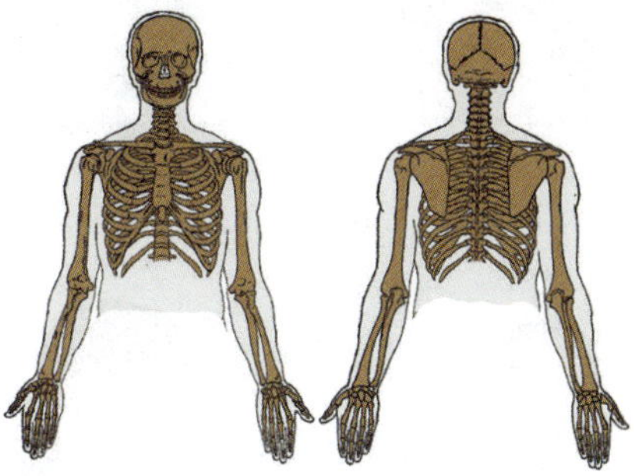

ROM & Joint Play: □ WNL

Cervical spine	Active L	Active R	Passive L	Passive R
Flexion (50°)				
Extension (60°)				
Lateral flexion (45°)				
Rotation (80°)				

Shoulder	L	R	L	R
Flexion (180°)				
Extension (50°)				
Abduction (180°)				
Adduction (30°)				
Internal rotation (90°)				
External rotation (80°)				
Scapulocostal rhythm				

TMJ	
Depression/elevation	
Lateral deviation	

Neurologic: □ WNL

Sensation □ WNL	L	R
Light touch		
Sharp/dull		
Vibration		

Reflexes (0-5) □ WNL	L	R
Biceps (C5)(musculocut.)		
Brachioradialis(C6)(radial)		
Triceps (C7)(radial)		

Motor (0-5) □ WNL	L	R
Cervical flexion (C1-C2)		
Cervical extension (C2, C3, XI)		
Cervical lat. flexion (C3)		
Cervical rotation (C1-4, XI)		
Trapezius (CN XI)(accessory)		
Deltoid (C5)(axillary)		
Biceps (C6)(musculocut.)		
Triceps (C7, C8)(radial)		
Wrist extensors (C6)(radial)		
Wrist flexors (C7)(med./ulnar)		
Interossei (C8, T1)(ulnar)		

Cranial nerves □ WNL	
□ I (smell)	□ VII (facial expres)
□ II (light, vision)	□ VIII (Weber, Rinne)
□ III, IV, VI (gaze)	□ IX, X (ahhh)
□ V (bite, sensation)	□ XI (trap/SCM)
□ V, VII (corneal ref.)	□ XII (tongue)

Orthopedic: □ WNL

Screening	L	R
Valsalva		
Cervical compression		
Max. compression		
Cervical distraction		
Soto Hall		
Jull's test		
Brachial stretch		
Shoulder depression		

TOS	L	R
Eden's		
Wright's		
Adson's		
Roo's		

L		R
	C0	
	C1	
	C2	
	C3	
	C4	
	C5	
	C6	
	C7	
	T1	
	T2	
	T3	
	T4	
	T5	
	T6	

Additional procedures: □ WNL

□ Abdominal exam: ______________________

□ Auscultation (heart, lungs): ______________________

□ Ophthalmoscopic exam: ______________________

□ Otoscopic exam: ______________________

□ Other: ______________________

DDx:

Signature: Date:

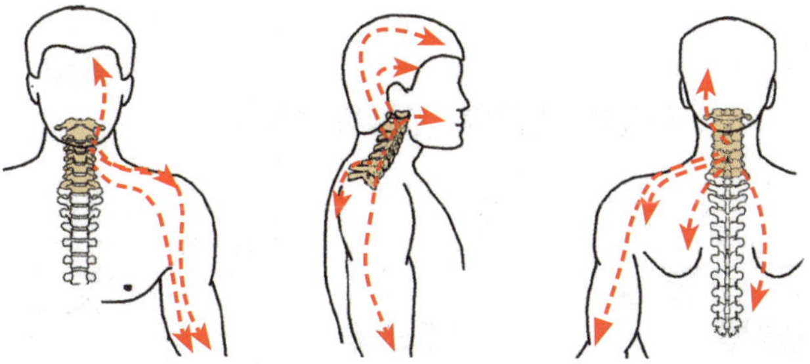

Introduction statement: "Try and move as far as possible, if any of the actions or movements are painful please let me know, do not do any action you feel will cause you further injury."

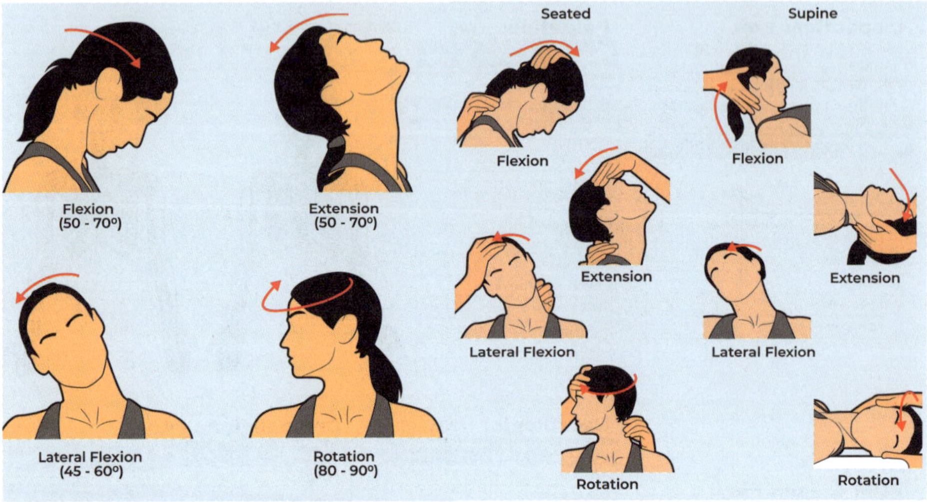

Muscle Testing

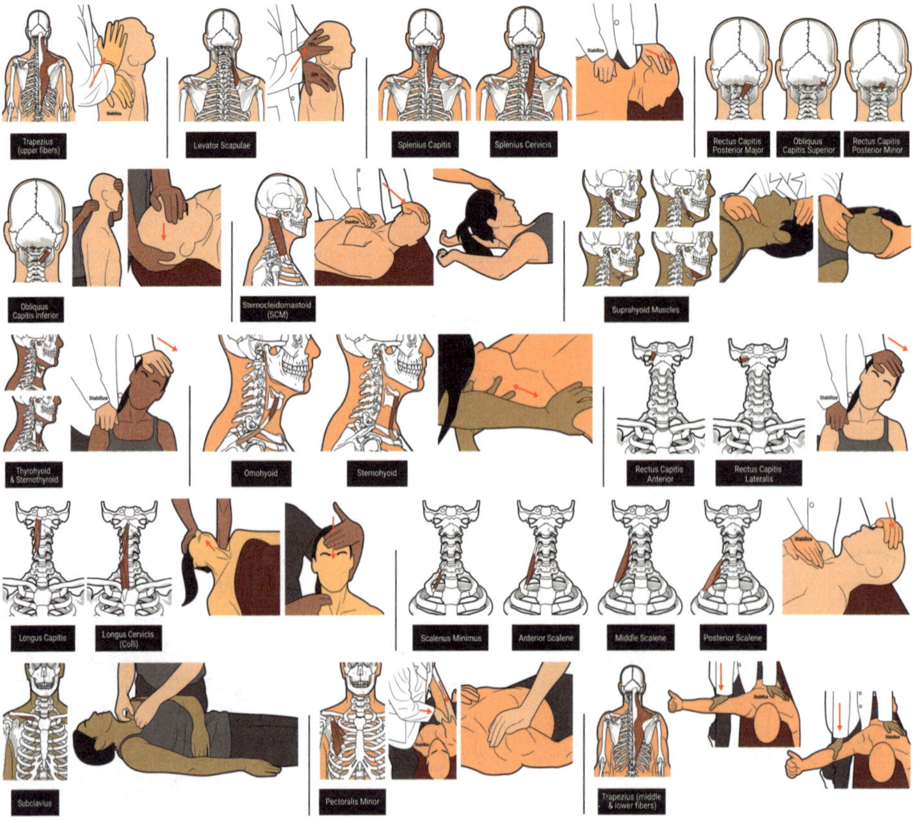

Realize that normal anatomical variation in bone size & shape may alter exact spinal levels being palpated.

- **C2** - first palpable SP below the occipital bone
- **C7 or T1** - most prominent SP at base of neck (C7 will usually move from a palpating finger with cervical flexion/extension)
- **T4** - level with the root of the spine of scapula or apex of axillary fold

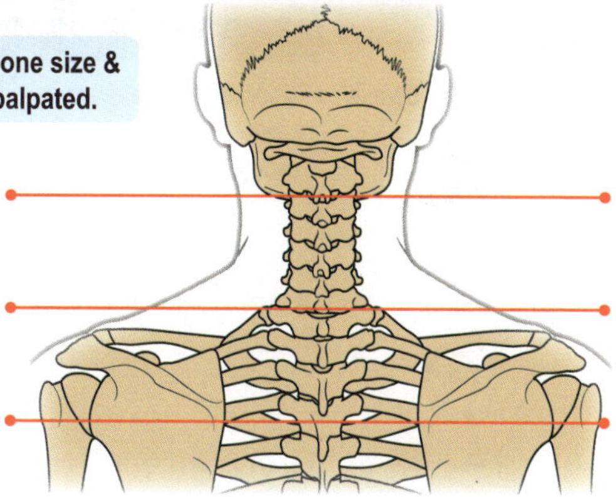

Structure	Location
EOP	midline of occipital base
C1 TP	~1 cm (½" inch) anterior & inferior to mastoid process (under earlobe)
C2 SP	1st prominent SP below EOP
C4 SP	hyoid bone
C5 SP	thyroid cartilage
C7 SP	usually second most prominent SP, slides anterior during cervical extension
T1 SP	most prominent SP (usually)

TP = transverse process, SP = spinous process

Trigger Points

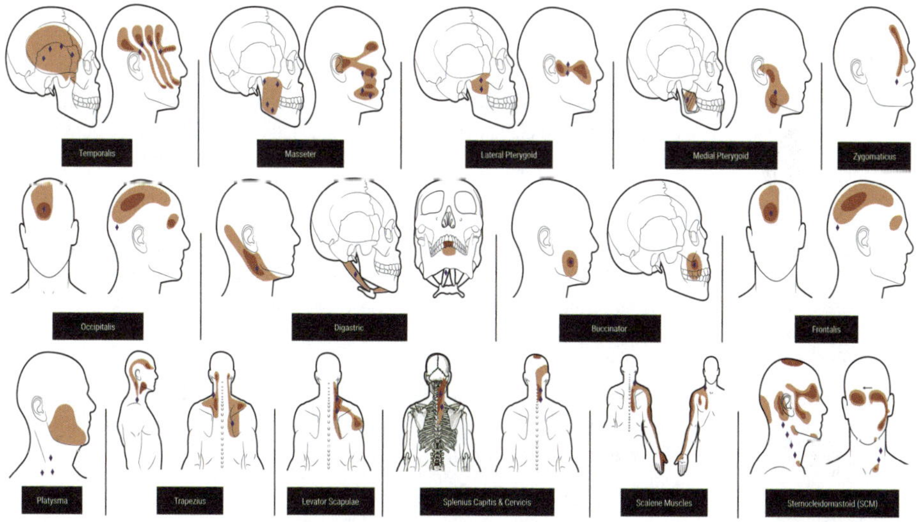

Test	Procedure	Interpretation	Clinical Notes
Alar Ligament Stress 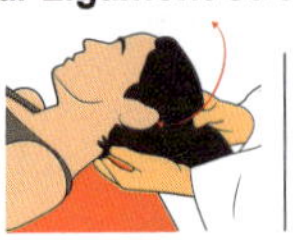	Patient supine, examiner stabilizes C2, rotates or side-bends head	(+) Pain or excessive motion → Alar ligament pathology	Use diagnostic imaging if positive. Assess end feel of C0-C1 joint
Bakody's Sign 	Patient places hand on top of head	(+) Pain relief → radiculopathy	Antalgic posture often seen in patients with radicular conditions
Brachial Stretch 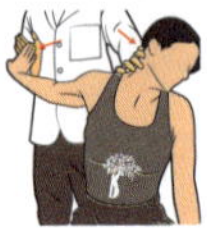	Patient seated, examiner applies compression to brachial plexus region	(+) Pain → Brachial plexus stretch or thoracic outlet syndrome (TOS)	Can add specific upper limb tension tests to get more specific
Cervical Comp. Test 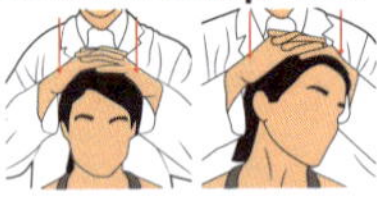	Patient seated, examiner applies downward pressure on the head	(+) Pain → Radiculopathy or IVF stenosis	Can also indicate facet joint irritation or subluxation
Cervical Distraction 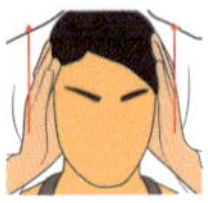	Examiner lifts patient's head while stabilizing under occiput or mandible	(+) Pain relief → Radiculopathy or IVF stenosis	Can be used as a treatment approach if positive
Dix-Hallpike Test 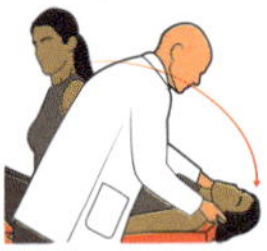	Patient lies back quickly with head rotated 30-45°, supported by the examiner	(+) Nystagmus or vertigo → Benign Paroxysmal Position Vertigo (BPPV)	Can also be used therapeutically to reposition otoliths
Jull's Flexor Endurance 	Patient supine, maintains chin tuck while lifting head	(+) Pain or inability → Deep neck flexor weakness or fatigue	Men: 120 sec, Women: 90 sec are normal values
Lateral Shear Test 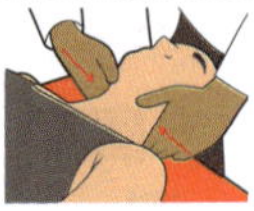	Examiner applies lateral shear force between C1 and C2 transverse processes	(+) Pain or instability → C1-C2 ligament instability	Use caution due to proximity to vascular structures
O'Donoghue 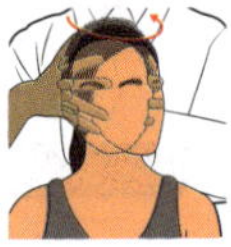	Examiner resists isometric cervical rotation, then performs passive cervical rotation	(+) Pain w resistance → Muscle strain; (+) Pain w passive motion → sprain	Differentiates muscle strain from ligament sprain

Test	Procedure	Interpretation	Clinical Notes
Scalene Cramp Test 	Patient tucks chin to supraclavicular fossa while rotating head to the same side.	(+) Pain or radicular symptoms → Scalene trigger points or TOS.	May reproduce pain referral patterns
Sharp-Purser Test 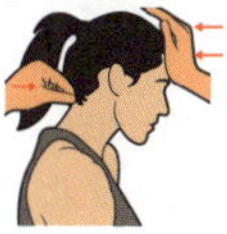	Patient seated, examiner stabilizes C2 and pushes the forehead posteriorly.	(+) Symptoms reduce → Atlantoaxial instability.	Perform after the Transverse Ligament Stress Test
Soto-Hall Test 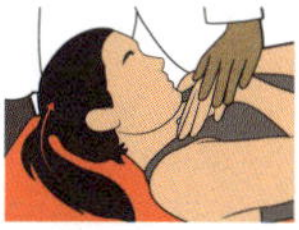	Patient supine, examiner flexes cervical spine with overpressure.	(+) Pain or stiffness → Cervical sprain, strain, or radiculopathy.	Passive ROM test for neck pain with overpressure
Swivel Chair Test 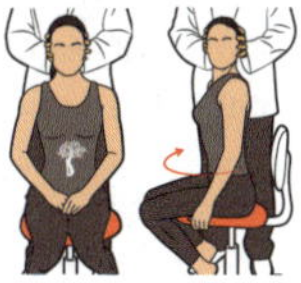	Patient rotates head while examiner stabilizes shoulders, then rotates body while stabilizing head.	(+) Symptoms in step 1 only → Cervicogenic vertigo. Symptoms in both → Vestibular vertigo.	Helps differentiate between cervicogenic and vestibular vertigo
Valsalva Maneuver 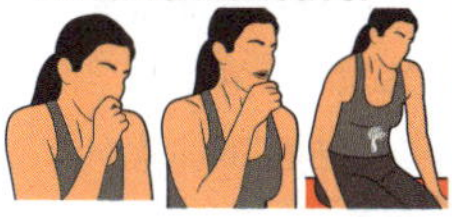	Patient bears down as if "straining at stool."	(+) Pain → Herniation, tumor, or IVF encroachment.	Increases intrathecal and intra-abdominal pressure De Jarine Triad - cough sneeze strain

Head & Neck

	Hx	SSx	Tx
Cervicogenic Headache (HA) 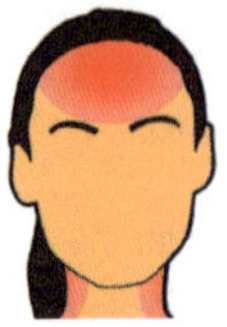	- Headache triggered by neck movement or poor posture	- **↓ ROM pain** - **Tenderness with palpation** - **(+) Cervical Flexion Rotation Test**	- Postural correction - ExRx (deep cervical flexors) - Stretch - METH
Cluster HA 	- Series of severe, one-side headache lasting 15 min to 3 hrs - Often triggered by alcohol or stress	- **Intense pain behind one eye** - **Lacrimation & rhinorrhea** - **Restlessness during attack**	- Oxygen therapy - Pharmacological treatment (triptans) - Avoid triggers
Migraine HA 	- Visual or sensory triggers (bright lights, strong smells, hormonal changes)	- **Unilateral throbbing** or pulsating pain - Photophobia & nausea - (+) Sensitivity to certain triggers	- Stress management - Pharmacological - Trigger avoidance (diet, environmental)
Muscle Tension Headache 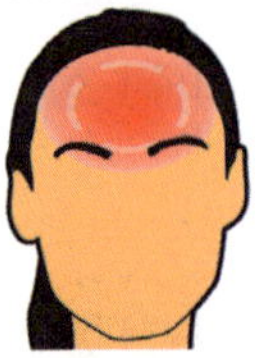	- Prolonged stress, poor posture, or inadequate sleep - Often episodic, may become chronic	- Bilateral tightness or pressure - **Neck & shoulder muscle tension** - (+) Palpable muscle tightness in shoulders or scalp	- Stress management - Postural correction - Stretching (neck & shoulder) - Relaxation tech.
Pathologic HA 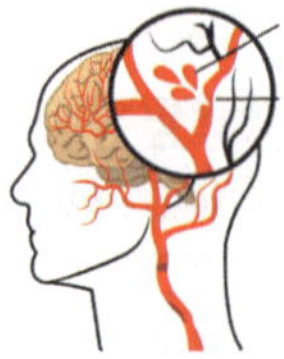	- Sudden onset in individuals over 50 - Associated systemics (fever, weight loss)	- Severe, new headache - ↑ intracranial pressure signs (vomiting, papilledema)	- Emergency medical eval. - Imaging (CT/MRI) - Treat underlying cause

Stroke / Vertebrobasilar Ischemia (VBI)

Hx: atherosclerosis, hypertension, diabetes, smoking, ligamentous hypermobility

SSx: Dizziness, D-LOC (decreased level of consciousness), Diplopia (or other visual disturbances), Dysarthria (difficulty speaking), Dysphagia (difficulty swallowing), Ataxia (motor control loss or unsteady gait), Nausea & vomiting, Numbness (unilateral over face), Nystagmus (lateral beating of the eyes)

DDx: stroke, transient ischemic attack, positional vertigo

Condition	Hx	SSx	Tx
Concussion 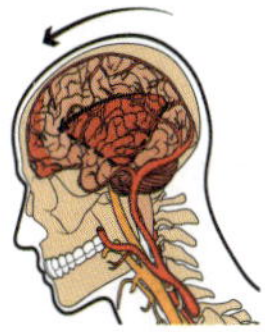	- **Trauma** to the head (falls, sports injuries, motor vehicle) - Direct impact or whiplash forces	- **Headache**, light/ noise sensitivity, dizzy, confusion - Possible loss of consciousness - (+) Cognitive issue	- **Immediate rest & medical evaluation** - Gradual activity guided by SSx - Avoid re-injury
Degenerative Joint Disease (DJD) 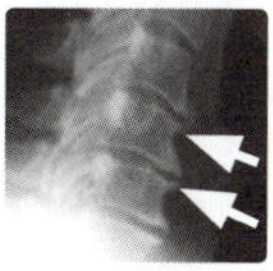	- Gradual onset, common in older adults - Associated with cervical disc degeneration	- Pain with movement - ↓ Cervical ROM - **Crepitus w/ ROM** - **Xray to confirm**	- Joint mobilize - ROM exercises - METH - Normal age related change
Radiculopathy 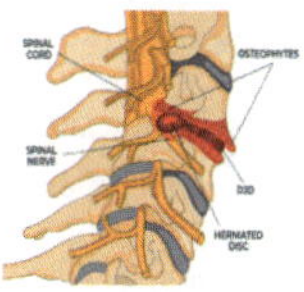	- Compression of cervical nerve roots (disc herniation, degeneration)	- Arm **Unilateral dermatomal**, numb, tingle, or shooting, ↓ reflex - Muscle weakness - (+) Spurling's Test	- Neural mobilization - Traction therapy - ROM ExRx for cervical stabilizers
TMJ Syndrome 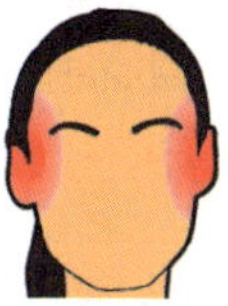	- **Jaw clicking, locking**, or pain - Linked to stress, teeth grinding, or trauma	- Jaw pain with eating - Tenderness to palpation over TMJ - (+) ↓ ROM, Joint Compression Test	- Oral appliances - Mandibular ROM - Posture ergo eval. correction
Torticollis (Wry Neck) 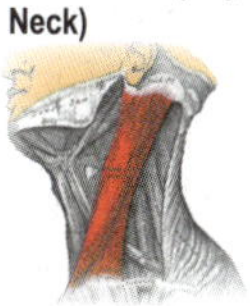	- Acute or gradual onset due to awkward sleeping posture, trauma, or muscle spasm	- **Head tilted** to side with limited ROM - Spasm of SCM - (+) **Palpable tightness in SCM** or traps	- Heat therapy - Stretching (SCM & upper traps) - Postural training
Whiplash (cervical sprain) 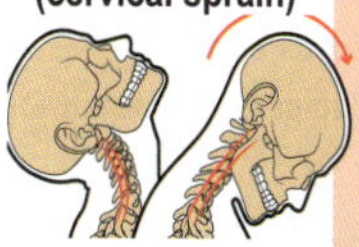	- **Trauma** from motor vehicle or sudden **acceleration-deceleration**	- **Neck pain & stiffness w/ ROM** - Headaches, dizzy - (+) Spurling's Test if radiculopathy	- Ice, METH - Gentle ROM - Strengthening cervical stabilizers

Head & Neck

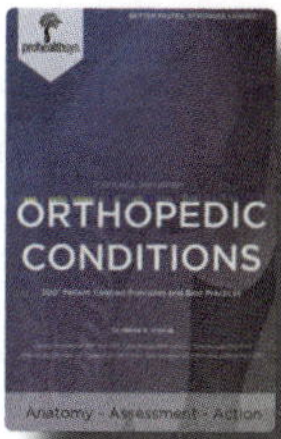

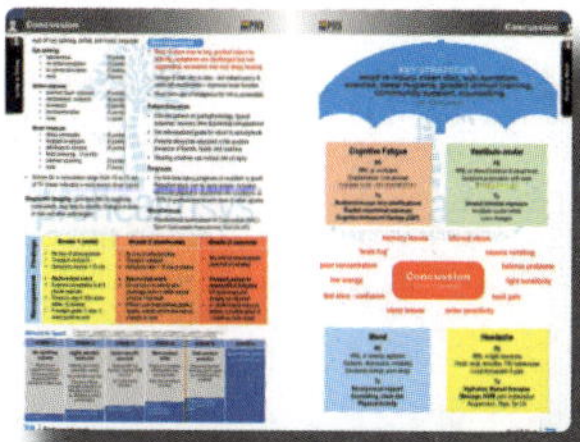

1. Which of the following muscles is responsible for cervical flexion?
a) Levator scapulae
b) Trapezius
c) Scalenes
d) Sternocleidomastoid

2. Which ligament stabilizes the cervical spine during flexion and extension?
a) Posterior longitudinal ligament
b) Ligamentum flavum
c) Alar ligament
d) Anterior longitudinal ligament

3. What type of end feel would you expect in the cervical spine during lateral flexion?
a) Bone-to-bone
b) Empty
c) Soft tissue stretch
d) Capsular

4. What type of pain is often associated with cervical radiculopathy?
a) Pain with deep breath
b) Dull, aching pain in the cervical region
c) Referred pain from the upper back
d) Sharp, electrical along a dermatomal pattern

5. In the case of a patient with TMJ syndrome, what is an important part of co-management?
a) Immediate spinal manipulation to relieve pressure
b) Surgical intervention for permanent relief
c) Complete rest and immobilization of the jaw
d) Posture correction for head and neck alignment

6. How should a clinician help a patient who expresses discomfort during a neck examination due to anxiety?
a) End the examination immediately
b) Proceed with the examination as planned
c) Force the patient to complete the examination
d) Offer reassurance and allow them to express their concerns before continuing

7. Which muscle is typically involved in neck pain from poor posture over time?
a) Trapezius
b) Pectoralis minor
c) Latissimus dorsi
d) Sternocleidomastoid

8. What is the primary goal when performing a muscle test on a patient with suspected cervical myopathy?
a) Measuring the patient's range of motion
b) Diagnosing the extent of a fracture
c) Identifying weakness or atrophy in cervical muscles
d) Strengthening the muscle to alleviate pain

9. During the cervical distraction test, what is typically the expected outcome if the test is positive?
a) No change in symptoms
b) Increased pain
c) Pain that radiates down the arm
d) Decreased pain

10. In a patient with whiplash, which type of pain is most commonly reported?
a) Aching pain that improves with movement
b) Mild, constant neck stiffness and ear pain
c) Radiating pain down the arm
d) Sharp pain that worsens with deep breaths

11. Which special test would you use to diagnose cervical radiculopathy?
a) Upper limb tension test
b) Spurling's test
c) Bakody's sign
d) Valsalva maneuver

12. What is the most likely diagnosis when a patient presents with dizziness, nausea, and positive results for the cervical flexion rotation test?
a) Meniere's disease
b) Cervicogenic headache
c) TMJ dysfunction
d) Stroke

13. What is the most effective treatment for a patient with a herniated disc in the cervical spine?
a) Spinal manipulation
b) Rest and NSAIDs only
c) Surgery for disc removal
d) Manual traction and posture correction

14. How would you address a patient with an acute onset of headache and neck stiffness after a fall?
a) Apply ice and rest
b) Encourage movement to prevent stiffness
c) Immediate spinal manipulation
d) Referral for imaging and possible concussion evaluation

15. What is the common characteristic of pain in a patient with torticollis?
a) Worse when head tilts to the unaffected side
b) Pain occurs in the upper back and shoulders
c) Pain radiates into the upper arm
d) Pain is localized to the sternocleidomastoid

16. In patients with chronic cervical spine pain, what is an appropriate co-management strategy?
a) Avoid any exercises until the pain subsides
b) Rely solely on manual therapy
c) Focus on pharmaceutical treatments alone
d) Combine spinal mobilizations and exercise program

17. What ethical consideration should be made when treating a patient who refuses a recommended treatment plan?
a) Discontinue the treatment altogether
b) Proceed with treatment regardless of their consent
c) Insist on the treatment to avoid worsening symptoms
d) Respect patient autonomy, provide alternative options

18. What type of pain would be indicative of a cervical disc herniation?
a) Pain that worsens with deep breathing
b) Dull pain with movement
c) Aching pain, worsened by flexion
d) Radiating, sharp pain in a specific dermatome

19. What is a common contributing factor to muscle tension headaches?
a) Poor posture and neck strain
b) Lack of sleep
c) Anxiety and stress
d) All of the above

20. Which of the following techniques would be most beneficial for improving ROM in the cervical spine?
a) Ice and rest
b) Postural correction exercises
c) Strengthening exercises for the neck
d) Spinal manipulation and stretching

PHS Certification

1. d
2. d
3. c
4. d
5. d
6. d
7. a
8. c
9. b
10. a
11. b
12. b
13. b
14. d
15. a
16. d
17. d
18. d
19. d
20. b

Case Study 1

A 55-year-old dentist presents with numbness, tingling, and weakness in their right arm, radiating down the forearm. They report that the symptoms began after lifting a heavy object two weeks ago. The patient also describes occasional neck pain and stiffness, with difficulty turning their head to the right.

Questions:

- What is the most likely differential diagnosis for this presentation?
- What treatment options, including manual therapy and ergonomic changes, would you recommend?
- How might the patient's occupation and physical activities contribute to the condition, and what preventive measures could help?

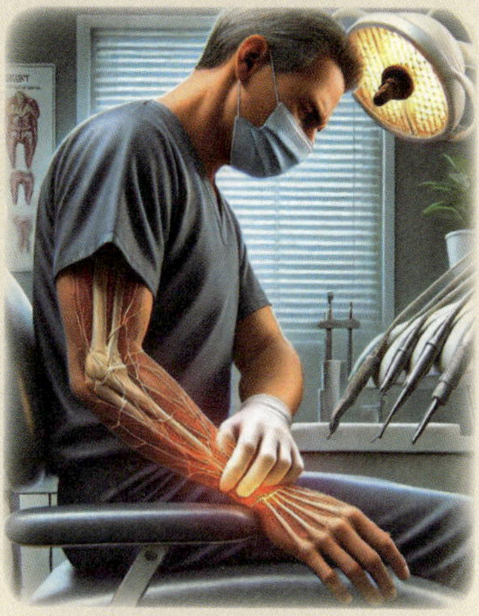

Case Study 2

A 30-year-old woman was involved in a rear-end car accident three days ago. She complains of neck pain, stiffness, and mild headaches. She reports difficulty moving her neck, especially when turning to the right, and her symptoms worsen with extended periods of sitting. There are no neuro deficits.

Questions:

- What is the most likely differential diagnosis for this presentation?
- What treatment options, including manual therapy and ergonomic changes, would you recommend?
- How might this patient's psychological response to the car accident impact her recovery, and what considerations should be made?

Case Study 3

A 62-year-old male presents with sudden dizziness, difficulty swallowing, and blurred vision. He experiences spinning and lightheadedness when turning his head left, especially when looking over his shoulder or driving. He also reports mild right-hand numbness, slurred speech, and hypertension.

Questions:

- What is the most likely differential diagnosis for this presentation?
- What immediate management steps should be taken, including medical referral?
- How might this patient's cardiovascular health contribute to the condition, and what lifestyle changes could reduce the risk of further complications?

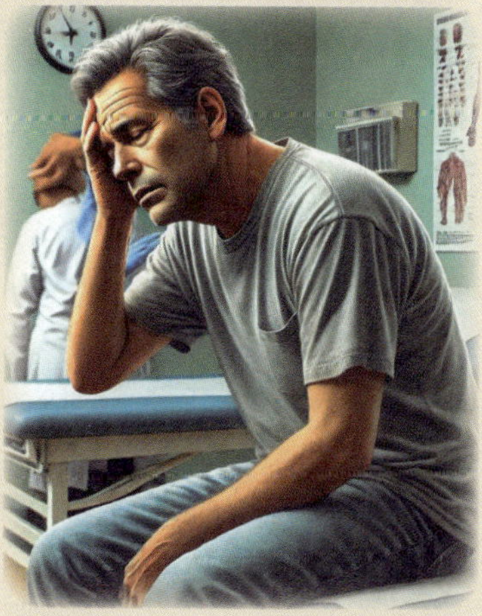

Head & Neck

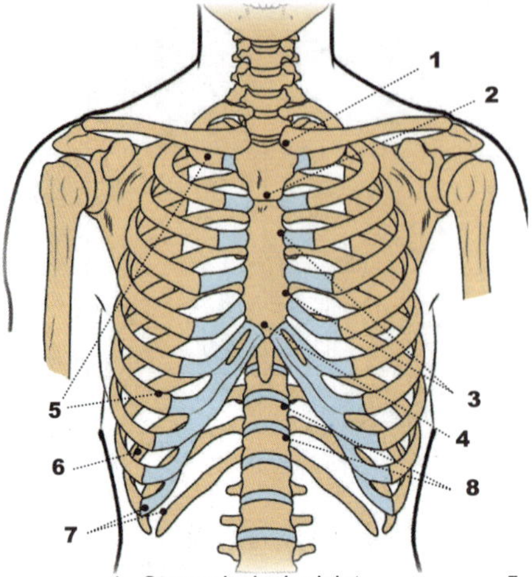

Ribs (costals)

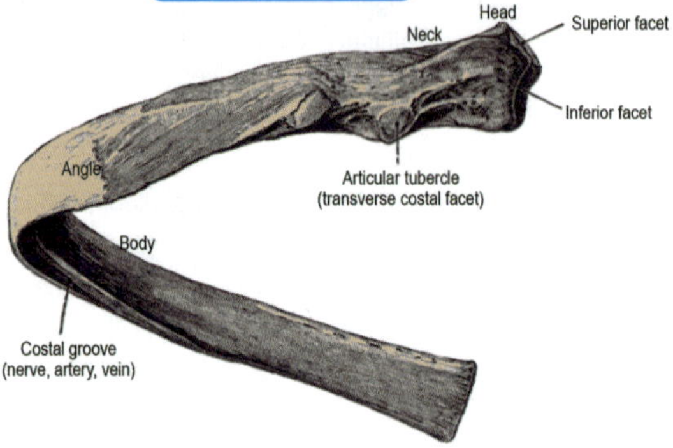

1. Sternoclavicular joint
2. Sternomanubrial joint
3. Sternocostal joint
4. Xiphisternal joint
5. True ribs (1-7)
6. False ribs (8-12)
7. Floating ribs (11-12)
8. Costovertebral joint

Thoracic Muscles

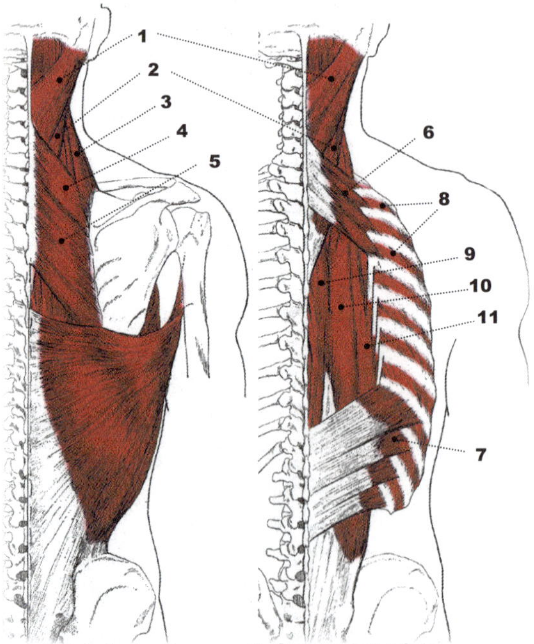

1. Splenius capitis
2. Splenius cervicis
3. Levator scapulae
4. Rhomboid minor
5. Rhomboid major
6. Serratus post. sup.
7. Serratus post. inferior
8. Intercostal muscles

Erector spinae (deep layer)

9. Spinalis
10. Longissimus
11. Iliocostalis

Rib Motions

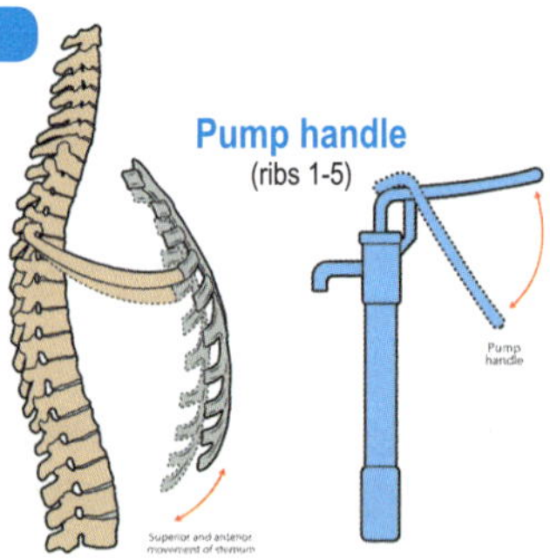

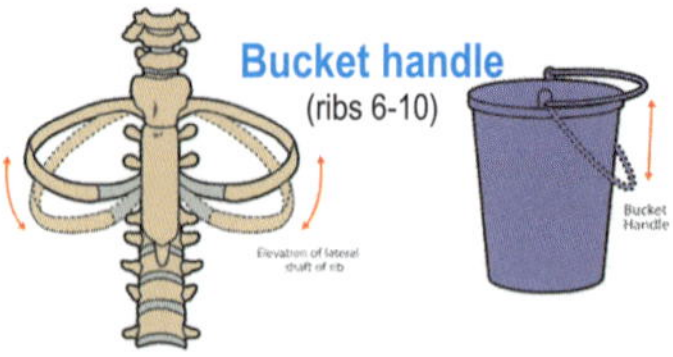

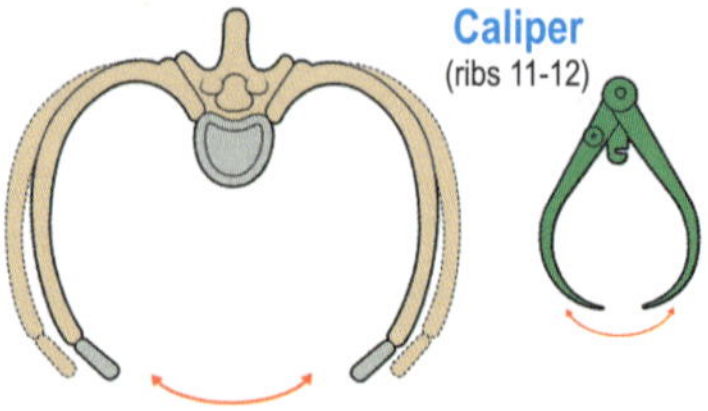

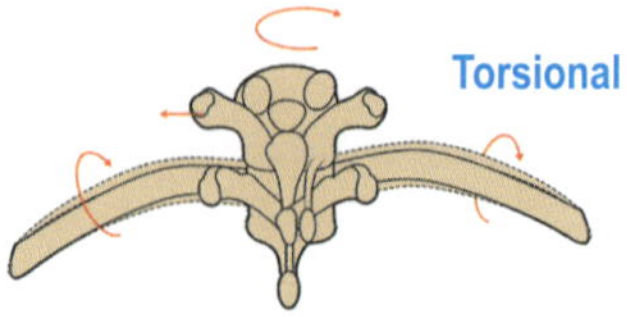

Thoracic & Torso

Heart-Lung & Abdominal Exam

☑ Check normal, circle & describe abnormal

CC & significant history: ______________________________

____

Temp: ________, Pulse: ______, Resp: ________, BP: L: ____/____, R: ____/____

Patient: ______________________ date: ________ (dd/mm/yr)

Insurance: ______________________

Date of birth: ______________________

Heart-Lung ☐ WNL

Observation

- ☐ Shape & symmetry, bony markings
- ☐ Spinal shape & curvature (kyphosis, lordosis, scoliosis)
- ☐ Skin: ______________________
- ☐ Effort of respiration (use of accessory muscles): ______________________
- ☐ Extremities: ______________________
  - ☐ Digital clubbing ______________________
  - ☐ Edema: ______________________
  - ☐ Cyanosis: ______________________
  - ☐ Trophic changes: ______________________

Lung Auscultation

- ☐ Wheeze (rhonchi): ______________________
- ☐ Crackles (rales): ______________________
- ☐ Basilar crackles: ______________________
- ☐ Crepitus: ______________________
- ☐ Stridor: ______________________

Heart Auscultation

- ☐ Point of maximal impulse: ______________________
- ☐ Carotid arteries: ______________________
- ☐ Abdominal aorta: ______________________

Specific valves

- ☐ Aortic: ______________________
- ☐ Pulmonic: ______________________
- ☐ Erb's point: ______________________
- ☐ Tricuspid: ______________________
- ☐ Mitral: ______________________

Sounds

- ☐ S1 ('lub'): ______________________
- ☐ S2 ('dup'): ______________________
- ☐ Bruit: ______________________
- ☐ Click: ______________________
- ☐ Other: ______________________

Percussion

- ☐ Resonant: ______________________
- ☐ Flat: ______________________
- ☐ Dull: ______________________
- ☐ Hyperresonant: ______________________

Palpation

- ☐ Spine/rib tenderness: ______________________
- ☐ Anterior chest wall: ______________________
- ☐ Thoracic excursion: ______________________
- ☐ Fremitus: ______________________
- ☐ Diaphramatic excursion: ______________________
- ☐ Tracheal palpation/deviation: ______________________
- ☐ Abdominal aorta: ______________________

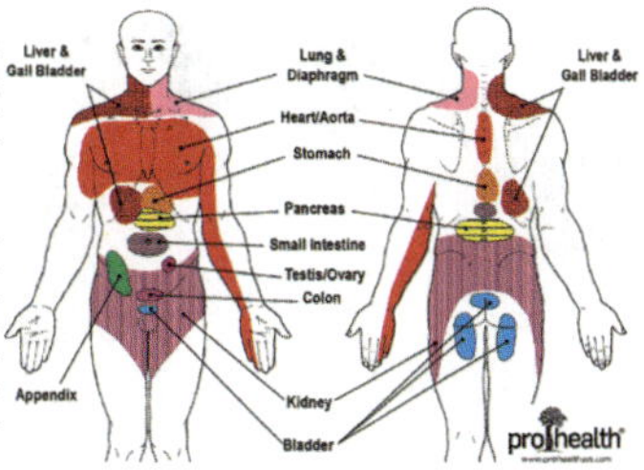

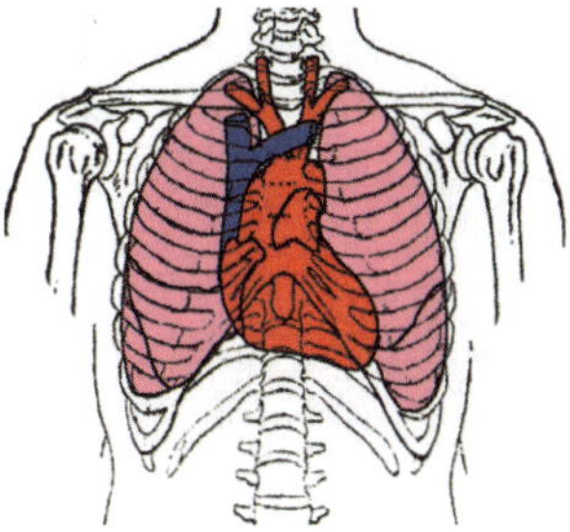

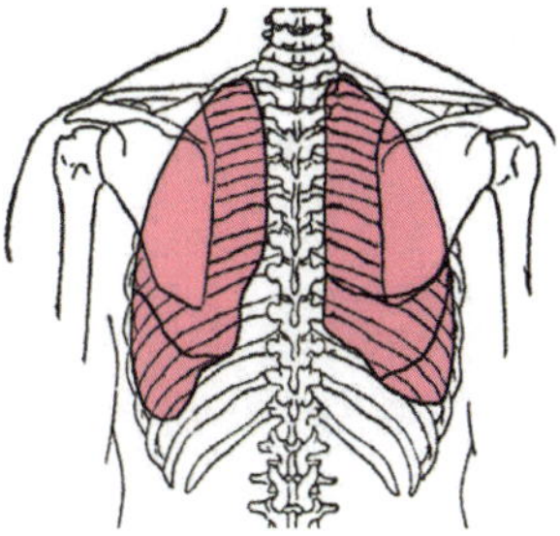

Abdomen ☐ WNL

Observation

- ☐ Skin: ______________________
- ☐ Symmetry/contour: ______________________
- ☐ Visible peristalsis: ______________________

Auscultation

- ☐ Upper left: ______________________
- ☐ Upper right: ______________________
- ☐ Lower right: ______________________
- ☐ Lower left: ______________________
- ☐ Vascular: ______________________
  - ☐ Aorta: ______________________
  - ☐ Renal: ______________________
  - ☐ Iliac: ______________________
  - ☐ Femoral: ______________________
- ☐ Bowel sounds: ______________________

Percussion

- ☐ Liver: ______________________
- ☐ Spleen: ______________________
- ☐ Murphy's punch: ______________________
- ☐ Percussion note: ______________________

Palpation (light then deep)

- ☐ Abdominal tone: ______________________
- ☐ Cutaneous hypersentitivity: ______________________
- ☐ Light palpation: ______________________
- ☐ Deep palpation: ______________________
- ☐ Inguinal lymphnodes: ______________________
- ☐ Other: ______________________

Hernia evaluation

- ☐ Umbilical: ______________________
- ☐ Inguinal direct: ______________________
- ☐ Inguinal indirect: ______________________
- ☐ Femoral: ______________________

Strength

- ☐ Resisted flexion: ______________________
- ☐ Reisisted L/R rotation: ______________________

Acute abdomen special tests

- ☐ Rigid abdomen: ______________________
- ☐ Rebound tenderness: ______________________
- ☐ Valsalva: ______________________
- ☐ Murphy's sign (GB): ______________________
- ☐ Murphy's punch (kidney): ______________________
- ☐ Carnett's test: ______________________
- ☐ Other: ______________________

Right Upper Quadrant

Liver
Gall bladder
Duodenum
Head of pancreas
Right adrenal gland
Portion of right kidney
Hepatic flexure of colon
Ascending colon
Transverse colon

Right Lower Quadrant

Lower pole of right kidney
Cecum & appendix
Portion of ascending colon
Ovary & salpinx
Uterus
Right spermatic cord
Right ureter

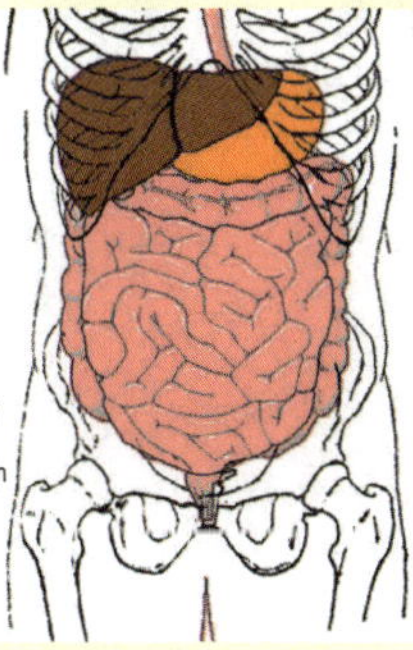

Left Upper Quadrant

Left lobe of liver
Spleen
Stomach
Body or pancreas
Left adrenal gland
Portion of left kidney
Splenic flexure of colon
Transverse colon
Descending colon

Left Lower Quadrant

Lower pole of left kidney
Sigmoid colon
Portion of descending colon
Ovary & salpinx
Uterus
Left spermatic cord
Left ureter

Signature: Date:

Full sized download & printing for personal & classroom use on website

Video demonstrations at:

prohealthsys.com

Compare bilaterally; prior to ROM the examiner makes an introduction statement:
"Try and move as far as possible, if any of the actions or movements are painful or uncomfortable please let me know, do not do any action you feel will cause you further injury."

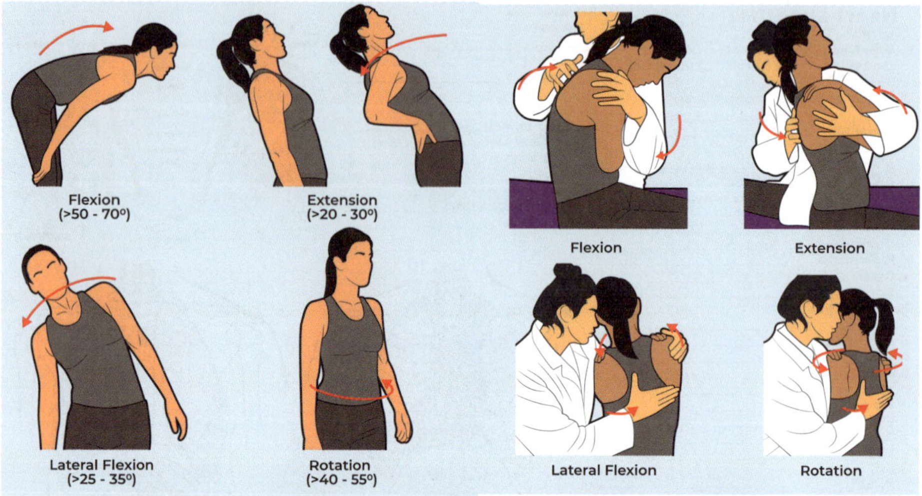

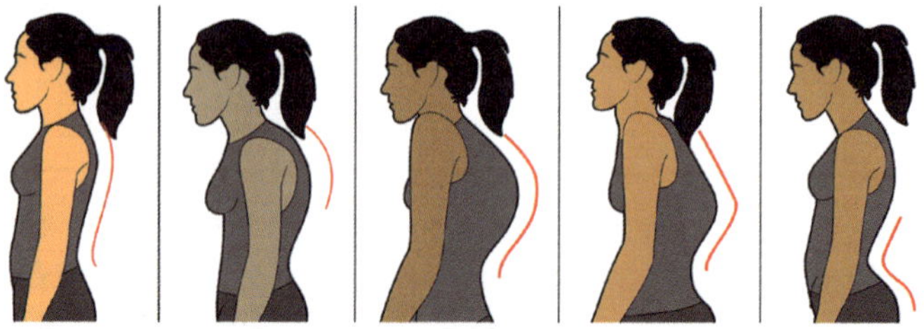

shape variations

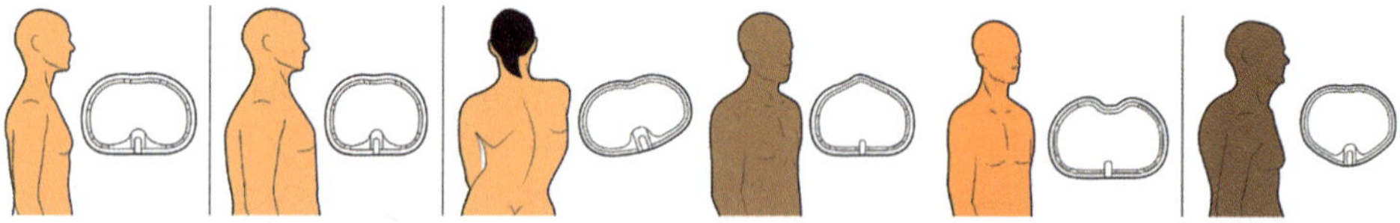

common surgical scars

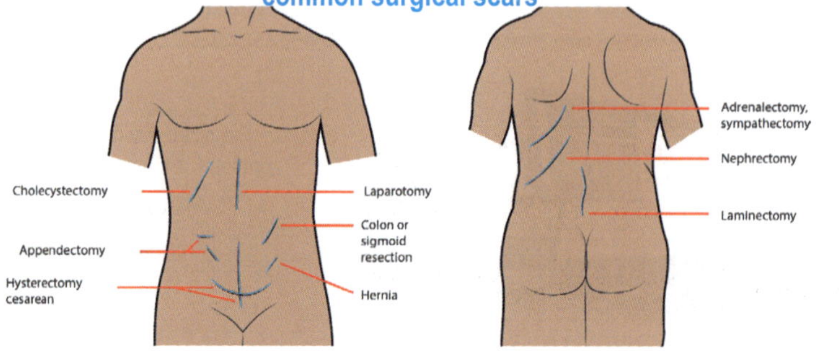

Chest Pain DDx

	Condition	History	Physical exam	Diagnostic tests
Cardiovascular	Angina pectoris	Substernal pressure Lasts 2-3 min, Exert/emotion Relieved: rest/nitroglycerine	Usually transient SSx Tachycardia, hypertension Systolic murmur	Stress ECG, Coronary arteriogram
Cardiovascular	Mycardial infarction	Chest pain or pressure, shortness of breath Pain into left neck & arm	Patient may be pale, sweating or anxious ↑ or irregular heart rate	ECG, PET scan exercise stress test Ultrasound
Cardiovascular	Mitral valve prolapse	Young F>M, non-exertional Unpredictable	Mid-systolic click Late systolic murmur	ECG
Chest wall	Rib fracture	Sharp, local pain following trauma or prolonged cough	Palpable crepitus Possible discoloration Pain with chest motion	x-ray
Chest wall	Rib sublux	Sharp local pain on near spine with inspiration	Palpatory tenderness & local myospasm	Joint play & passive ROM
Chest wall	Breast disorder	Tender mass, family history breast CA, large breasts Vague chest wall pain	Palpable, unilateral mass Non-supportive bra	Mammogram, biopsy
GI	Peptic ulcer	Burning, epigastric pain, ↑ by fasting, stress ↓ by food & antacids	Usually WNL	Barium swallow
GI	Biliary colic	Epigastric ache, nausea, vomiting, restlessness	↑ by fatty meals Usually WNL	Oral cholecysto-gram, ultrasound
Respiratory	Pleuritis	Sharp, lateral chest pain, Increased inspiratory effort Precipitated by cough	Possible: fever, dull percussion, bronchial breath sounds, friction rub	Chest x-ray, CBC
Respiratory	Bronchitis/ Asthma/ COPD	Vague recurrent chest pain Prolonged coughing Asthma/infection	Possible: rales, rhonchi, wheezing, ↑ with chest motion, cough, respiration	Chest x-ray

Other

Herpes Zoster (Hx: dermatomal pain, prolonged duration, PE: rash)
Biomechanical, Myofascial Trigger Points, Thoracic outlet syndrome

↑ = increase pain, ↓ = decrease pain

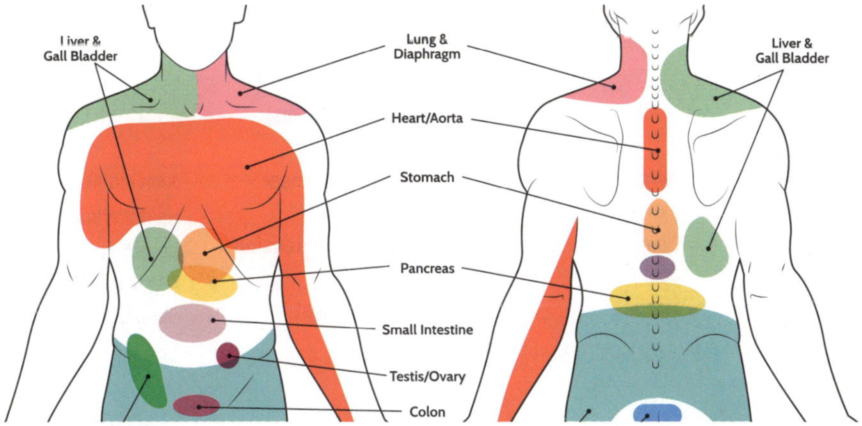

	Hx	SSx	Tx
Angina 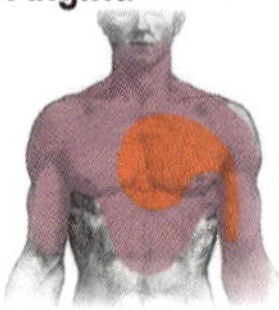	- History of coronary artery disease, hypertension, or stress - Triggered by exertion or emotional stress	- Chest pain radiating to jaw, arm, or neck - Pain ↓ with rest or nitroglycerin - Shortness of breath, nausea	- Rest immediate - Nitroglycerin or aspirin (per physician) - Lifestyle mods (stop smoking, diet, exercise)
Costo-chondritis 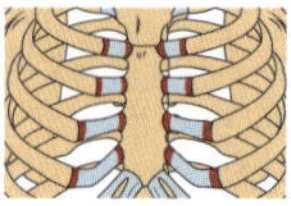	- Recent upper body strain, repetitive movements, or trauma (chest compression).	- Localized chest wall pain - Tenderness over costosternal joints - Pain ↑ with deep breaths	- Ice, METH - Postural correction - Stretching (pec stretches)
Heart Attack (Myocardial Infarction) 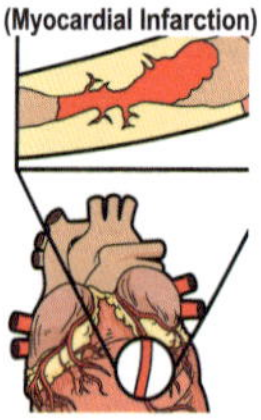	- Hypertension, smoking, or diabetes - Sudden intense stress or physical exertion	- Crushing chest pain radiating to arm, jaw, or neck - Shortness of breath, sweating, nausea - (+) ECG changes, ↑ cardiac enzymes	- Emergency (911) - Oxygen, aspirin, nitroglycerin as directed - Cardiac rehab. post-event
Kyphosis (Postural) 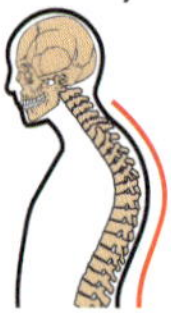	- Prolonged sitting or poor posture - Common in desk workers and adolescents	- Rounded upper back - Forward head posture - Pain & stiffness in thoracic spine	- Postural retraining - ExRx (rows, scapular retraction) - Foam roller
Scheuermann's Disease 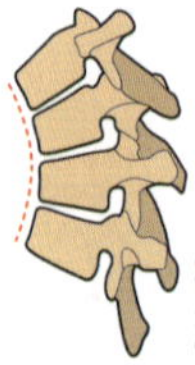	- Adolescent with progressive kyphosis - Family history of spinal deformities	- **Rigid thoracic kyphosis** - Tenderness over vertebrae - Pain with activity - Xray to confirm (3+ wedged segments)	- Bracing for severe cases - ExRx & flexibility exercises (spinal extension)
Thoracic Facet Syndrome 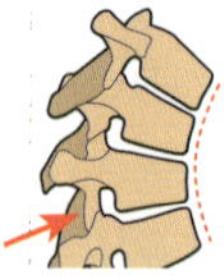	- Twisting or extension movements - Often sedentary or with poor posture	- Localized pain near spine - **Pain ↑ with extension & rotation** - (+) Kemp's Test	- Joint mobilize - Heat therapy - Stretching (cat-cow stretches) - Hang from a pull up bar

	Hx	SSx	Tx
Thoracic Outlet Syndrome (TOS) 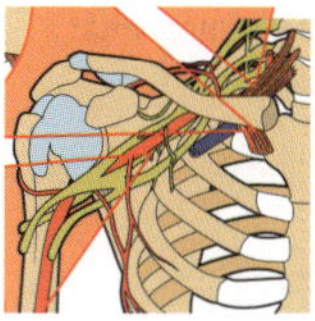	- Poor posture, repetitive overhead activity, carrying heavy loads	- Numbness, tingling in arm, weak grip, coldness in hands - **(+) Roo, Adson Costoclavicular maneuver**	- Postural correction - Neural mobilization - Strengthening, chin tucks
Rib Dysfunction 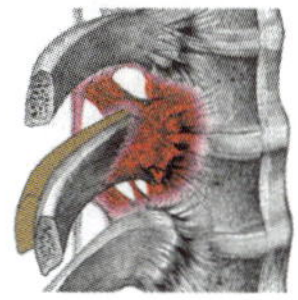	- Recent trauma, prolonged coughing, or poor posture	- **Sharp pain around costal joints** - **Pain ↑ with deep breaths** or movement - Tender to palpation	- Rib mobilization - Breathing exercises - Heat therapy
Scoliosis 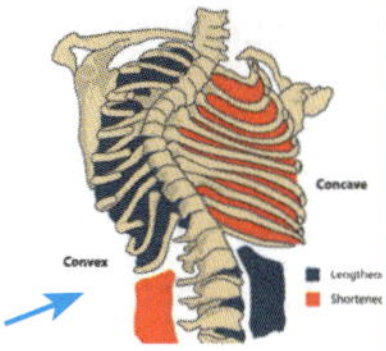	- **Adolescent females** more commonly affected - Family history of scoliosis	- Lateral curvature of the spine - **Uneven shoulders or hips** - **Rib hump on forward flexion** - Xray (cobbs angle)	- Bracing for moderate cases - Strengthening (core) - Postural correction

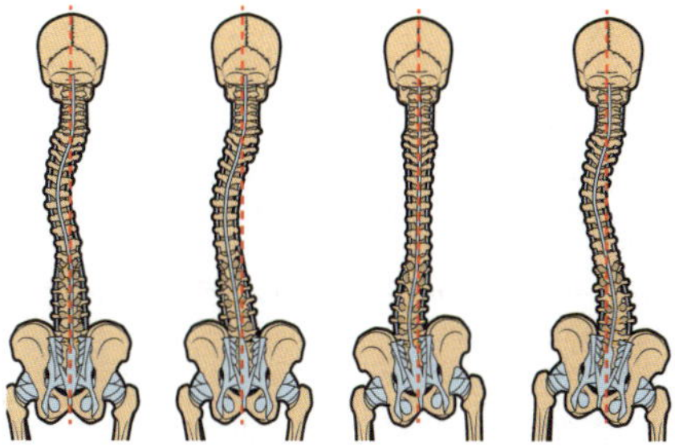
Thoracic Scoliosis | Thoracolumbar Scoliosis | Lumbar Scoliosis | Double Curve Scoliosis

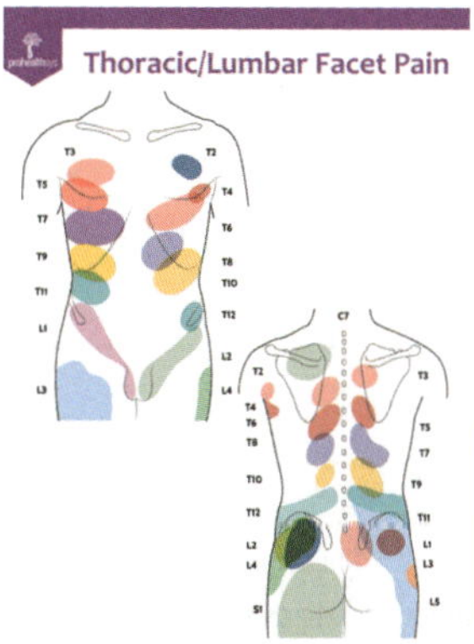

1. **Muscle primarily assists in thoracic extension?**
   a) Splenius cervicis
   b) Erector spinae
   c) Serratus anterior
   d) Rhomboid major
2. **Which ligament connects the costal cartilage of the ribs to the sternum?**
   a) Xiphisternal ligament
   b) Sternocostal ligament
   c) Costotransverse ligament
   d) Intercostal ligament
3. **Normal end feel for thoracic spine rotation?**
   a) Soft
   b) Empty
   c) Firm
   d) Hard
4. **Thoracic facet syndrome commonly presents with:**
   a) Pain along the intercostal spaces
   b) Numbness and tingling in the arm
   c) Localized pain with twisting or extension
   d) Sharp chest pain radiating to the jaw
5. **For managing thoracic outlet syndrome, which co-management strategy is most appropriate?**
   a) Cardiovascular rehabilitation
   b) Immediate surgical referral
   c) Rib mobilization techniques
   d) Postural retraining and strengthening exercises
6. **Which ribs are classified as floating ribs?**
   a) Ribs 11–12
   b) Ribs 1–7
   c) Ribs 8–10
   d) None
7. **The bucket handle rib motion is primarily seen in which ribs?**
   a) Ribs 11–12
   b) Ribs 6–10
   c) All ribs
   d) Ribs 1–5
8. **What is the primary function of the serratus posterior inferior muscle?**
   a) Stabilize the thoracic spine
   b) Rotate the thoracic spine
   c) Elevate the ribs during inspiration
   d) Depress the ribs during exhalation
9. **Test commonly used to assess rib dysfunction?**
   a) Adson's Test
   b) Compression Test
   c) Kemp's Test
   d) Phalen's Test
10. **What would a firm end feel indicate in thoracic lateral flexion?**
    a) Ligamentous restriction
    b) Joint capsule adhesions
    c) Muscle spasm
    d) Fracture
11. **Scoliosis is most commonly associated with:**
    a) Middle-aged individuals with postural kyphosis
    b) Adolescent males with a family history of rib fractures
    c) Adolescent females with uneven shoulder heights
    d) Elderly patients with osteoporosis
12. **In thoracic kyphosis due to poor posture, what treatment is recommended?**
    a) Postural correction exercises
    b) Manual rib mobilization
    c) Immediate bracing
    d) Ice and anti-inflammatory medication
13. **Rib dysfunction typically presents with:**
    a) Numbness in the arms and hands
    b) Burning pain in the thighs and calves
    c) Pain with twisting motions
    d) Pain with deep breathing or coughing
14. **Which muscle is primarily responsible for elevation of the thoracic ribs?**
    a) Iliocostalis
    b) Splenius cervicis
    c) Rhomboid minor
    d) Intercostal muscles
15. **What is a key characteristic of Scheuermann's?**
    a) Generalized thoracic stiffness with scoliosis
    b) Localized thoracic pain with extension
    c) Rounded thoracic kyphosis with wedged vertebrae
    d) Sharp thoracic pain radiating to the jaw
16. **Which test would be most appropriate to confirm thoracic outlet syndrome?**
    a) Straight Leg Raise
    b) Kemp's Test
    c) Neer's Test
    d) Roo's Test
17. **Costochondritis is most likely to cause pain:**
    a) With thoracic spine rotation
    b) Along the intercostal spaces
    c) In the upper back and shoulders
    d) At the sternocostal joints
18. **What muscle group is activated during the pump handle rib motion?**
    a) Splenius capitis
    b) Scalenes
    c) Rhomboid major
    d) Erector spinae
19. **What co-management technique is recommended for angina as a thoracic condition?**
    a) Emergency oxygen and aspirin administration
    b) Postural correction
    c) Rib mobilization
    d) Effleurage
20. **Hyperkyphosis in older adults is most commonly associated with:**
    a) Rib dysfunction
    b) Osteoporosis
    c) Scoliosis
    d) Postural habits

PHS Certification

1. b	5. d	9. b	13. d	17. d
2. b	6. a	10. a	14. d	18. b
3. c	7. b	11. c	15. c	19. a
4. c	8. d	12. a	16. d	20. b

Case Study 1

A 34-year-old office worker presents with numbness and tingling in the left arm, particularly when carrying a heavy bag or sitting with poor posture. Symptoms improve when they adjust their posture or stretch their neck. On examination, the Adson's and Roo's tests are positive.

Questions:

- What is the most likely **differential diagnosis** for this presentation?
- What treatment options, including **manual therapy** and **ergonomic changes**, would you recommend?
- How might workplace ergonomics and **daily habits** contribute to this condition, and what strategies could help prevent recurrence?

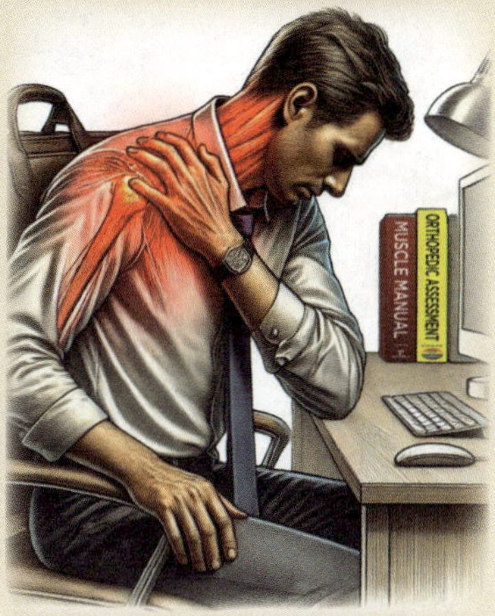

Case Study 2

A 50-year-old teacher reports sharp, localized chest pain that worsens with deep breaths and palpation near the sternum. The pain began after a vigorous cleaning session last week. ECG and other cardiac tests were normal, and the pain is reproducible on physical examination.

Questions:

- What is the most likely **differential diagnosis** for this patient's symptoms?
- What conservative **management options**, including manual therapy and home care, could alleviate this condition?
- How would you address patient concerns about the potential for cardiac issues, given the symptoms mimic heart-related pain?

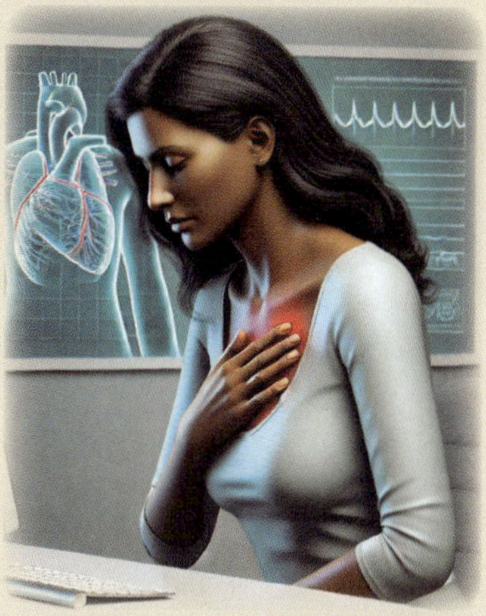

Case Study 3

A 68-year-old retired librarian has upper back stiffness and a hyperkyphotic rounded posture. They report mild pain and difficulty maintaining an upright posture while sitting or standing for long periods. The patient has no significant trauma history but has been sedentary for the past decade.

Questions:

- What is the most likely **differential diagnosis** for this condition?
- What interventions, including **posture training and physical therapy**, would be most beneficial?
- How might **psychosocial factors**, such as lifestyle and self-esteem, impact recovery and adherence to treatment?

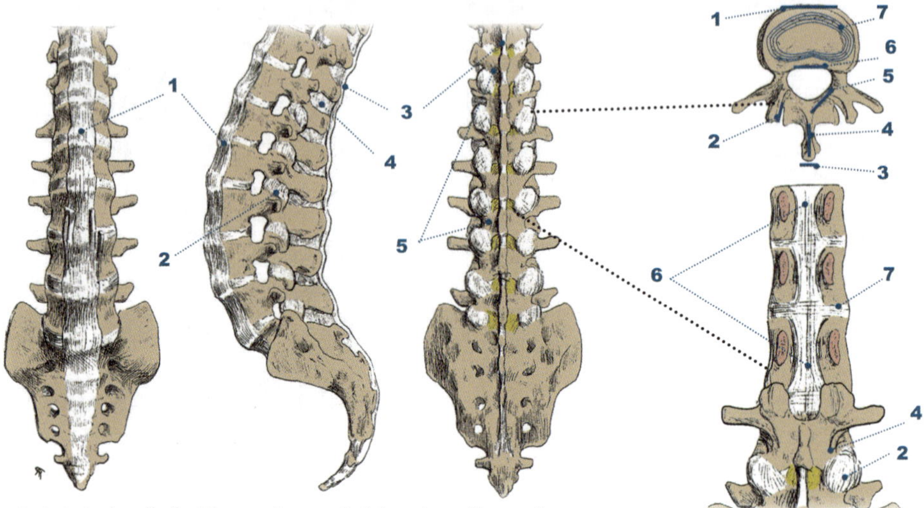

1. Anterior longitudinal ligament
2. Z-joint capsule
3. Supraspinous ligament
4. Interspinous ligament
5. Ligamentum flavum
6. Posterior longitudinal ligament
7. Annulus fibrosis (disc)

posterior view L1-L5 (pedicles have been cut to show posterior aspect of the lumbar vertebral bodies)

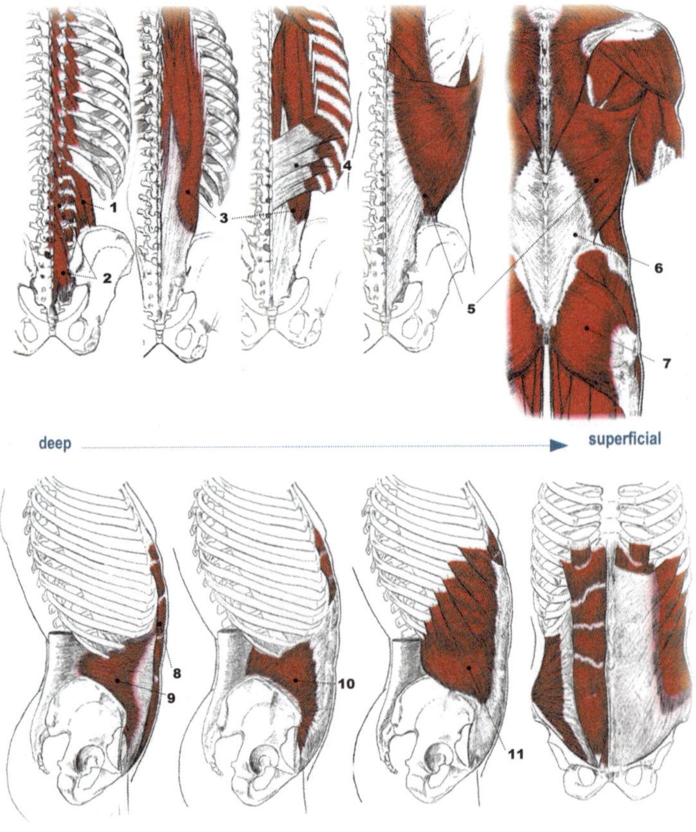

1. Quadratus lumborum
2. Multifidi lumborum
3. Erector spinae
4. Serratus posterior inferior
5. Latissimus dorsi
6. Thoracolumbar fascia
7. Gluteus maximus
8. Rectus abdominis
9. Transversus abdominis
10. Internal oblique
11. External oblique

Lumbopelvic Regional Exam

☑ Check normal, circle & describe abnormal

CC & significant history: ______________________

Patient: ______________ date: ________ (dd/mm/yr)
Insurance: ______________
Date of birth: ______________

Fracture screen (tuning fork, percussion, torsion test, 5-step test): □ WNL □ **Refer for X-ray:** ______________

Observation: □ WNL

Development: □ good, □ fair, □ poor
□ Posture: ______________
□ Skin (bruising, scars): ______________
□ Swelling: ______________
□ Asymmetry: ______________

Observation □ WNL	L	R
Antalgia		
Lordosis: hyper, normal, hypo		
Scoliosis		
Postural asymmetry		
Heel walk (L4)		
Toe raises, multiple (S1)		
Squat & rise		
Gait		

Palpation: □ WNL, □ pain (circle), □ spasm (s), □ edema (e), □ fibrotic (f), □ MFTP (x), □ ache (a), □ tingling (t)

Palpation	L	R
Abdomen		
Inguinal lymph nodes		
Skin temperature		
Pubic symphysis		
ASIS		
Iliac crest		
Paraspinal muscles		
Quadratus lumborum		
Sciatic notch		
PSIS		
Ischial tuberosities		
Hamstrings		
TFL		
Greater trochanter		

Palpation	L	R
Piriformis		
Sacrotuberous lig.		
Sacroiliac joint		
Sacrospinous lig.		
Gluteus maximus		
Gluteus medius		
Quadriceps		
Gastro-soleus		

Pulses (0-4)	L	R
Femoral pulse		
Tibial pulse		
Dorsal pedial		

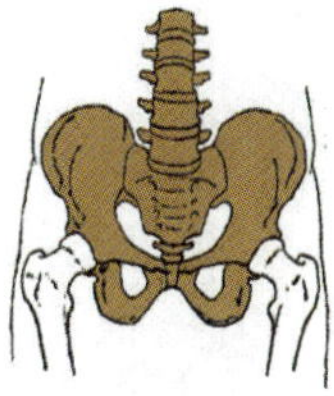

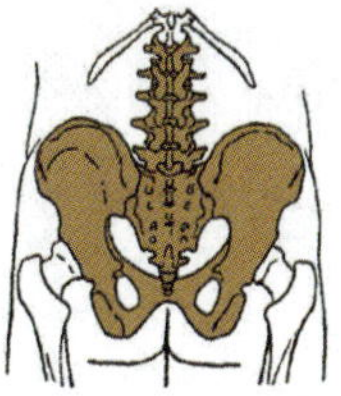

ROM & Joint Play: □ WNL

□ Pain at end ROM: ______________
□ Abnormal motion: ______________

Lumbar ROM	Active		Passive	
	L	R	L	R
Flexion (70°)				
Extension (30°)				
Lateral flexion (30°)				
Rotation (30°)				

Sacroiliac joint	L	R	L	R
Flex-ext (0-10°)				
Extern/intern (0-10°)				
Lumbopelvic rhythm				

Left	Joint Play	Right
	T12	
	L1	
	L2	
	L3	
	L4	
	L5	
	S1	
	SI	

Neurologic: □ WNL

Sensation, □ WNL	L	R
Light touch		
Sharp/dull		
Vibration		

Reflexes (0-5), □ WNL	L	R
Patellar (L4)		
Hamstring (L5)		
Achilles (S1)		
Babinski		

Motor (0-5), □ WNL	L	R
Abdomen (Beevor's sign)		
Resisted trunk rotation		
Resisted trunk lateral flexion		
Quadriceps (L2-L4)(femoral)		
Iliopsoas (L1-L3)(femoral)		
Tib. anterior (L4-L5)(deep f.)		
Ext. hal. long. (L4-S1)		
Flex. hallicus (L5-S2)		
Fibularis long. (L5-S1)		
Glut. max. (L5-S2)(inf. glut.)		
Hamstring (L4-S1)(sciatic)		
Glut. medius (L4-S1)		

Orthopedic: □ WNL

	L	R
Adam's sign		
Minor's sign		
Belt test		
Neri bowing		
Trendelenburg		
Lat. pelvic shift		
Valsalva		
Bechterew		
Slump test		
Deyerle		
Kemp's test		
Ober's		
Anvil test		
Allis' sign		

	L	R
SLR active/passive		
SLR maximal		
Bragard's		
Goldthwait's		
Patrick FABERE		
LaGuerre		
Hip circumduction		
SI compression		
SI distraction		
Thomas/Gaenslen		
Homan's		
Nachlas/Ely/Hibb		
Brudzinski's		
Leg length		

Additional procedures: □ WNL

□ Hip exam: ______________
□ Knee exam: ______________
□ Abdominal: ______________

The lumbar spine & soft tissues may refer pain to many regions including the lower thoracic spine, sacroiliac joint, thigh & leg, knee joint & foot. Pain referral down the leg may be secondary to a serious lumbar spine lesion (radiculopathy, trauma, cancer, infection, cauda equina) & careful consideration must be taken to differentially diagnose referred leg pain. Conversely, hip, sacroiliac, abdominal, & thoracic spine conditions may refer to the lumbar spine.

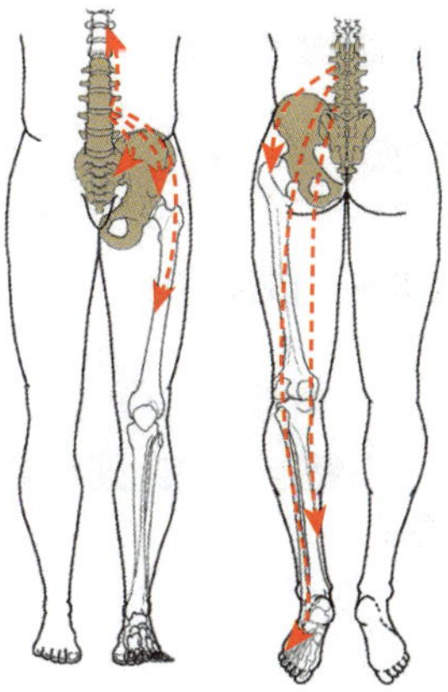

Compare bilaterally; prior to ROM examiner should make an introduction statement:
"Try and move as far as possible, if any of the actions or movements are painful or uncomfortable please let me know, do not do any action you feel will cause you further injury."

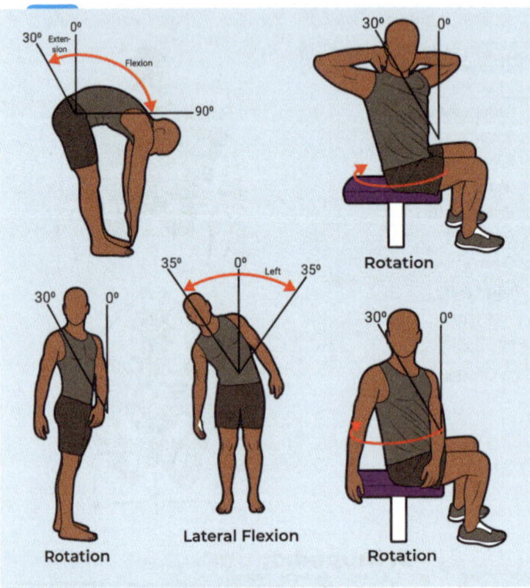

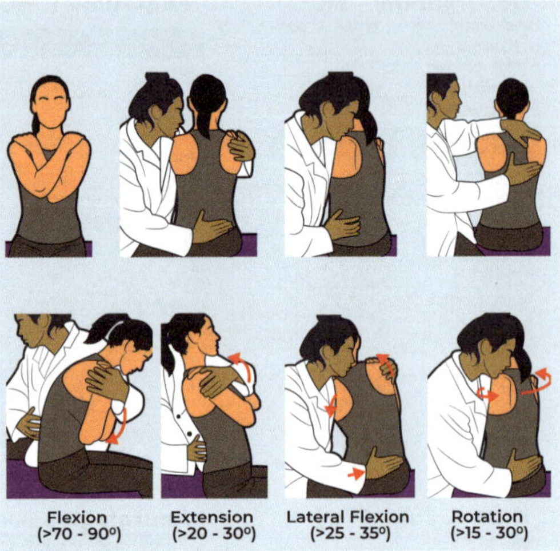

Muscle Testing

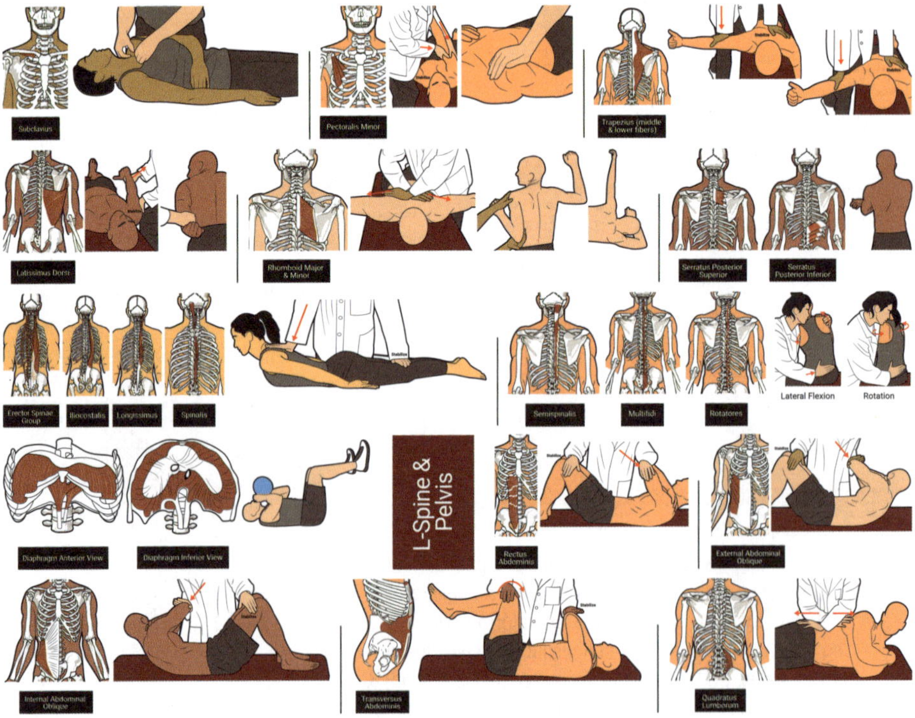

Lumbopelvic Rhythm

Realize the same muscles are involved in both flexion (eccentric) & extension (concentric) from a bent to standing position when upright

- When bending forward, a combined movement of the lumbar spine and the pelvis occurs
- Movement starts from the head and upper trunk
- The **pelvis shifts backwards** (counter-nutation) to keep the centre of gravity over the feet balancing the body
- For the first ~45° of flexion, the extensor muscles of the spine maintain the balance of the body (**eccentric stabilization**)

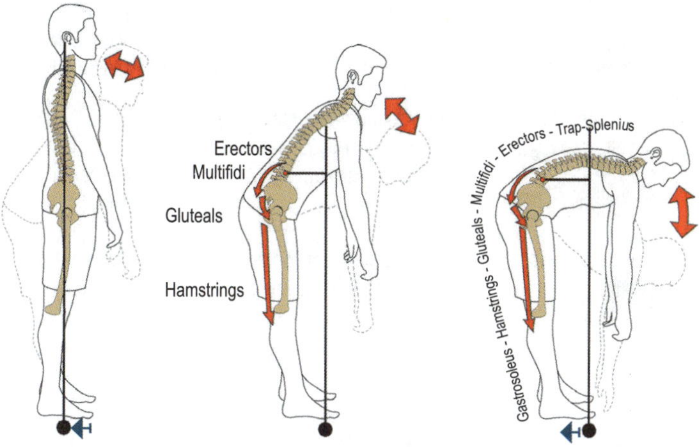

- The posterior ligaments become taut and the facet of the zygapophyseal joints come together (provides stability for the intervertebral joints)
- The pelvis will continue to rotate forward, until the muscles are at full length. **Range of motion depends on the flexibility of the back extensors, the ligaments/fasciae and hip extensors** (hamstrings, glutes, joint capsules)

- Ligaments tight include posterior IVD, PLL, Interspinous, supraspinous and ligamentum flavum & knee ligaments

The farther from midline the center of gravity, the greater force muscles (active stabilizers) and ligaments (passive stabilizers) have to resist (↑ injury risk).

'Keep your nose between your toes' when lifting to reduce strain on low back.

Disc Load (Pressure) with Activities

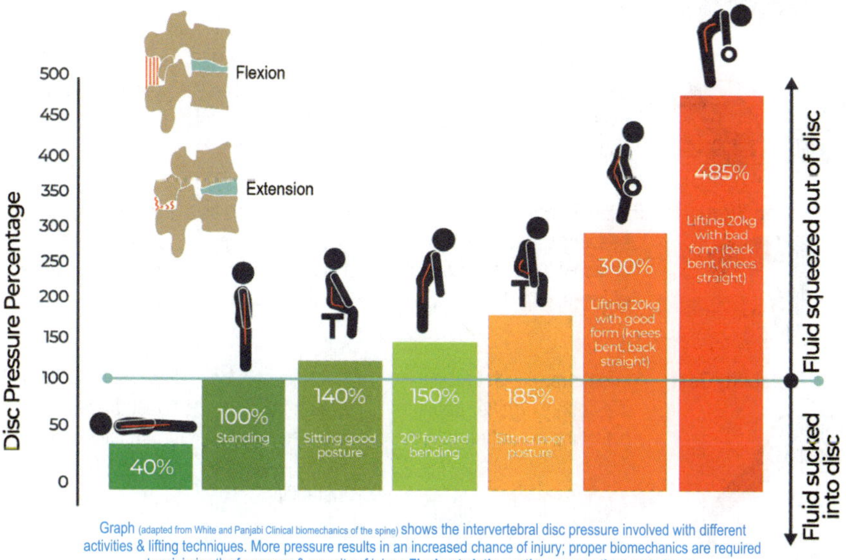

Graph (adapted from White and Panjabi Clinical biomechanics of the spine) shows the intervertebral disc pressure involved with different activities & lifting techniques. More pressure results in an increased chance of injury; proper biomechanics are required to minimize the frequency & severity of injury. **Flexing twisting actions cause the most stress.**

Test	Procedure	Interpretation	Clinical Notes
Active SLR Test 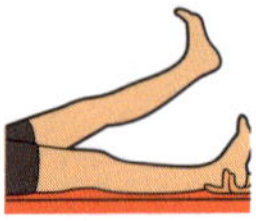	Patient raises one leg while keeping the other extended	(+) Pain or difficulty → Lumbar instability or SI joint dysfunction	Useful for assessing dynamic stability of the lumbar spine
Ant-Post Instability 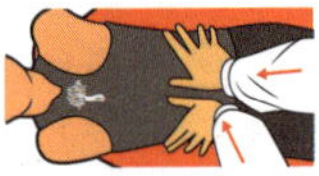	Pt prone, examiner stabilizes pelvis and applies anterior/ posterior pressure to the lumbar spine	(+) Pain or excess motion → Segmental instability	Focuses on identifying hypermobility or instability in specific segments
Bechterew's Test 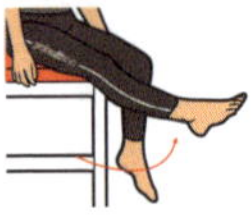	Patient seated, extends one leg at a time while keeping arms crossed	(+) Pain or inability → nerve root compression or radiculopathy	Combines with Slump Test for more comprehensive assessment
Belt Test 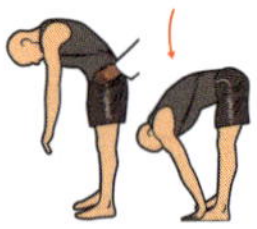	Patient stands and bends forward. Examiner stabilizes pelvis by holding iliac crests and sacrum	(+) Pain ↓ with stabilization → SI joint dysfunction	Differentiates between lumbar spine and SI joint involvement
Burn's Bench Test 	Patient kneels on a bench, bends forward, and attempts to touch the floor	(+) Inability to bend without pain → Non-organic or malingering pain	Useful for identifying functional disorders or malingering
Femoral Nerve Tract. 	Patient side-lying, hip extended, and knee flexed while examiner extends the hip further	(+) Pain in anterior thigh → Femoral nerve irritation	Targets upper lumbar nerve roots (L2–L4)
Kemp's Test 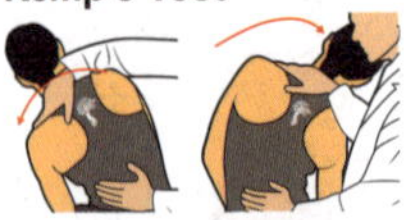	Patient seated, extends and rotates spine while examiner applies pressure on lumbar area	(+) Pain → Facet joint dysfunction or nerve root compression	Also used for identifying radicular symptoms
Neri Bowing Sign 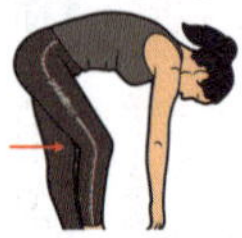	Patient bends forward, keeping knees straight. Observe for knee flexion on affected side	(+) Knee flexion or pain → Lumbar nerve root or sciatic irritation	Indicates tension or irritation in the sciatic nerve or associated lumbar structures
Prone Instability Test 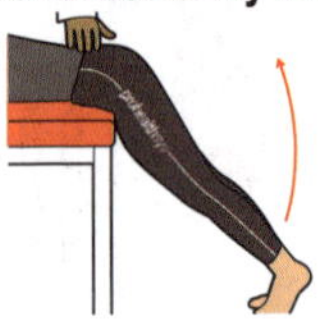	Patient prone with feet on the floor, examiner applies pressure to lumbar spine	(+) Pain when feet are on the floor, relieved when lifted → Lumbar instability	Indicates segmental instability in the lumbar spine

Test	Procedure	Interpretation	Clinical Notes
Schober's Test 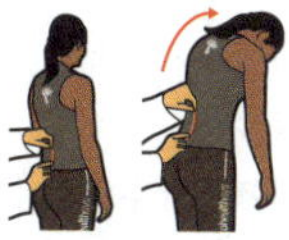	Mark lumbar spine landmarks, have patient bend forward, and measure change in distance	(+) Limited movement → Lumbar spine stiffness (**ankylosing spondylitis**)	A quantitative test for measuring lumbar spine flexion
Slump Test 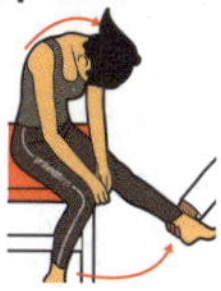	Patient seated, slumps forward with neck flexed and extends one leg at a time	(+) Pain or nerve symptoms → Sciatic nerve or lumbar root irritation	Combine with Bechterew's and Lasegue's (SLR) Test for more sensitivity
Sign of the Buttock 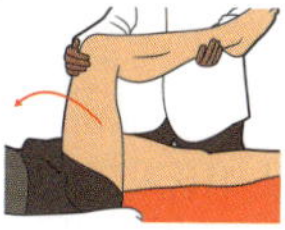	Perform SLR; if limited, flex the knee and attempt further hip flexion	(+) Hip flexion does not improve → Serious pathology (infection, tumor)	Indicates non-musculoskeletal pathology
Straight Leg Raise 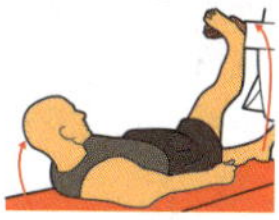	Patient supine, examiner raises one leg with knee extended	(+) Pain or radiating symptoms → Lumbar radiculopathy or sciatic nerve irritation	Gold standard for assessing sciatica or disc herniation aka - Lasegue's Test
Valsalva Maneuver 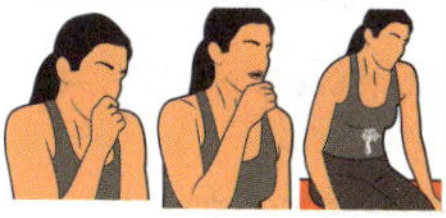	Patient bears down as if "straining at stool"	(+) Pain → Herniation, tumor, or IVF encroachment	Increases intrathecal and intra-abdominal pressure Dejerine Triad - cough sneeze strain

Lumbar & SI

Lumbar Pathology

	Hx	SSx	Tx
Ankylosing Spondylitis 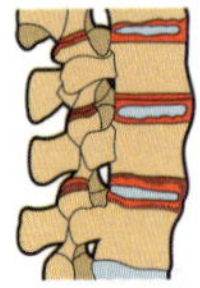	- **Onset 20–35 years**, more common men - Insidious low back pain, morning stiff, better w/ motion	- ↓ lumbar ROM (schober's test) - Pain & stiffness worse with prolonged rest - Starts in SI joint - **+ HLA-B^{27}**, ↑ ESR	- METH - ExRx (spinal ROM exercises) - Encourage regular movement - Rhumatologist consult
Cauda Equina Syndrome 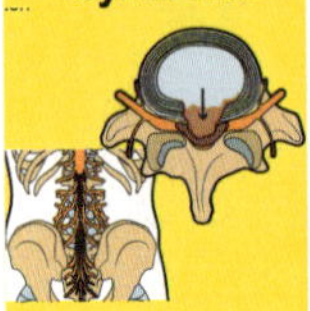	- Recent trauma, severe lumbar disc herniation, or spinal stenosis - **Medical emergency**	- **Bilateral** leg weakness, saddle anesthesia, bowel & bladder dysfunc - (+) Babinski reflex, ↓ DTRs	- Immediate surgical decompression - Pain management - Physical therapy post-surgery
Disc Herniation 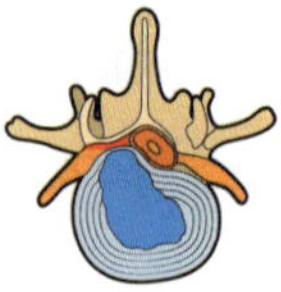	- Repetitive bending or heavy lifting - Common in younger adults	- Low back pain radiating to 1 leg - ↑ pain w/ flexion - **(+) Straight Leg Raise (SLR) test or Valsalva** (cough, sneeze, strain)	- Ice, METH - Extension or Flexion exercises - Avoid long sitting - Pool/hot tub time
Lumbar DJD (Osteoarthritis) 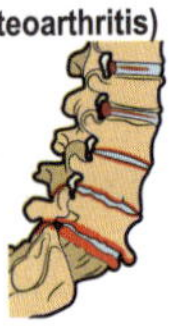	- Older adults with history of chronic LBP - Worse in morn, improves with activity	- Localized lumbar stiffness - Crepitus w/ motion - ↓ lumbar ROM - Normal age related change	- METH - ROM exercises (lumbar side bends) - Aquatic therapy
Lumbar Facet Syndrome 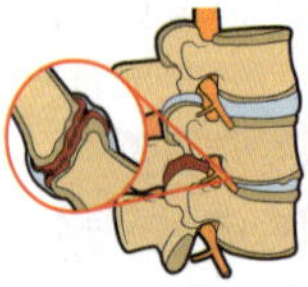	- Repetitive twist or extension movements - Sedentary individuals or older adults - May follow acute trauma	- Localized low back pain - **Pain ↑ with extension** & rotation - **(+) Kemp's Test**	- Joint mobilization - Heat therapy - Core strength (bird dog, planks, wood choppers)
Lumbar Joint Dysfunction 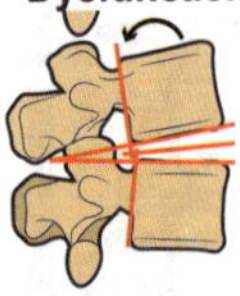	- History of twisting or repetitive strain - Often seen in sedentary individuals	- Localized pain near spine - Pain with AROM & PROM - **(+) Joint Play Test**	- Joint mobilization - ExRx (cat-cow stretches) - Postural retraining

	Hx	SSx	Tx
Lumbar Sprain/Strain 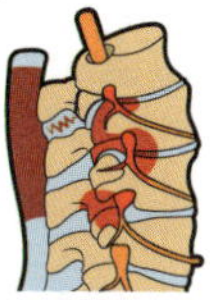	- **Sudden trauma** or overuse injury - Common in athletes or after heavy lifting	- **Localized lumbar pain** - Pain with active or resisted movements - **No neuro**	- Ice, heat application - Stretching (hamstring stretches) - Gradual ExRx
Piriformis Syndrome 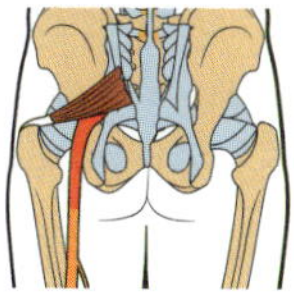	- **Prolonged sitting, trauma, or overuse** - May follow repetitive hip flexion activities	- Pain in buttocks, may radiate down thigh - Worse with sitting - (+) Piriformis Test	- Stretching (figure-4 stretch) - Postural correction - Avoid prolonged sitting
Sacroiliac Joint Dysfunction 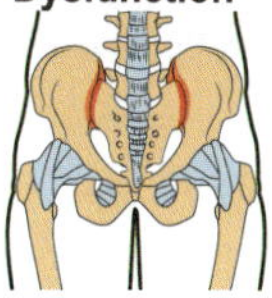	- Pregnancy, prolonged sitting, or repetitive impact activities - Often seen in active adults	- **Localized pain over SI joint** - Pain ↑ with stairs or prolonged standing - (+) FABER Test	- SI joint mobilization - Stretching (hip flexor stretches) - Core strengthen - SI belt
Spinal Stenosis 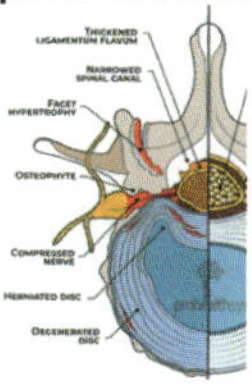	- Common in older adults - History of chronic low back pain	- **Pain ↑ w/ stand or walking** - **Pain ↓ with flexion** (shopping cart sign) - (+) Two-Stage Treadmill Test	- **Flexion-based exercises** (child's pose) - METH - Aquatic therapy
Spondylolisthesis 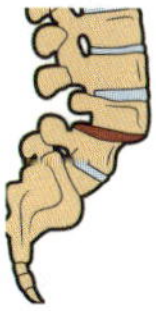	- Repetitive extension activities (rowing, gymnastics) - Common in younger athletes	- Low back pain with hyperlordosis - **Step-off deformity** palpable - Hypertonic tissue - (+) Stork Test	- Core ExRx (plank variation) - Postural correction - Avoid excessive extension

Lumbar & SI

Lumbar Quiz

1. What muscle is primarily responsible for lumbar spine extension?
a) Quadratus lumborum
b) Rectus abdominis
c) Transversus abdominis
d) Erector spinae

2. What ligament is the strongest spinal stabilizer?
a) Anterior longitudinal ligament
b) Ligamentum flavum
c) Annulus fibrosus
d) Supraspinous ligament

3. What is the normal end feel for lumbar flexion?
a) Hard
b) Firm
c) Soft
d) Empty

4. Pain down the leg, accompanied by a positive Straight Leg Raise test, indicates which condition?
a) Lumbar DJD
b) Piriformis syndrome
c) Disc herniation
d) Spinal stenosis

5. In managing lumbar DJD, which co-management strategy is recommended?
a) Surgical decompression
b) Heat therapy & aquatic exercises
c) NSAIDs with complete rest
d) Lumbar immobilization braces

6. Which muscle assists in stabilizing the lumbar spine during trunk movements?
a) Serratus posterior inferior
b) Multifidus
c) External oblique
d) Gluteus maximus

7. What is the primary function of the anterior longitudinal ligament in the lumbar spine?
a) Limit extension
b) Resist flexion
c) Support rotational movement
d) Connect adjacent vertebral arches

8. Expected end feel during lumbar rotation?
a) Soft
b) Firm
c) Hard
d) Empty

9. A patient with sharp, localized low back pain after lifting heavy objects most likely suffers from:
a) Ankylosing spondylitis
b) Lumbar sprain/strain
c) Spondylolisthesis
d) Facet syndrome

10. For managing lumbar facet syndrome, which co-management approach is most suitable?
a) Lumbar stabilization exercises & postural retraining
b) Aggressive joint mobilization
c) Bed rest for three weeks
d) Heat application with corticosteroid injections

11. Which test can help confirm disc herniation in a patient with radiating leg pain?
a) Straight Leg Raise test + Valslava
b) FABER test
c) Thomas test
d) Straight Leg Raise test

12. Function of posterior longitudinal ligament?
a) Support anterior vertebral stability
b) Prevent disc herniation
c) Limit hyperextension of the spine
d) Allow free vertebral motion

13. Pain worsened by standing or walking but relieved by sitting often suggests:
a) Lumbar DJD
b) Spinal stenosis
c) Facet syndrome
d) Spondylolisthesis

14. Which muscle group is critical for core stability in lumbar injury prevention?
a) Latissimus dorsi
b) Abdominals
c) Hamstrings
d) Gluteals

15. What biomechanical factor commonly contributes to lumbar facet syndrome?
a) Excessive lumbar extension
b) Poor thoracic mobility
c) Weak pelvic floor muscles
d) Hyperkyphosis

16. A positive FABER test is most indicative of:
a) Sacroiliac joint dysfunction
b) Lumbar disc herniation
c) Hip osteoarthritis
d) Ankylosing spondylitis

17. Which exercise is best suited for lumbar joint stabilization?
a) Side planks
b) Hamstring curls
c) Jumping lunges
d) Heavy squats

18. Which special test differentiates discogenic pain from facet syndrome?
a) Straight Leg Raise
b) Kemp's Test
c) Brudzinski's Test
d) Trendelenburg test

19. Postural corrections are most beneficial in managing:
a) Spinal stenosis
b) Sacroiliac joint dysfunction
c) Spondylolisthesis
d) Piriformis syndrome

20. Lumbar radiculopathy commonly results from which pathology?
a) Muscle strain
b) Disc herniation
c) Facet syndrome
d) Lumbar DJD

PHS Certification

Get certification badges for answering questions

1. d	5. b	9. b	13. b	17. a
2. c	6. b	10. a	14. b	18. b
3. b	7. a	11. a	15. a	19. c
4. c	8. b	12. b	16. a	20. b

Case Study 1

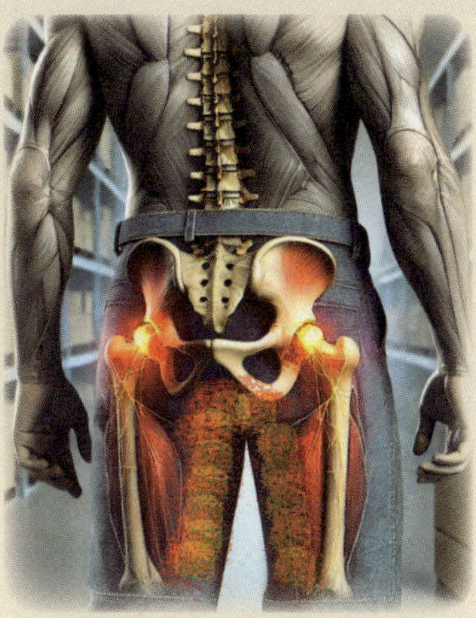

A 45-year-old warehouse worker presents with severe low back pain, difficulty urinating, and numbness in the inner thighs and perineal area over the past week. The pain radiates down both legs, accompanied by weakness and an unsteady gait. They report worsening symptoms after a heavy lifting incident two weeks ago.

Questions:

- What is the most likely **differential diagnosis** for this presentation?
- What are the immediate **management steps** and treatment options for this condition?
- How might the patient's **occupation and delay in seeking care** contribute to their presentation, and what can be done to prevent future occurrences?

Case Study 2

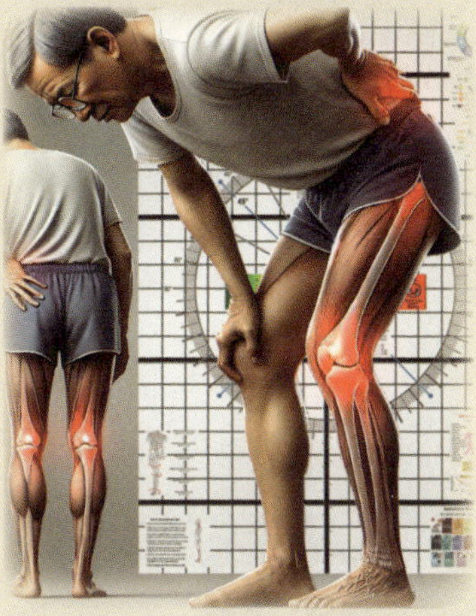

A 70-year-old retired teacher complains of chronic low back pain and bilateral leg discomfort that worsens when standing or walking for extended periods. They describe a burning sensation in both thighs and calves that improves with sitting or leaning forward. They have a history of degenerative arthritis but no recent trauma. Two-Stage Treadmill Test indicates reduced walking endurance with upright posture.

Questions:

- What is the most likely **differential diagnosis** for this presentation?
- What **treatment plan**, including manual therapy, exercise, and postural adjustments, would you propose?
- How could this patient's reduced mobility and fear of activity impact their **recovery**, and what strategies could address these issues?

Case Study 3

A 29-year-old construction worker reports acute lower back pain after lifting a heavy object with improper technique two days ago. The pain is localized to the lower lumbar region and worsens with movement, particularly bending forward or twisting. The patient denies any radiating pain, numbness, or tingling. Palpation reveals tenderness in the paraspinal muscles and limited range of motion due to pain.

Questions:

- What is the most likely **differential diagnosis** for this presentation?
- What **treatment options**, including manual therapy, exercise, and activity modifications, would you recommend?
- How could the patient's **physical workload and lifting techniques** contribute to this condition, and what preventative measures might be implemented?

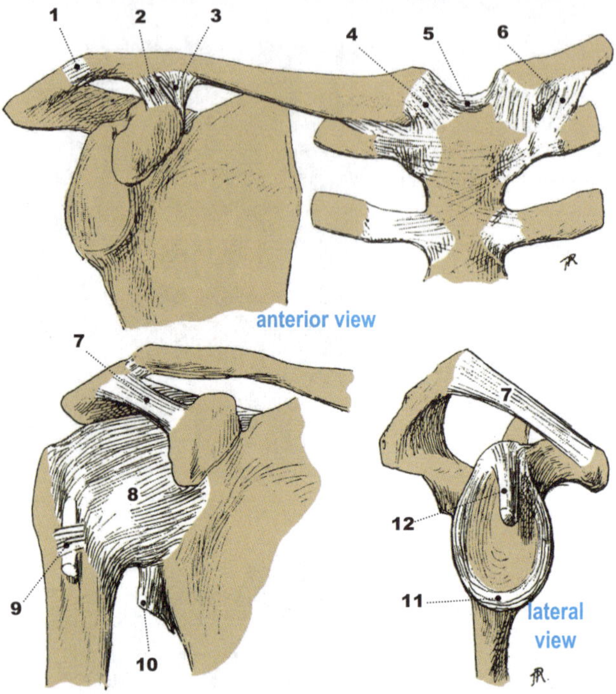

1. **Acromioclavicular (AC) joint**

Coracoclavicular ligaments

2. Trapezoid ligament
3. Conoid ligament

Sternoclavicular (SC) joint

4. Anterior SC ligament
5. Interclavicular ligament
6. Costoclavicular ligament

Glenohumeral (GH) joint

7. Coracoacromial ligament
8. GH ligaments (joint capsule)
9. Transverse humeral ligament
10. Triceps brachii long head tendon
11. Glenoid labrum
12. Biceps long head tendon

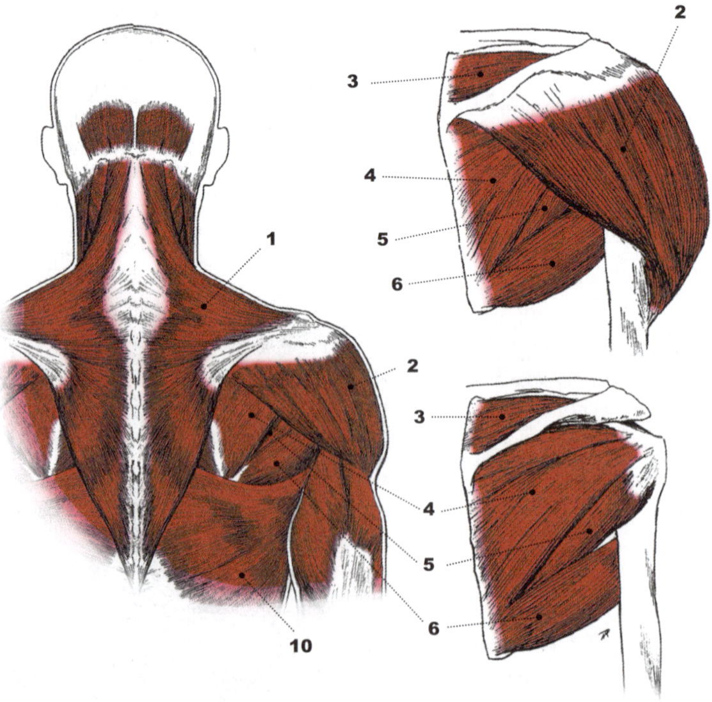

1. Trapezius
2. Deltoid
3. Supraspinatus
4. Infraspinatus
5. Teres minor
6. Teres major
7. Subscapularis
8. Serratus anterior
9. Pectoralis major
10. Latissimus dorsi

Shoulder Regional Examination

☑ Check normal, circle & describe abnormal

CC & significant history: ______________________

Patient: ______________________ date: ______ (dd/mm/yr)
Insurance: ______________________
Date of birth: ______________________ M/F

Fracture screen (tuning fork, percussion, torsion test, ultrasound): □ **WNL** □ **Refer for X-ray** **Pulses** (bilateral): □ **WNL** ______________

Inspection: □ WNL

Development: □ good, □ fair, □ poor
□ Posture: ______________
□ Skin (bruising, scars): ______________
□ Asymmetry: ______________

Observation □ WNL	L	R
Head tilt		
Head rotation		
Shoulder high		
Scapula		
Scapula winging		
Shoulder rounded		
Scapula rotated medial		
Scapula rotated lateral		
Humerus internally rotated		
Humerus externally rotated		
GH sulcus sign		
AC step defect		

Palpation: □ WNL, texture, tenderness, pain referral

Palpation	L	R
Middle trapezius		
Lower trapezius		
Rhomboids		
Thoracic spine		
Ribs 1-9 posterior		
Levator scapulae		
Upper trapezius		
Scalenes		
Thoracic outlet		
Cervical spine		
Supraspinatus		
AC joint		
Infraspinatus		
Teres minor		
AC step defect		
Rotator cuff post.		

Palpation	L	R
Rotator cuff sup.		
Rotator cuff ant.		
Teres major		
Latissimus dorsi		
Subscapularis		
Serratus anterior		
Triceps brachii		
Deltoid		
Deltoid tuberosity		
Pectoralis minor		
Coracoid process		
Coracobrachialis		
Biceps brachii		
Bicipital groove		
Pectoralis major		
SC joint		

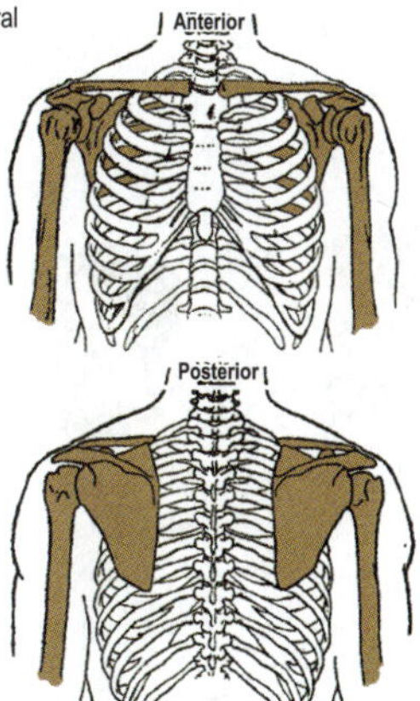

ROM & Joint Play: □ WNL

□ Painful arc: ______________
□ Pain at end ROM: ______________
□ Abnormal motion: ______________

ROM	Active L	Active R	Passive L	Passive R
Flexion (180°)				
Extension (50°)				
Abduction (180°)				
Adduction (35°)				
Internal rotation (90°)				
External rotation (80°)				
Horizontal abd. (30°)				
Horizontal add. (130°)				
Scapulocostal rhythm				

Joint Play	L	R	Comments
Scapula			
Glenohumeral			
Scapulocostal			
AC joint			
SC joint			

Neurologic: □ WNL

Reflexes (0-5), □ WNL	L	R
Biceps (C5)		
Brachioradialis (C6)		
Triceps (C7)		
General grip strength		

Motor (0-5), □ WNL	L	R
Pec major clavicular (C6-C8)		
Pec major sternal (C7-T1)		
Latissimus dorsi (C6-C8)		
Subscapularis (C5-C7)		
Supraspinatus (C4-C6)		
Infraspinatus/teres minor (C4-C6)		
Serratus anterior (C5-C7)		
Biceps brachii (C5-C6)		
Triceps brachii (C6-C8)		
Deltoid (anterior) (C5-C6)		
Deltoid (middle) (C5-C6)		
Deltoid (posterior) (C5-C6)		
Pectoralis minor (C8-T1)		
Teres major (C6-C7)		
Rhomboids (C4-C5)		
Trapezius (lower) (C3-C4)		
Trapezius (middle) (C3-C4)		
Trapezius (upper) (CN IX)		
Levator scapulae (C4-C5)		

*General sensation is done through palpation

Orthopedic: □ WNL

Screening	L	R
Apley superior		
Apley inferior		
Codman arm drop		
Dugas		

Impingement	L	R
Hawkins-Kennedy		
Impingement sign		
Painful arc		
Passive Neer's		

Bicep tendonitis	L	R
Yergason's		
Speed's		
Bicipital instab. test		
Empty can		

Labral tear	L	R
Hyperabduction		
Clunk		
Crank		
Obrien's		

Instability	L	R
Anterior apprehen.		
Posterior drawer		
Load & shift		
Faegan's		

Other	L	R

DDx:

Signature: Date:

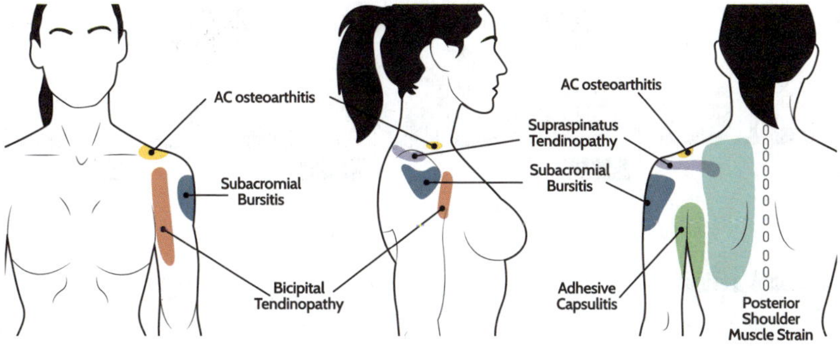

Compare bilaterally, examiner should make an introduction statement:
"Try to move as far as possible, if any of the actions or movements are painful or uncomfortable please let me know. Do not do any action you feel will cause you further injury."

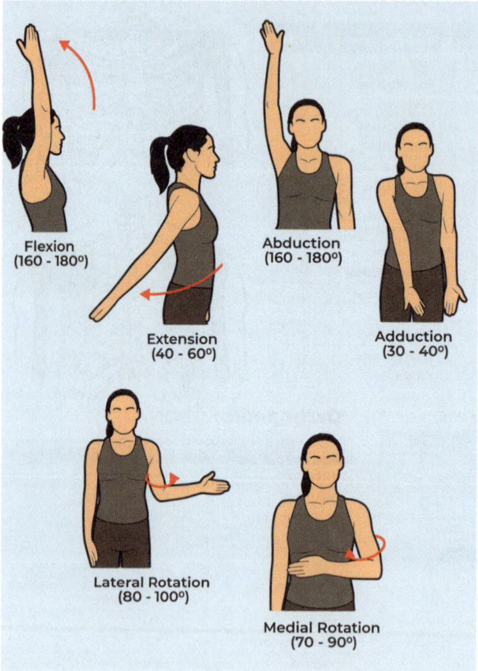

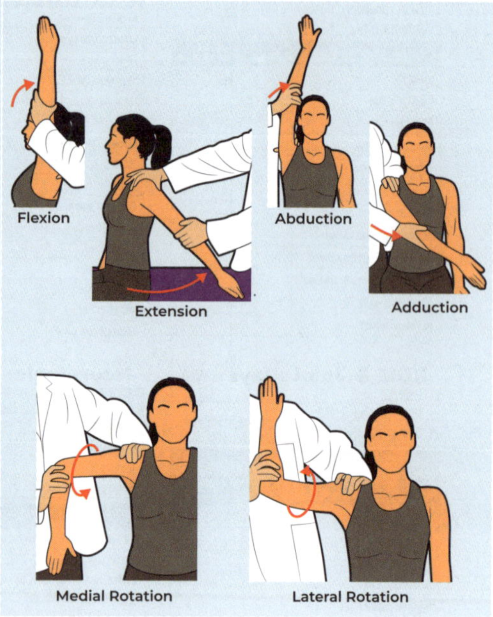

Muscle Testing

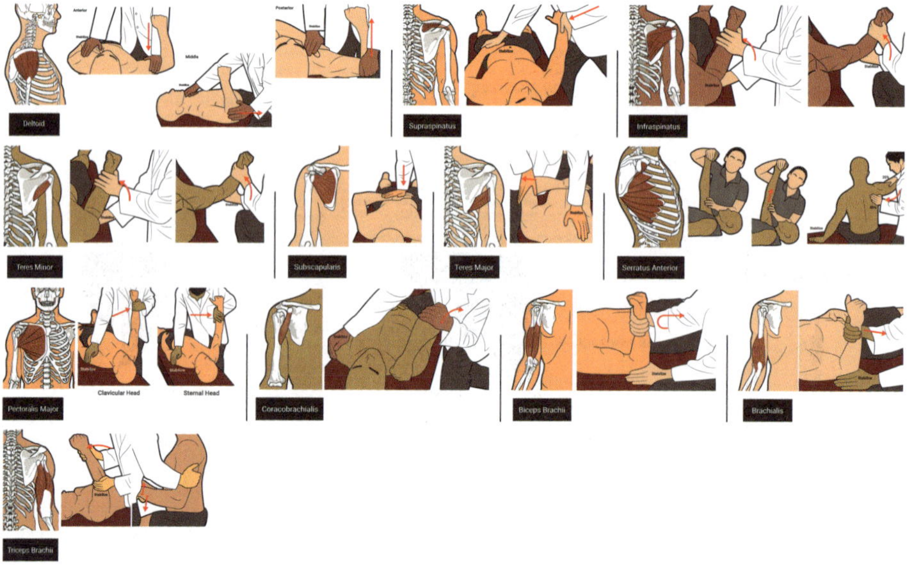

PHS PROFESSIONAL HEALTH SYSTEMS

Prepared for: ____________________

Prepared by: ____________________

Purpose of program: ____________________

Rotator Cuff & Shoulder Exercises

Recover Faster & Prevent Injury - After an injury or surgery, exercise, stretch and strengthen speed recovery and reduce future risks. **Regular activity improves mood, healing times, and slows aging.**

Warm-Up - Start with 5–10 minutes of low-impact activity like walking or biking.

Ask Questions
If unsure about an exercise or routine, consult your doctor, therapist, or trainer.

Strengthen - To build & stabilize joints, relieve pain, and prevent further injuries.

Stretch - to restore motion, reduce soreness, and prevent injuries.

prohealthsys PROFESSIONAL HEALTH SYSTEMS

Prescription (your doctor, therapist or trainer will circle desired exercises above and give appropriate directions on how to perform)

________ reps, ________ sets, ________ seconds to hold, ________ times/day or week

1000+ exercises on prohealthsys wall posters - body weight, kettle bell, foam roller, resistance bands, stretching strap, yoga, yoga block, suspension gym, staff, resistance bands.

"We've got your back."

By Dr. Nikita Vizniak. prohealthsys.com

PHS PROFESSIONAL HEALTH SYSTEMS

Prepared for: ____________________

Prepared by: ____________________

Purpose of program: ____________________

Rotator Cuff & Shoulder Stretches

Recover Faster & Prevent Injury - After an injury or surgery, exercise, stretch and strengthen speed recovery and reduce future risks. **Regular activity improves mood, healing times, and slows aging.**

Warm-Up - Start with 5–10 minutes of low-impact activity like walking or biking.

Ask Questions
If unsure about an exercise or routine, consult your doctor, therapist, or trainer.

Strengthen - To build & stabilize joints, relieve pain, and prevent further injuries.

Stretch - to restore motion, reduce soreness, and prevent injuries.

prohealthsys PROFESSIONAL HEALTH SYSTEMS

Prescription (your doctor, therapist or trainer will circle desired exercises above and give appropriate directions on how to perform)

________ reps, ________ sets, ________ seconds to hold, ________ times/day or week

1000+ exercises on prohealthsys wall posters - body weight, kettle bell, foam roller, resistance bands, stretching strap, yoga, yoga block, suspension gym, staff, resistance bands.

"We've got your back."

By Dr. Nikita Vizniak. prohealthsys.com

Trigger Points

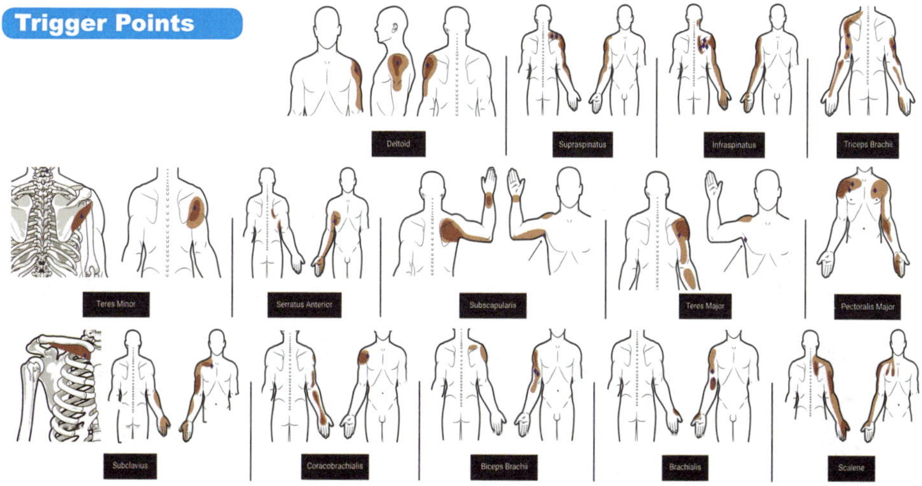

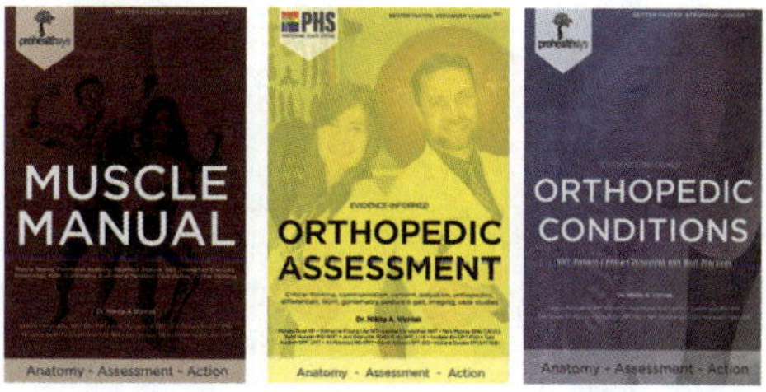

Shoulder Special Tests

Test	Procedure	Interpretation	Clinical Notes
Anterior Apprehen. 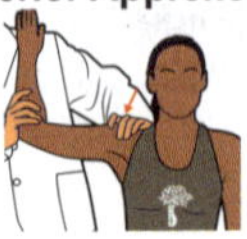	Patient supine; shoulder is abducted and externally rotated while observing for apprehension	(+) Apprehension → anterior instability or labral tear	Often combined with the Relocation Test
Clunk Test 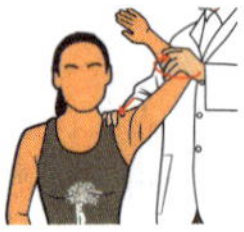	Examiner rotates humerus externally with anterior pressure on humeral head	(+) Pain or crepitus → labral tear or instability	Similar to the Anterior Apprehension Test
Crank Test 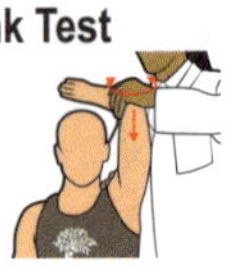	Examiner compresses and rotates humerus internally and externally in abduction	(+) Pain or grinding → labral tear or arthritis	A "scour test" for the GH joint.
Empty Can Test 	Patient abducts arm in scaption plane, internally rotates (thumb down), and resists pressure	(+) Pain or weakness → supraspinatus pathology	Alternative to Full Can Test
Full Can Test 	Same as Empty Can, but palm is up	(+) Pain or weakness → supraspinatus or suprascapular nerve pathology	Less painful alternative to Empty Can Test
Hawkins-Kennedy 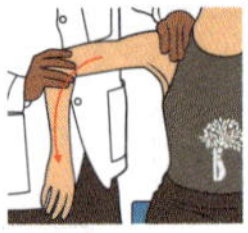	Patient seated; examiner flexes shoulder to 90° and applies internal rotation	(+) Pain → impingement or rotator cuff tear	Part of a cluster for impingement syndrome diagnosis
Lift-off Test 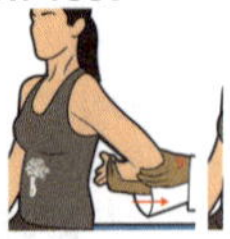	Patient places hand on lower back and attempts to lift it off	(+) Inability to lift → subscapularis tear or weakness	Belly Press Test may be used as an alternative for patients with limited motion
Load & Shift Test 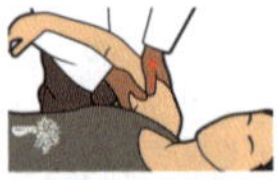	Examiner applies anterior and posterior pressure to humeral head in neutral position	(+) Excessive motion → GH instability or labral tear	Ensure shoulder muscles are relaxed to avoid false negatives
Neer's Test 	Patient seated; examiner passively elevates the arm while internally rotating it	(+) Pain → subacromial impingement or bursitis	Use to identify impingement syndrome

Test	Procedure	Interpretation	Clinical Notes
Painful Arc Test 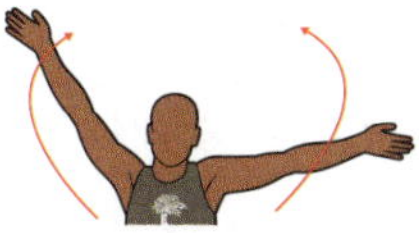	Patient abducts arm actively while examiner observes for pain between 60°–120°	(+) Pain → impingement or AC pathology	Effective as part of a cluster for subacromial impingement syndrome
Relocation Test 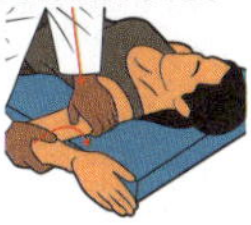	After anterior apprehension, examiner applies posterior force to humeral head	(+) Pain relief → anterior instability or labral tear	Followed by Surprise Test for comprehensive diagnosis
Speed's Test 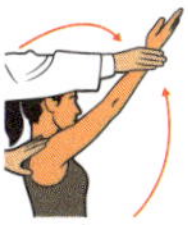	Pt flexes arm against resistance while examiner palpates bicipital groove	(+) Pain → bicipital tendonitis or SLAP lesion	Combine with Yergason's Test for bicipital instability
Sulcus Sign 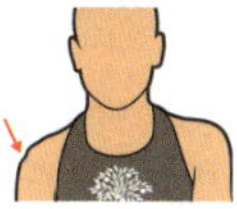	Examiner applies inferior traction to the humerus with the arm relaxed	(+) Depression below acromion → GH instability	Graded 1–3 based on the degree of inferior translation Strep defect = AC separation
Yergason's Test 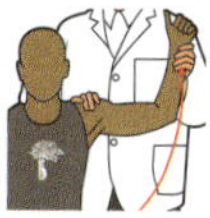	Patient resists supination while examiner palpates bicipital groove	(+) Pain → bicipital tendon instability	Useful in combination with Speed's Test

Shoulder & Arm

	Hx	SSx	Tx
AC Joint Separation 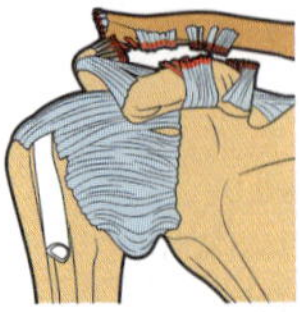	- Trauma (e.g., fall on outstretched arm or shoulder)	- Localized pain at AC joint - **Visible deformity ("step-off")** - (+) Cross-Body or AC Shear Test	- PRICE or METH - Gradual ROM & strengthening ExRx (scap retraction, pendulums) - Avoid overhead lifting
Biceps Tendinitis 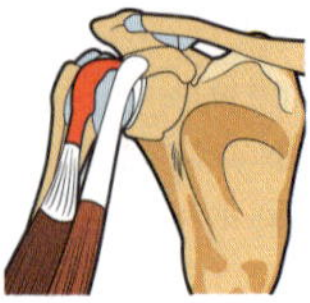	- Repetitive elbow flexion or overhead lifting - Common in athletes (lifters, swimmers).	- Pain at anterior shoulder - Tenderness over bicipital groove - (+) Speed's Test	- METH, METH - Strengthening of biceps & rotator cuff (iso-holds, band curls)
Calcific Tendonitis 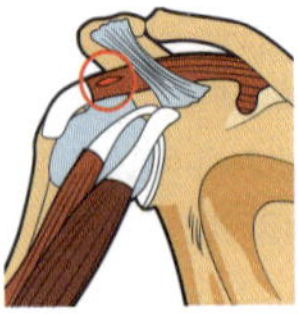	- Middle-aged adults - May follow repetitive shoulder strain or trauma	- Sudden severe pain at the rotator cuff - Pain w/ ROM - **Visible on Xray** - (+) Neer's Test	- Ice, METH - Ultrasound-guided aspiration - Pendulum ExRx, & gentle mobes, Avoid lifting
Frozen Shoulder (Adhesive Capsulitis) 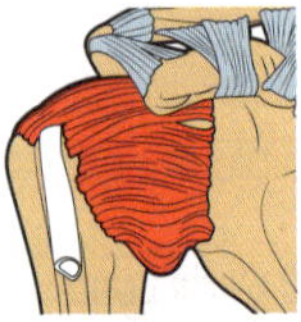	- Gradual onset - Common in diabetics and middle-aged adults, non-dominant arm	- **Limited AROM and PROM** - Pain at night and stiffness - (+) Apley's Scratch Test	- Joint mobilization - Stretching exercises (wall walks, PROM) - Heat therapy - Avoid prolonged immobility
Impingement Syndrome 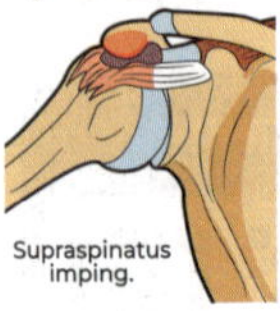	- Prolonged overhead activity - Common in swimmers and painters	- Pain with arm elevation - **(+) Hawkins-Kennedy Test**	- Postural correction - Anti-inflammatory therapy
Labral Tear (SLAP or Bankart) 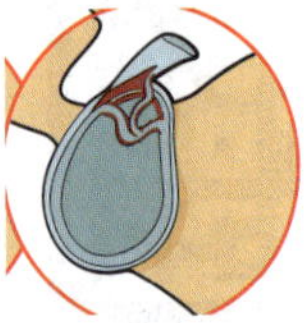	- Trauma or repetitive throwing activity - History of shoulder instability.	- Deep pain in shoulder joint - Clicking/popping sensation - **(+) O'Brien's & Biceprs Load II**	- Physical therapy - Scapular stabilization ExRx - Surgery if severe

Shoulder Rapid DDx

	Hx	SSx	Tx
Osteoarthritis (GH OA) 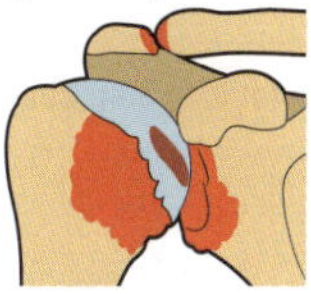	- History of previous shoulder injury or overuse - Common in older adults	- Joint stiffness - **Crepitus** with movement - Pain ↑ w/ activity & ↓ rest - **(+) GH Scour test**	- METH - ROM exercises (pendulum swings) - Modify lifting techniques
Rotator Cuff Tendinitis 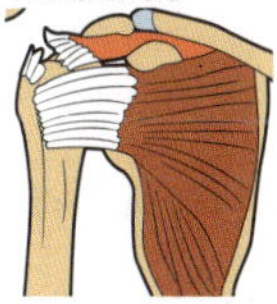	- Overhead activity (throwing, painting) - Repetitive shoulder strain	- Pain overhead motions - Tenderness at supraspinatus tendon - **(+) Empty Can**	- Ice, METH - ExRx (shoulder squeezes, rotator cuff ROM)
Shoulder Instability 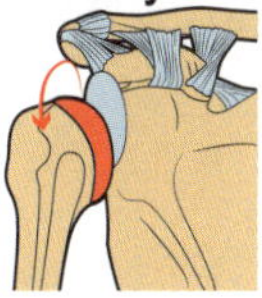	- History of dislocations or trauma - Young, active individuals at higher risk.	- Clicking or catching sensation - **(+) Apprehension Test**	- Strengthening rotator cuff muscles - Scapular stabilization exercises
Subacromial Bursitis 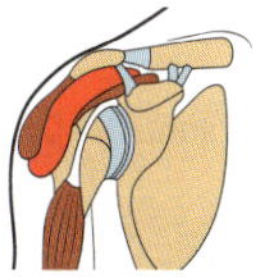	- Overuse or trauma to shoulder joint - Repetitive overhead motion	- Pain with arm elevation - Swelling and tenderness under acromion - **(+) Neer's Test**	- Ice, METH - Rest and ROM exercises - Avoid overhead lifting
Thoracic Outlet Syndrome (TOS) 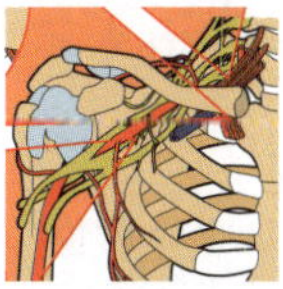	- Poor posture, repetitive overhead activity, carrying heavy loads.	- Numbness, tingling in arm, weak grip, coldness in hands - (+) Roo, Adson Costoclavicular	- Postural correction - Neural mobilization - Strengthening, chin tucks

1. **Muscle is involved in shoulder external rotation?**
   a) Subscapularis
   b) Infraspinatus
   c) Supraspinatus
   d) Pectoralis major

2. **Ligament stabilizes the acromioclavicular (AC) joint?**
   a) Coracoclavicular ligament
   b) Glenohumeral ligament
   c) Costoclavicular ligament
   d) Transverse humeral ligament

3. **What is the typical end feel for shoulder external rotation in a healthy individual?**
   a) Hard
   b) Soft
   c) Firm
   d) Empty

4. **Which test causes pain in subacromial bursitis?**
   a) Hawkins-Kennedy Test
   b) Speed's Test
   c) O'Brien's Test
   d) Full Can Test

5. **What comanagement strategy is recommended for frozen shoulder?**
   a) NSAIDs and stretching exercises
   b) Surgery and immobilization
   c) Manual therapy and scapular strengthening
   d) Friction massage and ice therapy

6. **Which muscle assists in shoulder abduction?**
   a) Infraspinatus
   b) Supraspinatus
   c) Teres minor
   d) Subscapularis

7. **The labrum helps which function in the shoulder?**
   a) Joint stability
   b) Muscle contraction
   c) Tendon attachment
   d) Blood supply

8. **Which structure is most often implicated in thoracic outlet syndrome?**
   a) Pectoralis minor
   b) Subclavius muscle
   c) Costoclavicular ligament
   d) Biceps long head tendon

9. **Characteristic symptom of calcific tendinitis?**
   a) Severe pain with arm elevation
   b) Painless weakness in the shoulder
   c) Swelling at the AC joint
   d) Clicking with overhead movement

10. **Which special test is used to confirm rotator cuff pathology?**
    a) Neer's Test
    b) Finkelstein's Test
    c) Apprehension Test
    d) Tinel's Sign

11. **Which ligament provides primary support to the sternoclavicular (SC) joint?**
    a) Anterior SC ligament
    b) Acromioclavicular ligament
    c) Coracoacromial ligament
    d) Transverse humeral ligament

12. **Test reproduces symptoms of shoulder instability?**
    a) Apprehension Test
    b) Speed's Test
    c) O'Brien's Test
    d) Yergason's Test

13. **Which condition commonly presents with pain during resisted flexion of the biceps?**
    a) Subacromial bursitis
    b) Biceps tendinitis
    c) Impingement syndrome
    d) Labral tear

14. **Best initial treatment for acute AC joint separation?**
    a) Strengthening exercises
    b) PRICE (Protect, Rest, Ice, Compress, Elevate)
    c) Deep tissue massage
    d) Corticosteroid injection

15. **Typical pain pattern in rotator cuff tendinitis?**
    a) Pain with rest and at night
    b) Pain with overhead activities
    c) Constant dull ache
    d) Pain radiating into the hand

16. **Structure Hawkins-Kennedy Test compresses?**
    a) Subacromial bursa
    b) Labrum
    c) Biceps tendon
    d) Rotator cuff tendons

17. **What is the typical presentation of shoulder DJD?**
    a) Joint stiffness with crepitus
    b) Sharp pain with arm elevation
    c) Swelling over the scapula
    d) Numbness radiating down the arm

18. **Muscle that primarily supports scapula protraction?**
    a) Serratus anterior
    b) Trapezius
    c) Pectoralis major
    d) Deltoid

19. **What is the primary goal of manual therapy for frozen shoulder?**
    a) Pain relief and joint mobilization
    b) Muscle strengthening
    c) Fracture healing
    d) Tendon repair

20. **What imaging modality is most useful for confirming a rotator cuff tear?**
    a) Ultrasound
    b) X-ray
    c) CT scan
    d) MRI

PHS Certification

Get certification badges for answering questions

1. b	5. c	9. a	13. b	17. a
2. a	6. b	10. a	14. b	18. a
3. c	7. a	11. a	15. b	19. a
4. a	8. a	12. a	16. a	20. d

Case Study 1

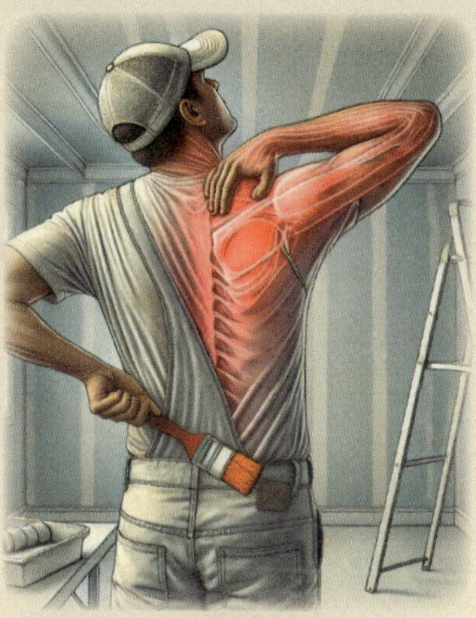

A 42-year-old painter with pain and weakness in their right shoulder that worsens with overhead activities, particularly painting ceilings. The patient reports no trauma but has had persistent symptoms for three months. Examination reveals pain with abduction and a positive Empty Can Test.

Questions:

- What is the likely **differential diagnosis** for this presentation?
- What **treatment options**, including strengthening exercises and manual therapy, would you recommend to address this condition?
- How could the patient's occupation and repetitive overhead work contribute to this condition, and what **strategies** might help reduce its impact?

Case Study 2

A 50-year-old teacher experiences a gradual loss of shoulder mobility and pain, especially at night, over the past four months. The patient reports difficulty reaching overhead or behind their back. Examination reveals limited active and passive range of motion (ROM), with a firm end feel in multiple planes and a positive Apley's Scratch Test.

Questions:

- What is the **differential diagnosis** for these symptoms?
- What **interventions**, including joint mobilizations and stretching exercises, would best address this patient's restricted ROM?
- How might the patient's **stress levels** and sedentary lifestyle influence the progression of this condition?

Case Study 3

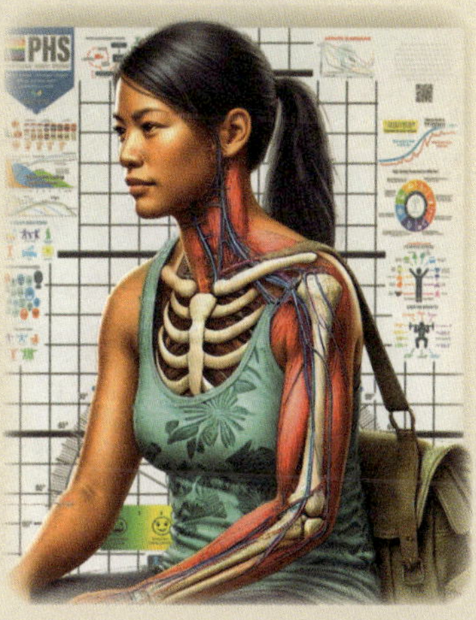

A 34-year-old office worker presents with tingling and numbness in their right arm, particularly when carrying a heavy bag or sitting with poor posture. Symptoms improve when they correct their posture. Physical examination reveals a positive Adson's Test and mild tenderness in the scalene muscles.

Questions:

- What are the likely **differential diagnoses** for this presentation?
- What combination of **postural correction, manual therapy, and strengthening exercises** could help resolve this issue?
- How could **workplace ergonomics** and stress management impact the patient's recovery?

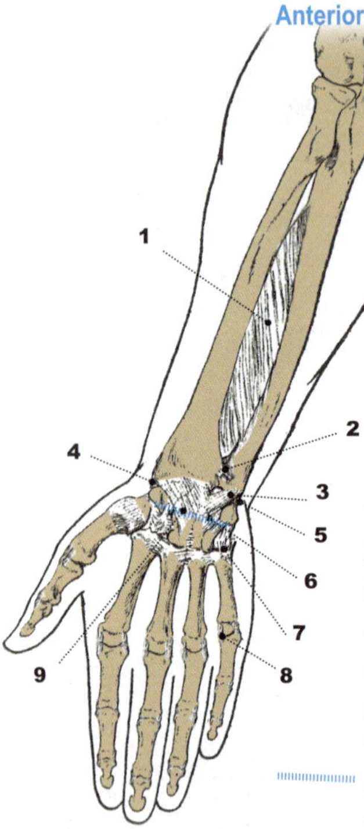

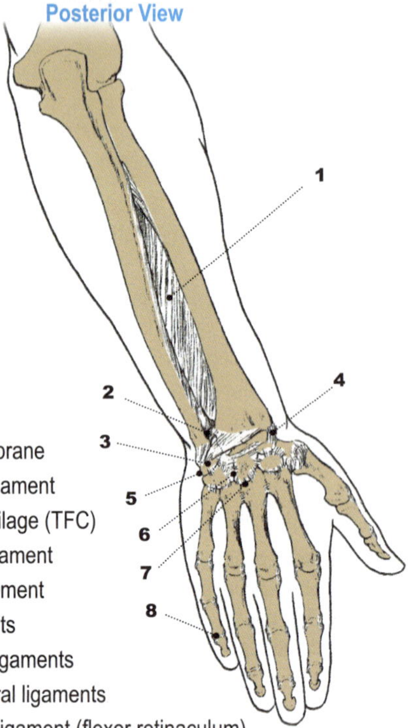

1. Interosseous membrane
2. Distal radioulnar ligament
3. Triangular fibrocartilage (TFC)
4. Radial collateral ligament
5. Ulnar collateral ligament
6. Intercarpal ligaments
7. Carpometacarpal ligaments
8. Phalangeal collateral ligaments
9. Transverse carpal ligament (flexor retinaculum)

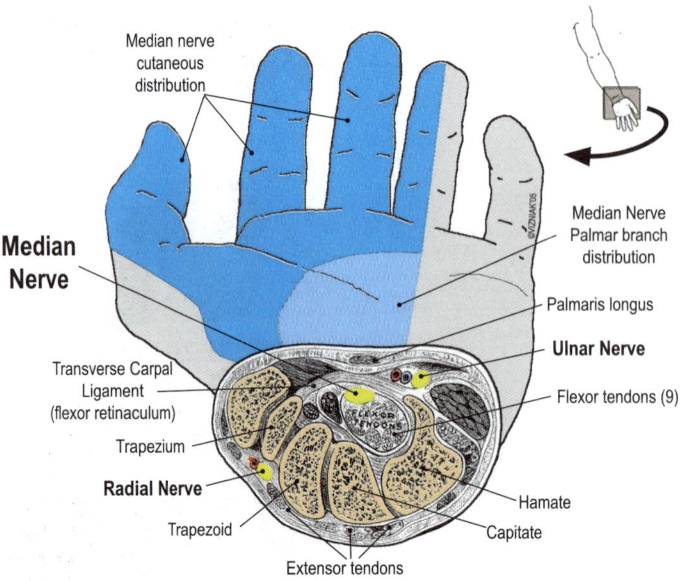

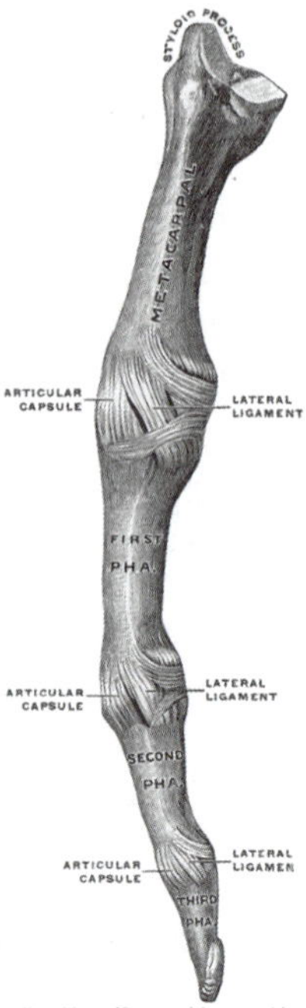

Forearm Muscles

1. Brachioradialis
2. Extensor carpi radialis longus
3. Anconeus
4. Extensor digitorum
5. Extensor carpi radialis brevis
6. Extensor digiti minimi
7. Extensor carpi ulnaris
8. Abductor pollicis longus
9. Extensor pollicis brevis
10. Flexor carpi ulnaris
11. Supinator
12. Extensor pollicis longus
13. Extensor indicis

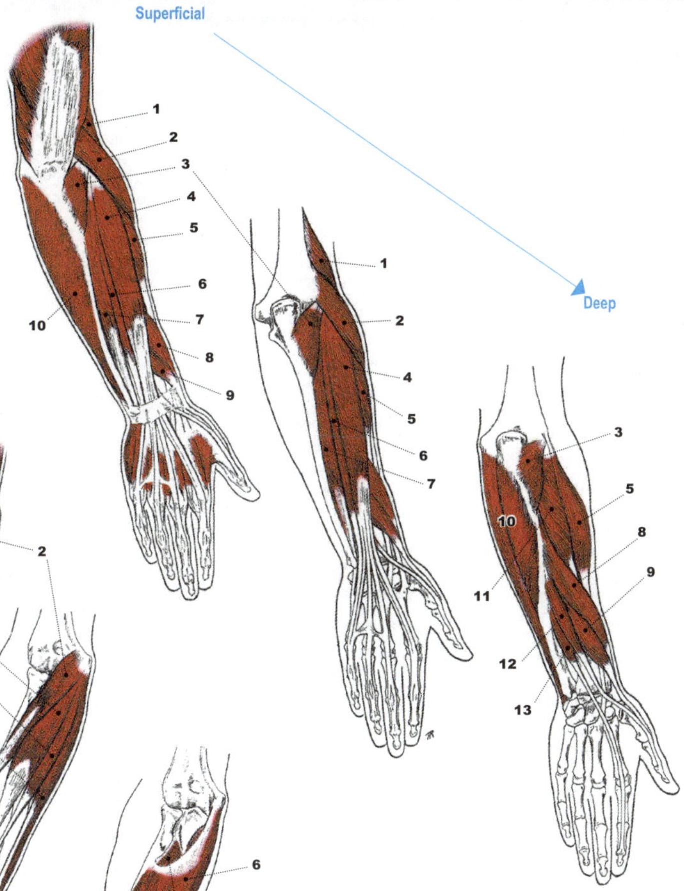

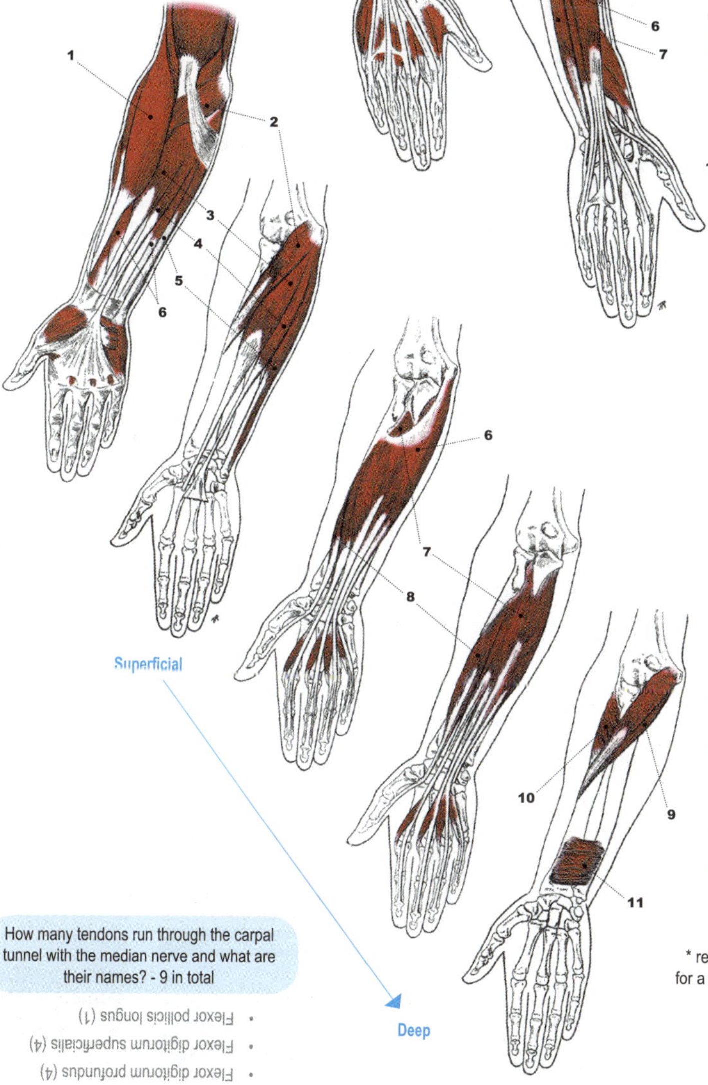

1. Brachioradialis
2. Pronator teres (superficial head)*
3. Flexor carpi radialis*
4. Palmaris longus*
5. Flexor carpi ulnaris*
6. Flexor digitorum superficialis
7. Flexor digitorum profundus
8. Flexor pollicis longus
9. Pronator teres (deep head)
10. Supinator
11. Pronator quadratus

* remember Pass Fail Pass Fail for a mnemonic of the 4 superficial forearm flexors

How many tendons run through the carpal tunnel with the median nerve and what are their names? - 9 in total

- Flexor digitorum profundus (4)
- Flexor digitorum superficialis (4)
- Flexor pollicis longus (1)

Elbow Regional Examination

☑ Check normal, circle & describe abnormal

Patient: ______________ date: ______ (dd/mm/yr)

Insurance: ______________

Date of birth: ______________

CC & significant history: ______________

Fracture screen (tuning fork, percussion, torsion test, grip strength): □ WNL, □ Refer for X-ray: ______________

Inspection: □ WNL

Development: □ good, □ fair, □ poor

□ Antalgia: ______________

□ Skin (bruising, scars): ______________

□ Asymmetry: ______________

Observation □ WNL	L	R
Head tilt		
Head rotation		
Shoulder high		
Shoulder rounded		
Humerus rotated		
Elbow flexed		
Elbow hyperextended		
Valgus forearm		
Varus forearm		
Forearm pronated		
Forearm supinated		
Hand/finger deformity		

Palpation: □ WNL, texture, tenderness, pain referral

Palpation	L	R
Medial epicondyle		
Ulnar groove		
Med. collateral ligament		
Common flexor tendon		
Flexor carpi ulnaris		
Palmaris longus		
Flexor carpi radialis		
Pronator teres		
Biceps tendon		
Head of radius		
Radial tunnel		
Lateral epicondyle		
Lat. collateral ligament		
Lat. supracondylar ridge		

Palpation	L	R
Common exten. tendon		
Anconeus		
Brachioradialis		
Extensor carpi ulnaris		
Extensor carpi rad longus		
Extensor carpi rad brevis		
Extensor digitorum		
Supinator		
Triceps tendon		
Triceps muscle		
Olecranon		
Olecranon bursa		
Cubital fossa		

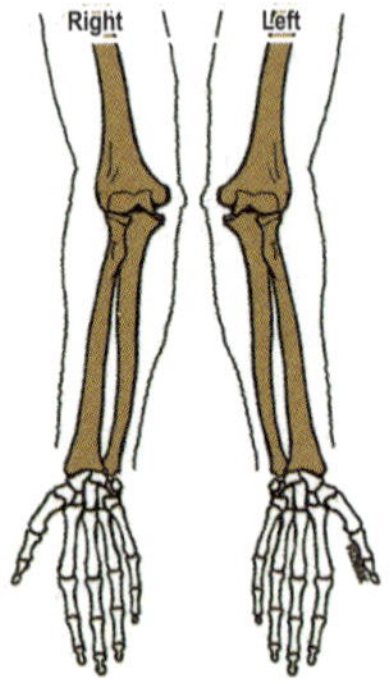

Vascular Screen: □ WNL

Pulses (0-4)	L	R
Brachial pulse		
Radial pulse		
Ulnar pulse		
Blanch test		
Allen's test		
Temperature		

ROM & Joint Play: □ WNL

□ Pain at end ROM: ______________

□ Abnormal motion: ______________

ROM	Active		Passive	
	L	R	L	R
Flexion (150°)				
Extension (0°)				
Supination (90°)				
Pronation (90°)				

Joint Play	L	R
Ulnohumeral		
Radiohumeral		
Proximal radioulnar		

Neurologic: □ WNL

Reflexes (0-5), □ WNL	L	R
Biceps (C5)		
Brachioradialis (C6)		
Triceps (C7)		
General grip strength		

Motor (0-5), □ WNL	L	R
Shoulder flexors		
Shoulder extensors		
Biceps brachii (musc.)		
Brachialis (musc.)		
Brachioradialis (radial)		
Triceps brachii (radial)		
Wrist extensors (radial)		
Wrist flexors (median/ulnar)		
Wrist abductors (median/radial)		
Wrist adductors (ulnar/radial)		
Pronator teres (median)		
Supinator (radial)		
Finger flexors (median/ulnar)		
Finger extensors (radial)		

Girth*, □ WNL	L	R
Mid arm		
Elbow		
Mid forearm		
Carrying angle		

*Atrophy, swelling, dominant vs. non-dominant

**General sensation is done through palpation

Orthopedic: □ WNL

Instability	L	R
Valgus stress (0°)		
Valgus stress (30°)		
Varus stress (0°)		
Varus stress (30°)		

Lateral epicondylitis	L	R
Book lift test		
Cozen's		
Mill's		
Kaplan's test		

Medial epicondylitis	L	R
Reverse Cozen's		
Reverse Mill's		
Reverse book lift		

Neuropathy	L	R
Tinel's (elbow)		
Tinel's (wrist)		
Elbow flexion test		
Pronator stretch test		

Dynamometer	L	R	L	R	L	R
Repeat 3 times						

Serial # ______________ Setting: ______________

Neck evaluation: ______________

Shoulder eval: ______________

Wrist/hand eval: ______________

DDx:

Signature: Date:

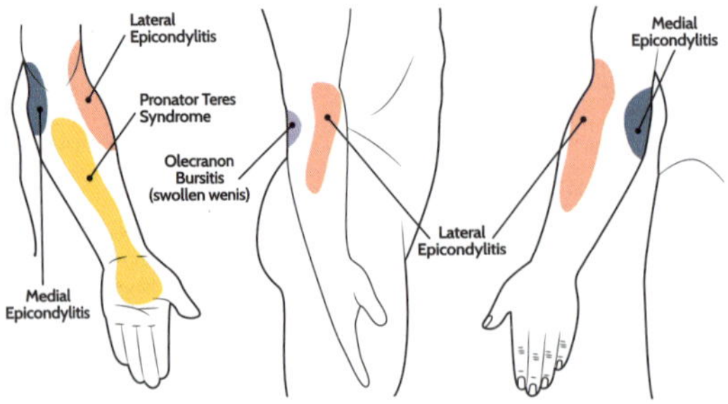

Palpation

Muscle Testing

Range of Motion

Orthopedics

Treatment

Nutrition

Exercises

Video prohealthsys.com

Wrist/Hand Regional Examination

☑ Check normal, circle & describe abnormal

CC & significant history: ______________________________

Patient: ____________________ date: ________ (dd/mm/yr)
Insurance: ____________________

Fracture screen (tuning fork, percussion, torsion test, grip strength): □ **WNL,** □ **Refer for X-ray:** ____________________

Inspection: □ WNL

Development: □ good, □ fair, □ poor
□ Antalgia: ______________
□ Skin (bruising, scars): ______________
□ Asymmetry: ______________

Observation □ WNL		L	R
Head position			
Shoulder position			
Elbow position			
Hand pronated/supinated			
Fingers flexed/extended			
Deformities	Boutonniere deformity		
	Swan neck deformity		
	Mallet finger		
	Heberden's nodes		
	Bouchard's nodes		
	Other:		

Palpation: □ WNL, texture, tenderness, pain referral

Palpation	L	R
Wrist flexors		
Pronator teres		
Wrist extensors		
Supinator		
Thumb extensors		
Interossei		
Thenar pad		
Hypothenar pad		
Carpal tunnel		
Tunnel of Guyon		
Anatomic snuff box		
Metacarpals		
Thumb (#1)		
Index finger (#2)		

Palpation	L	R
Middle finger (#3)		
Ring finger (#4)		
Little finger (#5)		
Scaphoid		
Lunate		
Triquetrum		
Pisiform		
Hamate		
Capitate		
Trapezoid		
Trapezium		
Ulnar/radial styloids		
Triangular complex		

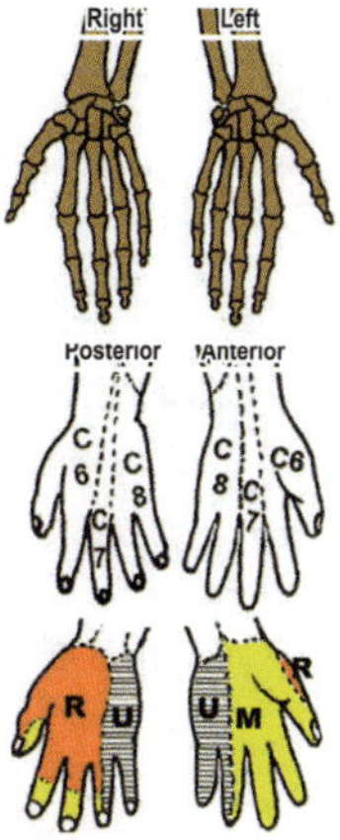

ROM & Joint Play: □ WNL

ROM & Joint play		Active L	Active R	Passive L	Passive R
Wrist	Flexion (80°)				
	Extension (70°)				
	Ulnar flexion (30°)				
	Radial flexion (20°)				
MP joint	Flexion (90°)				
	Extension (40°)				
	Abduction (20°)				
	Adduction (20°)				
PIP	Flexion (70°)				
	Extension (0°)				
DIP	Flexion (80°)				
	Extension (20°)				
Thumb	MP flexion (60°)				
	MP extension (20°)				
	IP flexion (90°)				
	IP extension (20°)				

Joint Play	L	R
Distal radioulnar		
Individual carpals		

* Most joint play is done with passive ROM for

Vascular Screen: □ WNL

Pulses (0-4)	L	R
Radial pulse		
Ulnar pulse		
Blanch test		
Allen's test		

Neurologic: □ WNL

Reflexes (0-5), □ WNL	L	R
Biceps (C5)		
Brachioradialis (C6)		
Triceps (C7)		
General grip strength		

Motor (0-5), □ WNL	L	R
Pronator teres (median)		
Pronator quadratus (median)		
Supinator (radial)		
Wrist extensors (C6)		
Wrist flexors (C7)		
Finger extensors (C7)		
Finger flexors (C8)		
Finger abductors (T1)		
Finger adductors (T1)		

*Atrophy, swelling, dominant vs. non-dominant
**General sensation is done through palpation

Orthopedic: □ WNL

Neuro-injury	L	R
Phalen's (median)		
Wrist drop (radial)		
Froment's cone (uln)		
Opposition (median)		
Thumb adduction		
Pinch grip test		
Tinel's (median)		
Tinel's (ulnar)		
Tourniquet test		
Wartenberg's sign		

Other injury	L	R
Scaphoid fracture test		
Thumb abd. stress		
Thumb grind test		
Finger stress test		
Bracelet test		
Lunotriquetral ballot.		
Bunnel-Littler test		
Retinaculum test		
Finkelstein's		
Wringing test		

Dynamometer	L	R	L	R	L	R
Repeat 3 times						
Serial #________			Setting: ________			

Neck evaluation: ______________________
Shoulder eval: ______________________
Elbow evaluation: ______________________

DDx:

Signature: Date:

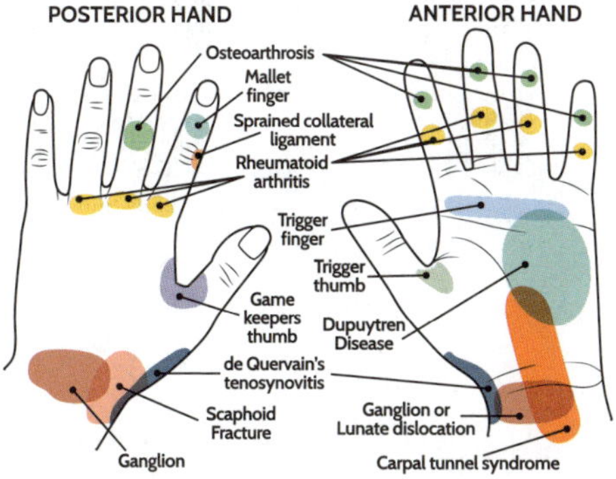

Compare bilaterally; prior to ROM the examiner makes an introduction statement:
"Try and move as far as possible, if any of the actions or movements are painful or uncomfortable please let me know, do not do any action you feel will cause you further injury."

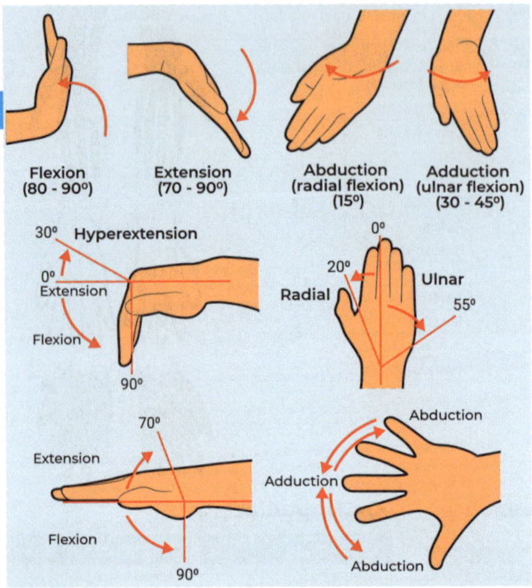

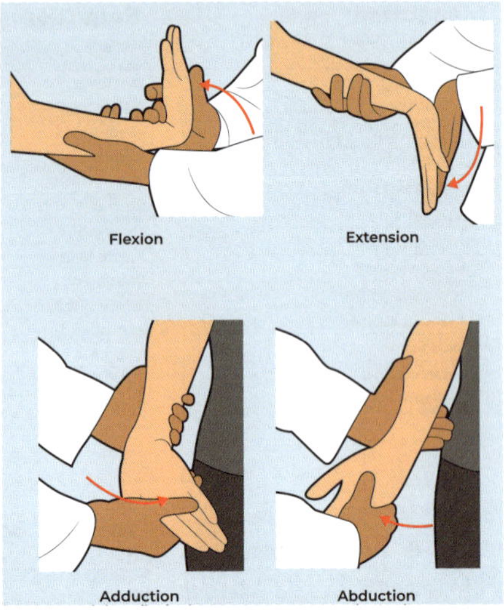

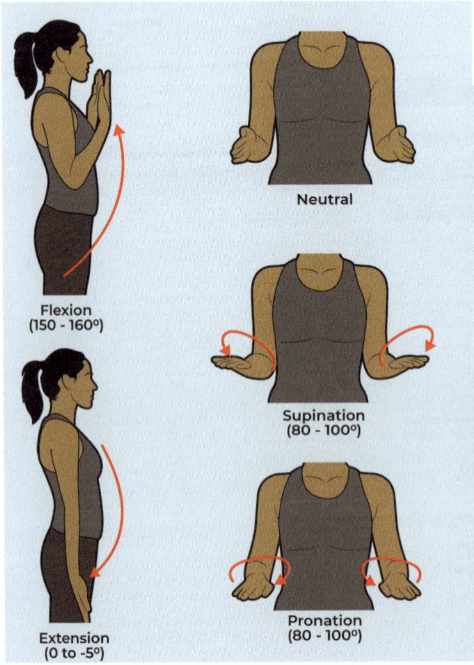

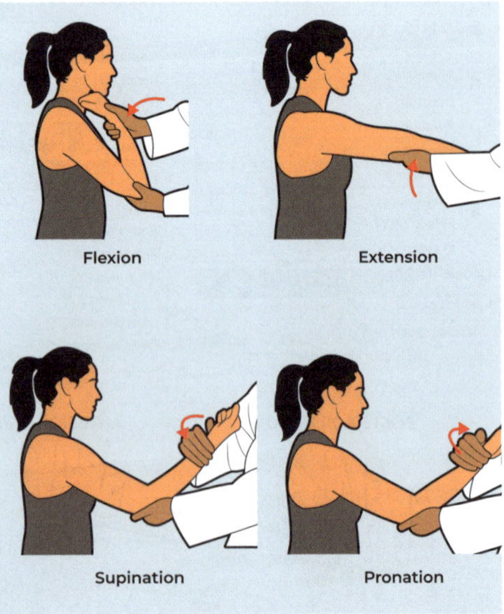

Muscle Testing

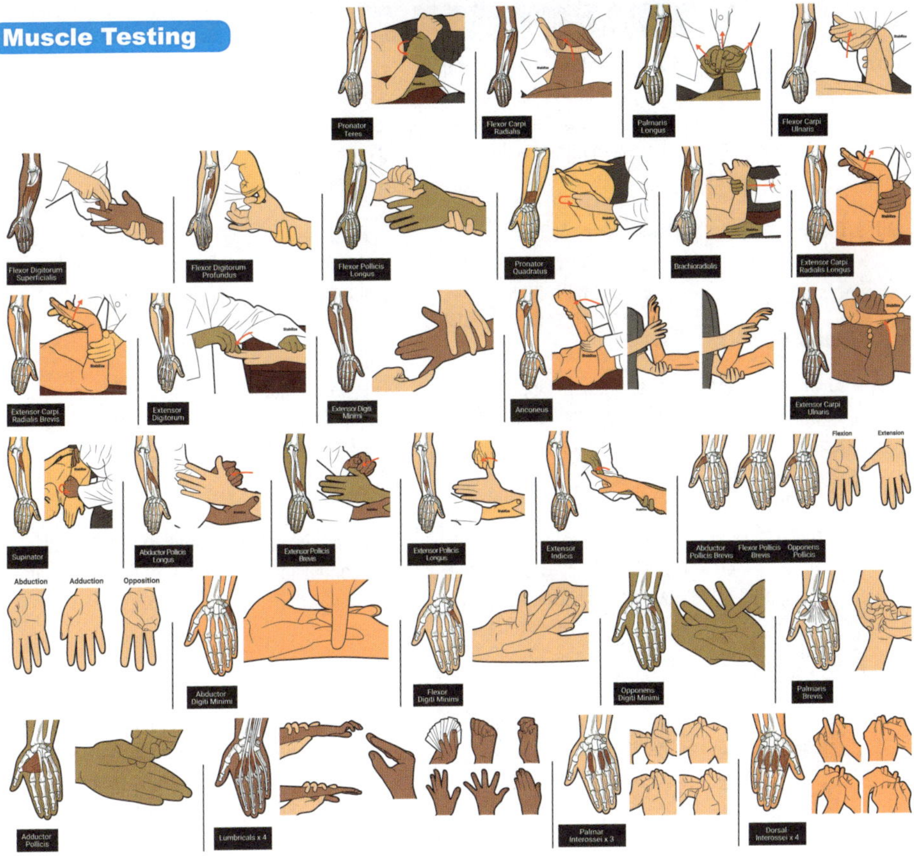

Trigger Points

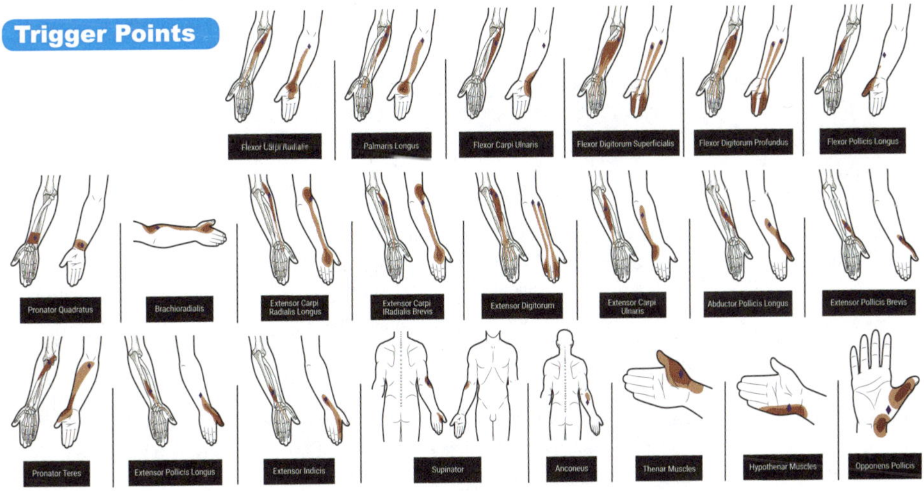

Test	Procedure	Interpretation	Clinical Notes
Cozen's Test 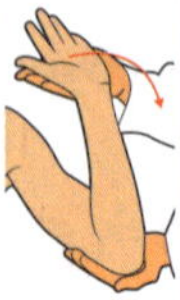	Patient makes a fist (or open hand) and resists wrist extension while examiner palpates lateral epicondyle	(+) Pain → Lateral epicondylitis (Tennis elbow)	Indicates extensor carpi radialis brevis involvement
Mill's Test 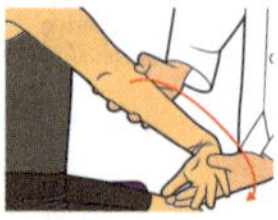	Passively stretch wrist extensors by extending elbow and pronating forearm while flexing wrist	(+) Pain → Lateral epicondylitis.	Stretch isolates common extensor tendon pathology
Reverse Cozens Test 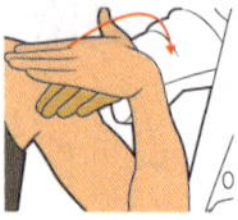	Patient resists wrist flexion while examiner palpates medial epicondyle	(+) Pain → Medial epicondylitis (Golfer's elbow)	Assesses flexor-pronator muscle group
Reverse Mill's Test 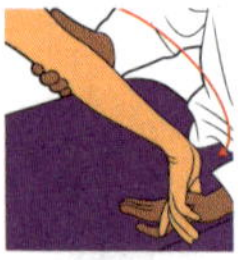	Passively stretch wrist extensors by extending elbow and supinating forearm while extending wrist	(+) Pain → Medial epicondylitis	Similar to Mill's Test but for flexor-pronator group
Phalen's Test 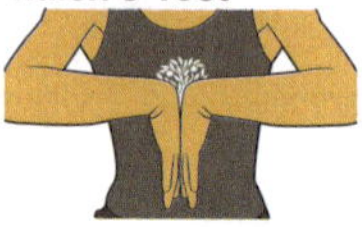	Patient places dorsum of hands together, flexing wrists for 60 seconds	(+) Tingling in median nerve distribution → Carpal Tunnel Syndrome	Compression of median nerve. Reverse phalens (prayer) stretches nerve
Finkelstein's Test 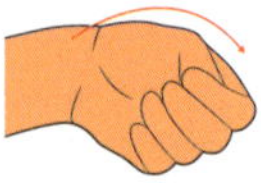	Patient makes a fist around thumb and ulnarly deviates wrist	(+) Pain → De Quervain's tenosynovitis	Indicates abductor pollicis longus/ extensor pollicis brevis inflammation
Tinel's Sign at Wrist 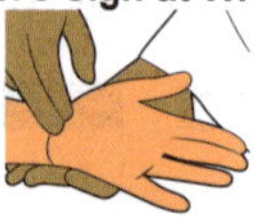	Tap over median & ulnar nerve at wrist (Carpal Tunnel Syndrome)	(+) Tingling → Median nerve compression	Localized tingling may indicate nerve compression severity
Lunotriquetral Ballottement 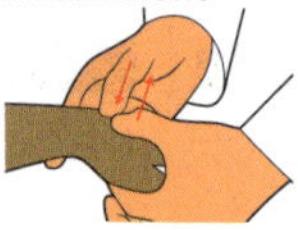	Stabilize lunate, move triquetrum dorsally and palmarly.	(+) Pain or crepitus → Lunotriquetral instability.	Assesses ligamentous integrity between lunate and triquetrum
Sweater Sign 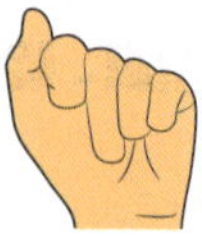	Patient flexes fingers; observe inability to flex distal phalanx of ring finger	(+) Inability to flex DIP → FDP rupture	Often associated with avulsion injuries

Test	Procedure	Interpretation	Clinical Notes
Press Test 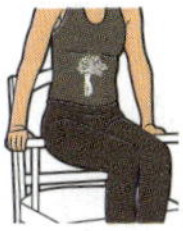	Patient pushes off a chair using their palms	(+) Pain → Triangular fibrocartilage complex (TFCC) injury	Indicates TFCC damage or instability
Froment's Sign 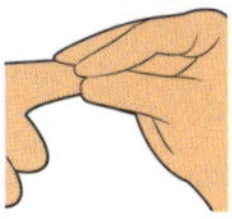	Patient pinches paper (or examiner finger) between thumb and index finger; examiner pulls paper away	(+) Thumb flexion → Ulnar nerve dysfunction	Weakness of adductor pollicis indicates ulnar nerve pathology
Reverse Phalen's 	Patient places palms of hands together, flexing wrists for 60 seconds	(+) Tingling in median nerve distribution → Carpal Tunnel Syndrome	Reverse phalens (prayer) stretches median nerve
Scaphoid Fracture 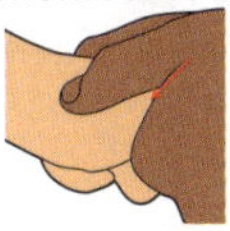	Apply pressure to the anatomical snuffbox or compress the scaphoid with axial loading of the thumb	(+) (+) Pain → Scaphoid fracture or injury	High risk for avascular necrosis; consider imaging if positive or if pain persists after initial assessment
Thumb Grind Test 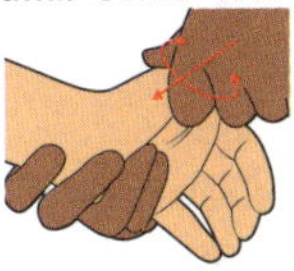	Apply axial compression and rotate thumb at CMC joint	(+) Pain or grinding → CMC arthritis	Assesses joint surface integrity and cartilage damage

Elbow Wrist Hand Pathology

PHS

	Hx	SSx	Tx
Carpal Tunnel Syndrome 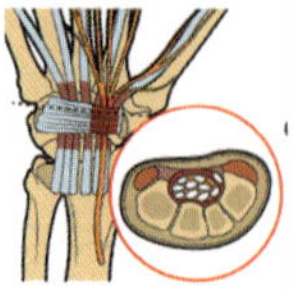	- Repetitive wrist movements (typing, cashier) - More common in middle-aged women	- Numbness, tingle in thumb, index, & middle fingers - Weak grip - **(+) Phalen's Test, Tinel's Sign**	- Splinting - METH - Neural gliding exercises - Avoid aggravating activities
Cubital Tunnel Syndrome 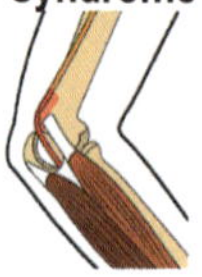	- Repetitive elbow flexion (e.g., desk work, sleeping positions)	- Numbness, tingle in ring & small fingers - Weakness grip - **(+) Tinel's Sign at the elbow**	- Splinting - Neural mobes - Avoid prolonged elbow flexion
De Quervain's Tenosynovitis 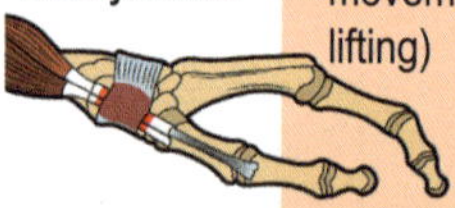	- Repetitive thumb movements (texting, lifting)	- **Pain & swelling** near thumb base - Difficulty gripping - **(+) Finkelstein's Test**	- Splinting, taping - Ice therapy - Stretching for thumb abductors
Dupuytren's Contracture 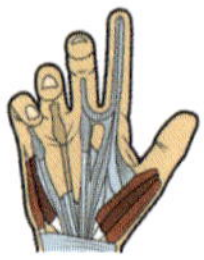	- Gradual thickening of the palmar fascia - Family history or manual labor	- Nodules or thick cords in palm - Progressive finger flexion contracture (ring & little finger) - Limited extension	- Stretching & ROM exercises - Steroid injections for inflammation - Surgical release for severe cases
Ganglion Cyst 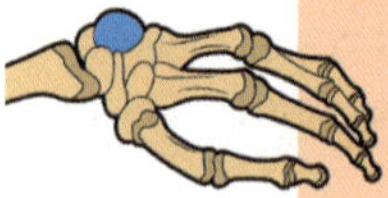	- Repetitive wrist motion, trauma or spontaneous	- Visible or palpable **lump over dorsal** or volar wrist - Pain or discomfort during wrist movement	- Observation if asymptomatic - Aspiration or surgical removal if symptomatic
Golfer Elbow (Med Epicondylit) 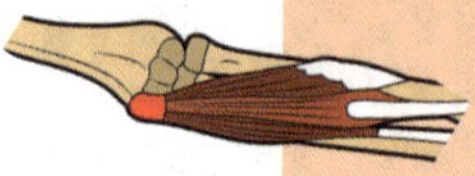	- **Repetitive wrist flexion** (golf, heavy lifting)	- Pain over medial epicondyle - ↑ Pain w/ resisted wrist flexion - **(+) Reverse Mill's/ Cozen's**	- Ice, METH - Stretching (wrist extensors) - ExRx eccentric wrist flexors
Pronator Teres Syn. 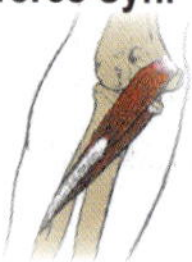	- **Repetitive pronation/ supination** movements (racket sports, manual labor)	- Numbness, tingle in palm & thumb - Weakness in grip - **(+) Pronator Compression Test**	- Neuro mobilization - Stretching (pronators & supinators) - Activity modification

	Hx	SSx	Tx
Scaphoid Fracture 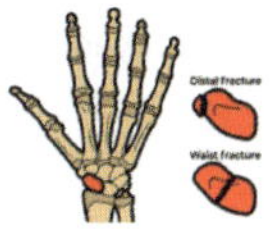	- **Fall on an outstretched hand** (FOOSH)	- **Tender in snuffbox** - Xray/CT/MRI to confirm - (+) Scaphoid Compression Test	- Immobilization in a thumb spica splint - Surgical fixation if displaced - Gradual ROM post-immobilize
Tennis Elbow (Lat Epicondylitis) 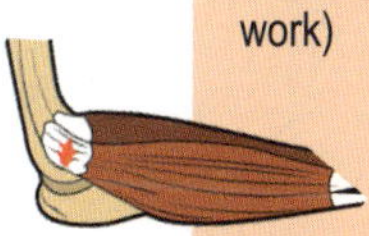	- Repetitive wrist extension (tennis, desk work)	- **Pain over lateral epicondyle** - Pain ↑ w/ resisted wrist extension - **(+) Cozen's, Mills's Test**	- Ice, METH - Stretching (wrist flexors) - Strengthening eccentric wrist extensors
Toddler Elbow (Nursemaid's Elbow) 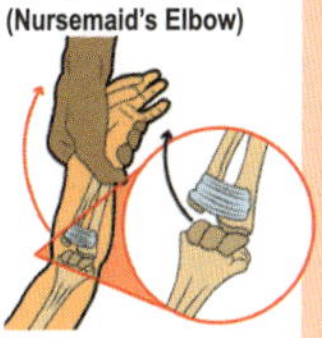	- Sudden **traction on child's arm** (pulling arm during play)	- Pain in elbow - Arm held flexed & close to body - **Refusal to move arm**, no redness or swelling	- Reduction maneuver - Avoid pulling mechanisms in the future
Trigger Finger 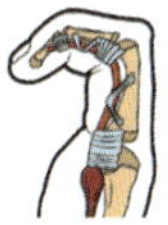	- Repetitive gripping or manual labor - Common in middle-aged	- **Finger locking** or **catching** w/ ROM - Tenderness over affected tendon - (+) Palpable node	- Splinting, taping - METH - Stretching for finger flexors - Corticosteroid
Triangular Fibrocartilage 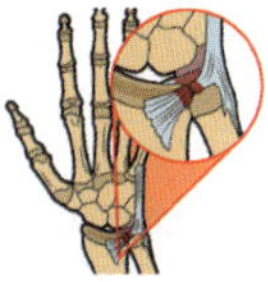	- Trauma to wrist or repetitive axial loading (gymnastics, weightlifting)	- **Pain on ulnar side of wrist** - Click or catching sensation - **(+) TFCC Load Test**	- Immobilization with a wrist brace - Surgical repair if severe - ExRx wrist stabilizers
Wrist Sprain 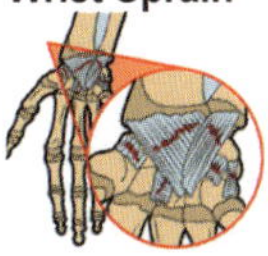	- Fall on an outstretched hand or direct trauma	- Swelling, tender over wrist joint - Pain with wrist movement	- Ice, splinting - Gentle ROM - Strengthening wrist stabilizers

PHS PROFESSIONAL HEALTH SYSTEMS

1. Primary muscle involved in Golfer's Elbow?
a) Extensor carpi radialis longus
b) Flexor carpi radialis
c) Pronator teres
d) Biceps brachii

2. Ligament most likely affected in Scaphoid Fracture?
a) Annular ligament
b) Ulnar collateral ligament
c) Scapholunate ligament
d) Radial collateral ligament

3. Typical end feel for wrist extension in a healthy joint?
a) Hard
b) Firm
c) Guarding
d) Empty

4. Pain is associated with Carpal Tunnel Syndrome?
a) Numbness in the thumb, index, & middle fingers
b) Sharp pain localized to the ulnar side of the wrist
c) Dull ache in the dorsal wrist
d) Tingling and weakness in the forearm

5. What comanagement strategy is recommended for Dupuytren's Contracture?
a) Immediate surgical referral
b) Splinting and neural gliding exercises
c) Observation or steroid injections
d) Strengthening wrist extensors

6. Which test is used to diagnose De Quervain's?
a) Phalen's Test
b) Reverse Mill's Test
c) Finkelstein's Test
d) Froment's Test

7. Which muscle is tested during Pinch Grip Strength assessment?
a) Opponens pollicis
b) Flexor pollicis longus
c) Lumbricals
d) Extensor digitorum

8. What is the likely injury mechanism for a Triangular Fibrocartilage Complex (TFC) Tear?
a) Direct trauma to the dorsal wrist
b) Repetitive axial loading of the wrist
c) Sudden twisting of the elbow
d) Falling on an outstretched hand

9. What ligament stabilizes the medial elbow?
a) Ulnar collateral ligament
b) Radial collateral ligament
c) Annular ligament
d) Transverse humeral ligament

10. Contraindication to massage for Trigger Finger?
a) Recent steroid injections
b) Local tenderness in the tendon
c) Acute inflammation with swelling
d) Pain with resisted finger flexion

11. Nerve is involved in Pronator Teres Syndrome?
a) Radial nerve
b) Ulnar nerve
c) Median nerve
d) Axillary nerve

12. Muscle commonly tight in Cubital Tunnel Synd?
a) Flexor carpi ulnaris
b) Biceps brachii
c) Extensor carpi radialis
d) Triceps brachii

13. Which structure can develop a ganglion cyst due to repetitive trauma?
a) Carpal bones
b) Scaphoid
c) Extensor retinaculum
d) Joint capsule

14. Primary management for an acute Wrist Sprain?
a) MFR for forearm stabilizers
b) Rest, ice, and gentle ROM exercises
c) Strengthening exercises for the extensors
d) Immediate surgical stabilization

15. Clinical sign of Carpal Tunnel Syndrome in wrist?
a) Positive Tinel's Sign
b) Negative Finkelstein's Test
c) Positive Froment's Test
d) Negative Allen's Test

16. Which of the following muscles is a wrist flexor?
a) Extensor digitorum
b) Palmaris longus
c) Pronator quadratus
d) Abductor pollicis longus

17. What is the characteristic motion affected in De Quervain's Tenosynovitis?
a) Gripping and pinching
b) Supination of the forearm
c) Flexion of the wrist
d) Extension of the fingers

18. What imaging modality is often used to confirm a Scaphoid Fracture?
a) MRI
b) X-ray
c) CT Scan
d) Ultrasound

19. Which special test can help diagnose Tennis Elbow?
a) Cozen's Test
b) Finkelstein's Test
c) Reverse Mill's Test
d) Froment's Test

20. Which group of muscles is involved in stabilizing the wrist during extension?
a) Flexor digitorum profundus
b) Extensor carpi radialis & ulnaris
c) Lumbricals & interossei
d) Flexor carpi radialis & ulnaris

PHS Certification

1. b 2. c 3. b 4. a
5. c 6. c 7. b 8. b
9. a 10. c 11. c 12. a
13. d 14. b 15. a 16. b
17. a 18. b 19. a 20. b

Case Study 1

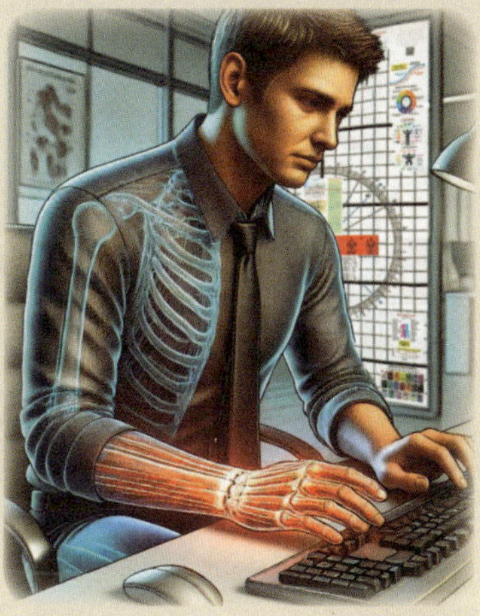

A 32-year-old office worker has numbness and tingling in the thumb, index, and middle fingers for the past three months. Symptoms worsen at night and with typing or using a mouse. Phalen's Test reproduces the symptoms, and there is mild thumb weakness. The patient denies any history of trauma.

Questions:

- What is the most likely **differential diagnosis** for this condition?
- What **treatment options**, including manual therapy and ergonomic adjustments, would you recommend?
- How could **workplace stress** and setup impact the condition, and what strategies might help?

Case Study 2

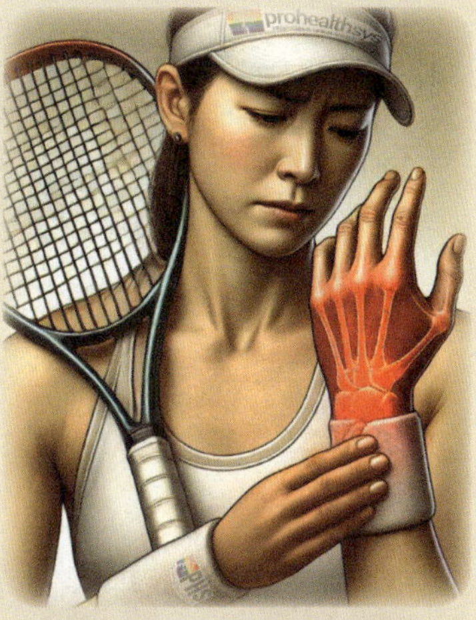

A 48-year-old recreational tennis player reports pain and swelling on the radial wrist, worsening with gripping and lifting. Symptoms began after a long tennis session three weeks ago. Finkelstein's Test is positive, and tenderness is noted along the radial wrist. There is no history of trauma.

Questions:

- What is the likely **differential diagnosis** for this presentation?
- What **treatments**, including taping, manual therapy, and exercises, would aid recovery?
- How might this condition affect recreational activities, and what **modifications** would you suggest?

Case Study 3

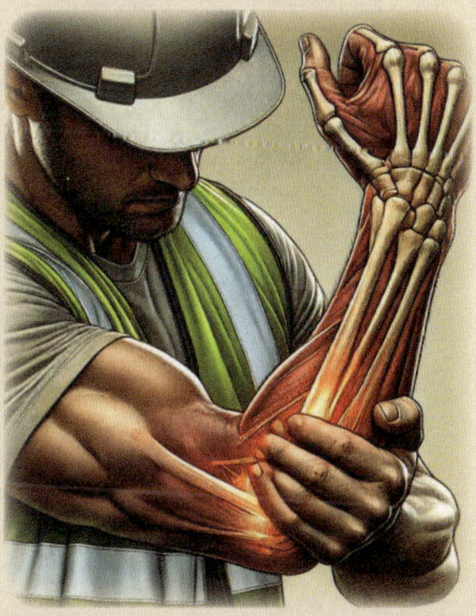

A 55-year-old construction worker has lateral elbow pain and weakness that began two months ago. The pain is sharp with wrist extenion against resistance and worsens during the workday. Mill's Test is positive, and tenderness is localized to the medial epicondyle.

Questions:

- What is the **differential diagnosis** for this condition?
- What **treatments**, including strengthening exercises and workplace modifications, would you recommend?
- How might **repetitive job tasks** contribute to this condition, and what preventative measures could help?

Anterior View

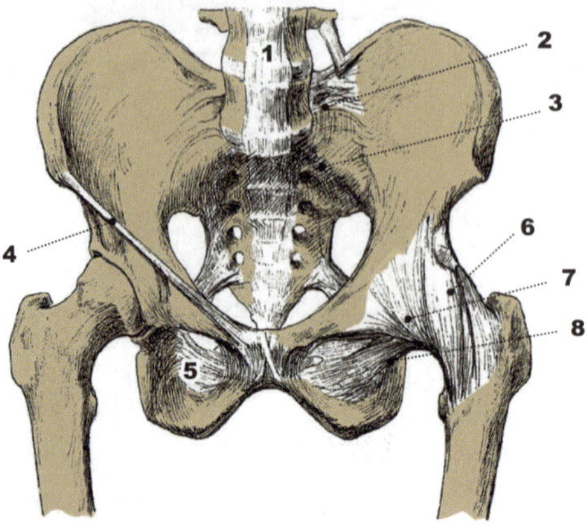

Posterior View

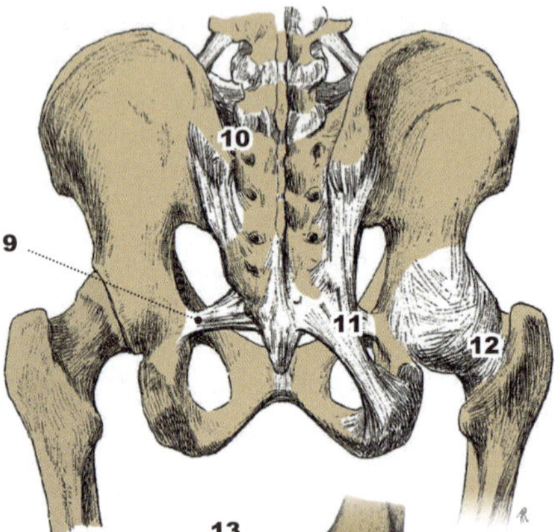

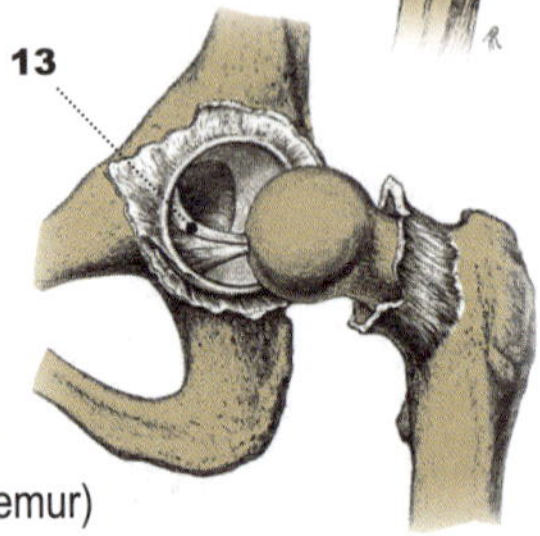

Pelvis & Hip

1. Anterior longitudinal ligament
2. Iliolumbar ligaments
3. Anterior sacroiliac ligaments
4. Inguinal ligament
5. Obturator membrane
6. Iliofemoral ligament
7. Pubofemoral ligament
8. Ischiofemoral ligament
9. Sacrospinous ligament
10. Posterior sacroiliac ligament
11. Sacrotuberus ligament
12. Acetabulofemoral joint capsule
13. Ligamentum teres (to head of femur)

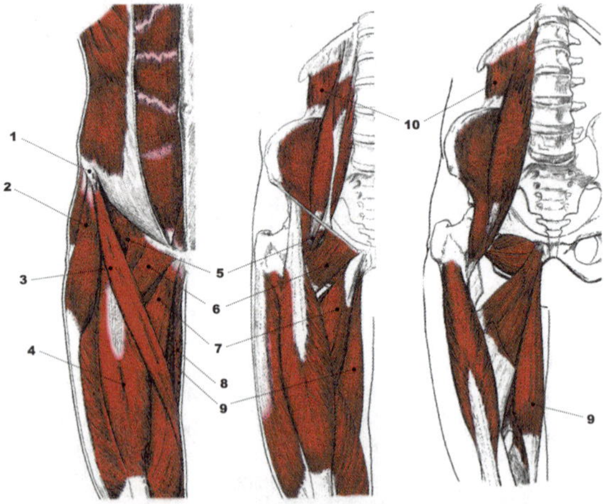

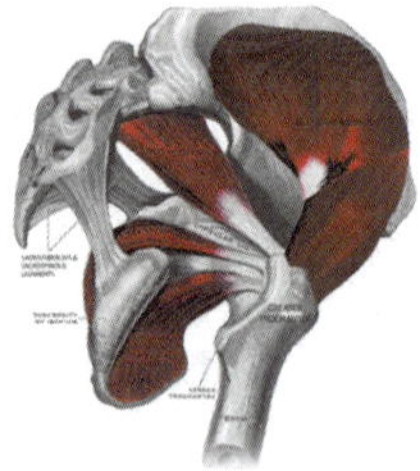

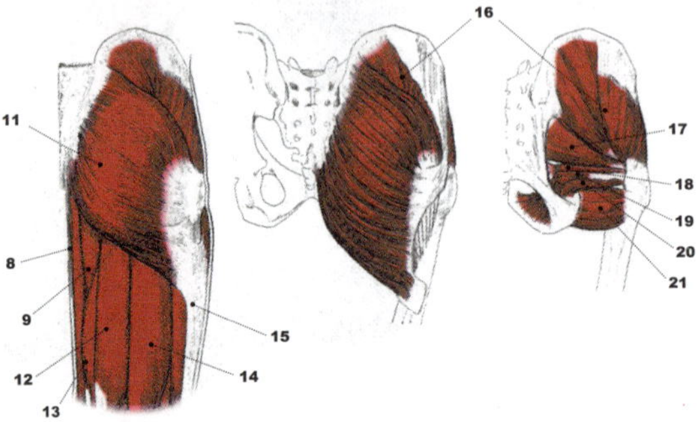

1. ASIS
2. Tensor fasciae latae
3. Sartorius
4. Rectus femoris
5. Iliopsoas
6. Pectineus
7. Adductor longus
8. Gracilis
9. Adductor magnus
10. Quadratus lumborum
11. Gluteus maximus
12. Semitendinosus
13. Semimembranosus
14. Biceps femoris (long head)
15. Iliotibial band
16. Gluteus medius
17. Piriformis
18. Superior gemellus
19. Obturator internus
20. Inferior gemellus
21. Quadratus femoris

Hip Regional Examination

☑ Check normal, circle & describe abnormal

Patient: ______________________ date: ________ (dd/mm/yr)
Insurance: ______________________
Date of birth: ______________________ M/F

CC & significant history: ______________________

Fracture screen (tuning fork, percussion, torsion test, 5-step test): □ WNL □ Refer for X-ray: ______________________

Observation: □ WNL

Development: □ good, □ fair, □ poor
□ Posture: ______________
□ Skin (bruising, scars): ______________
□ Asymmetry: ______________

Observation □ WNL	L	R
Leg length		
Q-angle		
Genu varum		
Genu valgum		
Iliac crest height		
Gluteal fold height		
Lumbar lordosis		
Lumbar scoliosis		
Toe in/out		
Femur int/external rotation		
Gait analysis		

Palpation: □ WNL

Palpation	L	R
ASIS/iliac crest		
TFL/ITB		
SI joint		
Sacrotuberous lig.		
Greater trochanter		
L-spine/sacrum		
Hip joint/capsule		
Gluteus max./med.		
Piriformis		
Sciatic nerve		
Ischial tuberosity		
Hamstrings		
Anterior thigh		
Iliopsoas		
Pubic symphysis		
Inguinal lig./nodes		
Femoral triangle		
Greater saph. vein		
Adductor muscles		

Mark on drawing □ pain (circle), □ spasm (s), □ edema (e), □ fibrotic (f), □ MFTP (x), □ ache (a), □ burning (b), □ tingling (t)

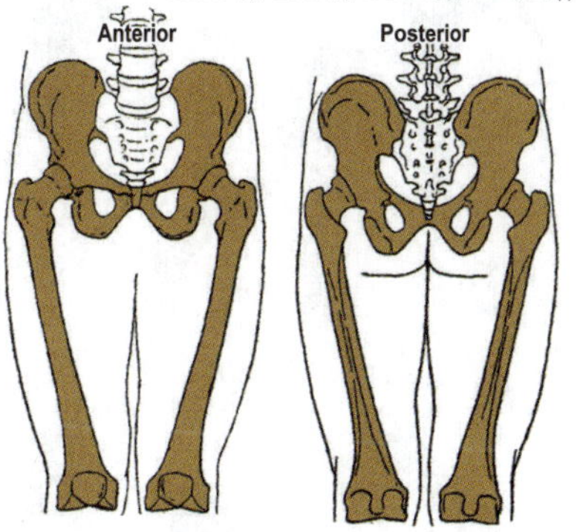

Hip & Thigh

ROM & Joint Play: □ WNL

□ Pain at end ROM: ______________
□ Abnormal motion: ______________

ROM	Active L	Active R	Passive L	Passive R
Flexion (120°) bent knee				
Flexion (80°-90°) SLR				
Extension (30°)				
Abduction (50°)				
Adduction (30°)				
Internal rotation (40°)				
External rotation (50°)				

Joint Play*	L	R	Comments
Long axis distraction			
Internal rotation (40°)			
External rotation (50°)			
SI joint			

Vascular Screen: □ WNL

Pulses (0-4)	L	R
Femoral pulse		
Tibial pulse		
Dorsal pedial		
Blanch test		

Neurologic: □ WNL

Reflexes (0-5), □ WNL	L	R
Patellar (L4)		
Hamstring (L5)		
Patellar (S1)		
Babinski		

Motor (0-5), □ WNL	L	R
Hip flexion (L2)		
Hip extension (L3-S1)		
Abduction (L4-S1)		
Adduction (L2-L4)		
Ext. rotation (L4-S1)		
Int. rotation (L4-S1)		
Knee flexion (L4-S1)		
Knee extension (L2-L4)		

Orthopedic: □ WNL

	L	R
Trendelenburg		
Heel walk (L5)		
Toe walk (S1)		
Toe touch		
Squat & rise		
Alli's sign		
Anvil		
Patrick FABERE		
Laguere		
Scour		
SI distraction		
SI compression		

	L	R
SLR active		
SLR passive		
Bragard's		
SLR maximal		
Valsalva		
Ober/Nobel/Rinné		
Thomas/Gaenslen's		
Nachlas		
Ely's		
Hibb's		
Yoeman's		
Kemp's		

Additional procedures: □ WNL

□ Abdominal exam: ______________
□ Knee exam: ______________
□ Lumbosacral exam: ______________

DDx:

Signature: Date:

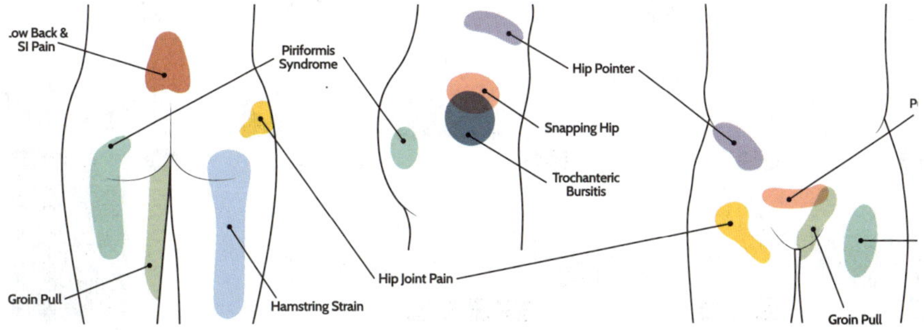

Compare bilaterally; prior to ROM the examiner makes an introduction statement:
"Try and move as far as possible, if any of the actions or movements are painful or uncomfortable please let me know, do not do any action you feel will cause you further injury."

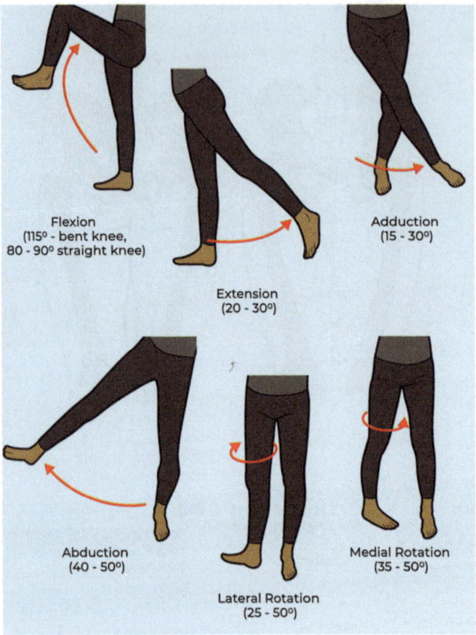

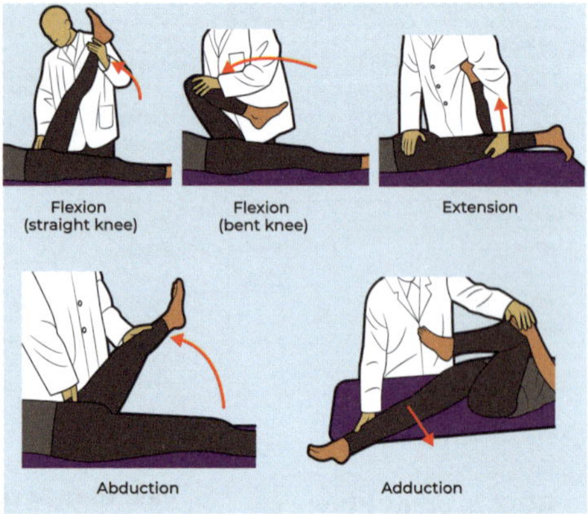

Muscle Testing

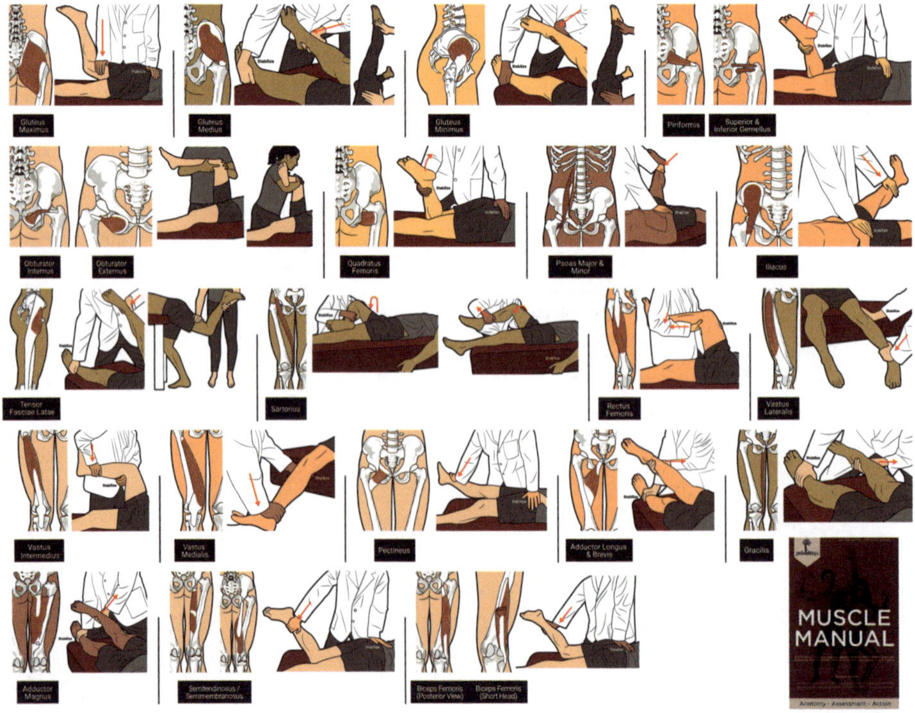

Coxa varus & valgus

- During growth it is possible for the femoral neck and acetabulum to have changes in orientations and the deepness of the joint socket
    - **Coxa valgus > 135°**
    - **Coxa varus < 120°**

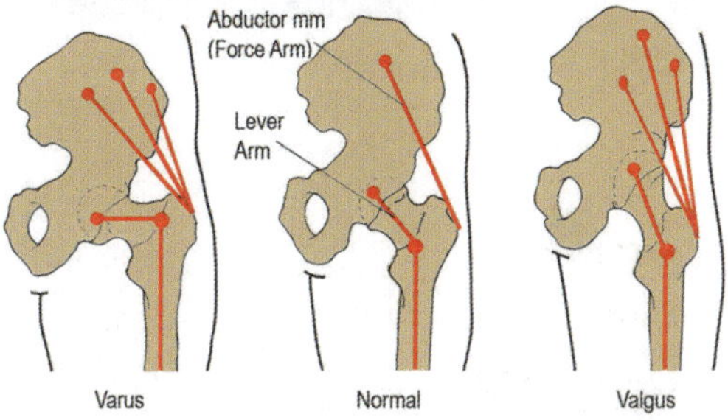

Anteversion & retroversion

- During growth it is possible for the femur and tibia to have anatomical variation in their long axis causing a rotational variation in alignment
    - **Medial rotation = anteversion**
    - **Lateral rotation = retroversion**

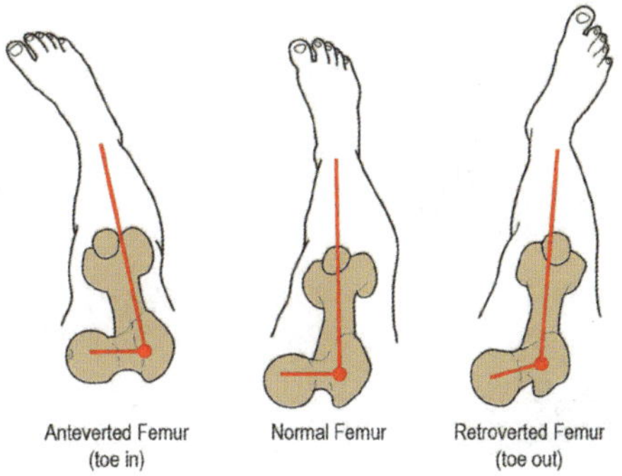

Trigger Points

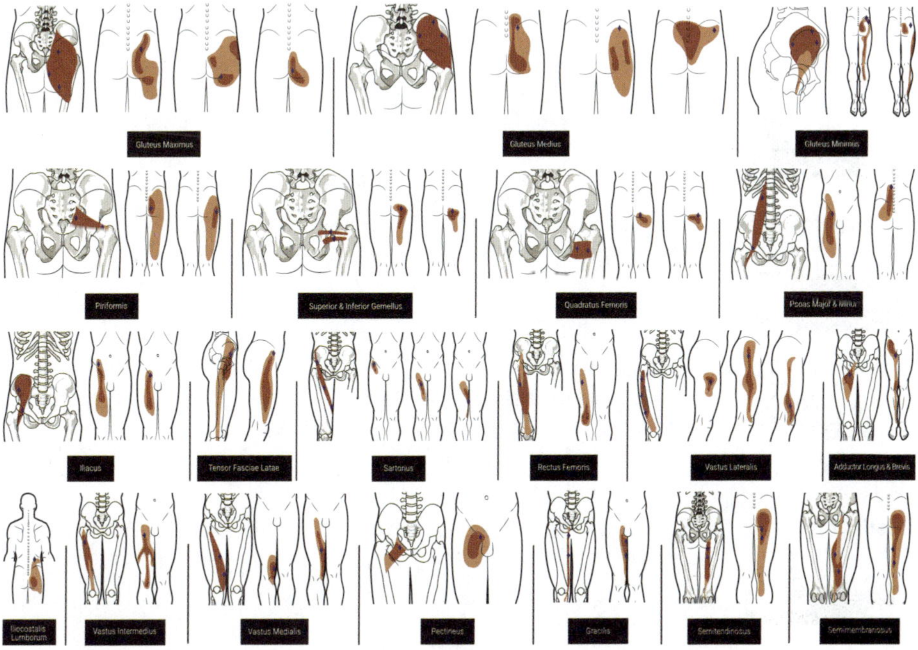

Test	Procedure	Interpretation	Clinical Notes
90-90 SLR Test 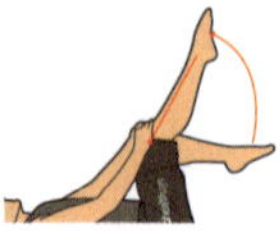	Patient supine, hips flexed to 90°. Extend each knee maximally	(+) Knee flexion >20° → Tight hamstrings	Useful for assessing hamstring flexibility. Also consider straight leg raise (SLR)
Abd/Adduction Tests 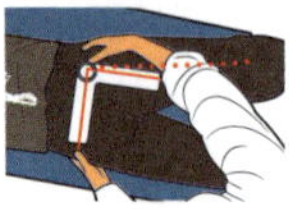	Patient supine, examiner evaluates leg angle relative to ASIS alignment	(+) Angle deviates from 90° → Abd/Adductor contracture	Assesses for muscle tightness affecting hip alignment. Can also use PROM
Allis' (skyline) Sign 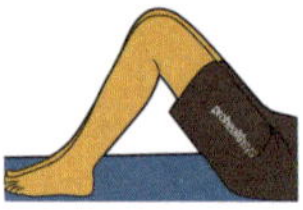	Patient supine, knees flexed to 90°, observe patella height differences	(+) Height difference → Tibial/ femoral length discrepancy	Indicates potential leg length inequality
Anvil Test 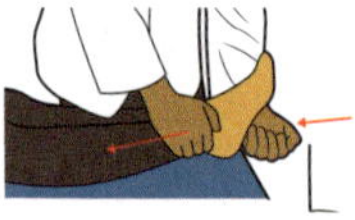	Tap patient's heel with a fist with gradually increasing intensity	(+) Pain in hip or femur → Fx or pathology in region	May also indicate infection or inflammation
Barlow & Ortolani 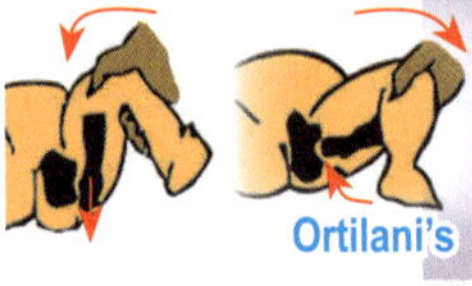	Infant supine, assess hip dislocation via posterior and anterior pressures	(+) Hip instability → Developmental hip dysplasia	Best used before 2–3 months of age
Craig's Test 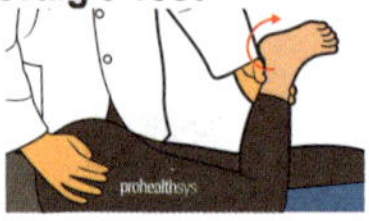	Pt prone, internally/externally rotate hip to find greater trochanter parallel to table	(+) Increased/ decreased anteversion → Hip alignment abnormality	Assesses femoral anteversion or retroversion
Dial (Log Roll) Test 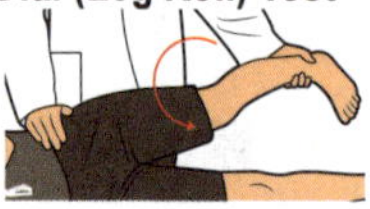	Pt supine, rotate hip internally and externally	(+) Excess ROM → Joint capsule laxity	Useful for identifying hip instability
Femoral Neck Stress 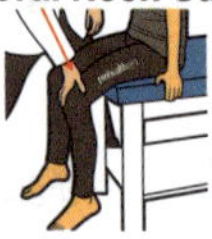	Pt seated femoral shaft on edge of table, examiner applies downward pressure on distal femur	(+) Pain → Femoral neck stress fracture	Consider female athlete triad/RED-S syndrome
Ober's Test 	Patient side-lying, extend and adduct hip with knee flexed	(+) Limited motion → IT Band tightness	Caution in patients with knee pathologies

Test	Procedure	Interpretation	Clinical Notes
Patrick's/FABERE 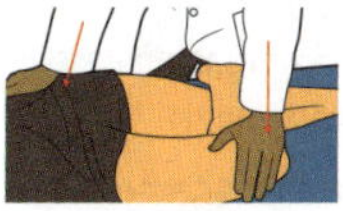	Patient supine, leg placed in **figure-4** position and pressure applied	(+) Pain → Hip pathology, tight adductors, or SI joint involvement	General screening test for hip issues
Piriformis/FAIR Test 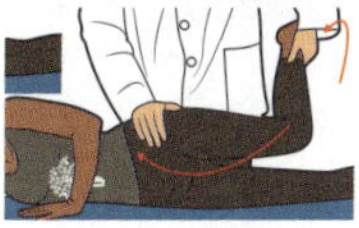	Flex, adduct, and internally rotate hip to stretch piriformis	(+) Pain → Piriformis syndrome or sciatic nerve compression	May also assess for femoral acetabular impingement
Scour (Quadrant) Test 	Apply compression and circumduction through hip ROM	(+) Pain → Labral tear, impingement, or osteoarthritis	Follow up with imaging if positive
Thomas Test 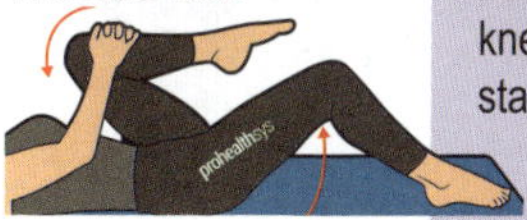	Pt supine, bring one knee to chest, other leg stays extended (straight)	(+) Straight leg elevation → Tight hip flexors	Modified Thomas test evaluates rectus femoris tightness
V (W) Test 	Pt prone, knees together. Observe femoral rotation (ante/retro) via hip alignment	(+) Ante or retro - version → Tight hip rotators, femoral ante or retroversion	Anteversion decreases from ~30° at birth to 8–15° in adulthood Increased angles may affect gait patterns

Hip & Thigh Rapid DDx

	Hx	SSx	Tx
Avascular Necrosis 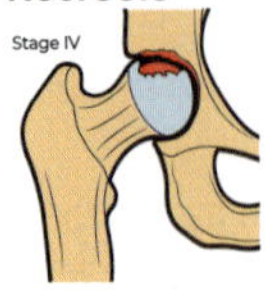	- Repetitive hip trauma, corticosteroid use, alcohol, diabetes; sickle cell anemia or atherosclerosis	- Pain/stiffness in hip joint - Antalgic limp - Limited ROM - Pain persists with rest	- Surgical (core decompression or joint replacement) - Pain management - Weight-bearing modifications
Acetabular Labral Tear 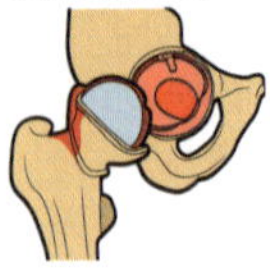	- Prior trauma or repetitive hip flexion (dancers, athletes)	- Sharp groin pain - Audible click with motion, pain with full hip flexion - (+) Flexion-Add.-Int. Rotation Test	- METH - Physical therapy - Arthroscopic repair if severe
Femoroacetabular Impingement (FAI) 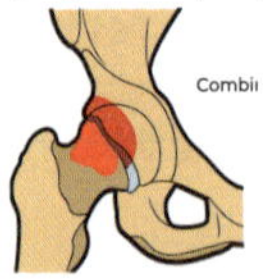	- Repetitive hip flexion or twisting motions (athletes, dancers)	- Groin pain worsens with hip flexion & rotation - ↓ ROM in flexion/ abduction - (+) FADIR Test	- METH, physical therapy). - Arthroscopic surgery if severe
Hernia (Inguinal or Femoral) 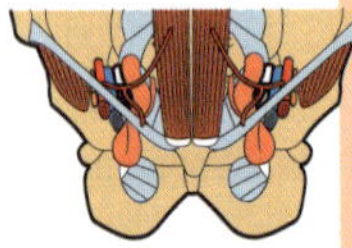	- **Heavy lifting** or activities with **Valsalva maneuver** - Males (inguinal) - Female (femoral)	- **Groin pain** worsened with straining or heavy lifting - Visible bulge in groin area	- Surgical repair - Avoid heavy lifting post-surgery - Gradual return to activity - May be reducible
Hip DJD (Osteoarthritis) 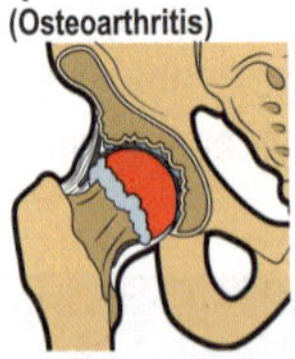	- Groin pain worsened with weight-bearing or cold weather - Morning stiffness	- **Antalgic gait** - ↓ ROM - **(+) Scour Test** - **Visible on x-ray** (joint space narrowing, sclerosis, osteophytes)	- Pain management (METH, Heat) - Weight control - Joint mobilization - ROM exercises

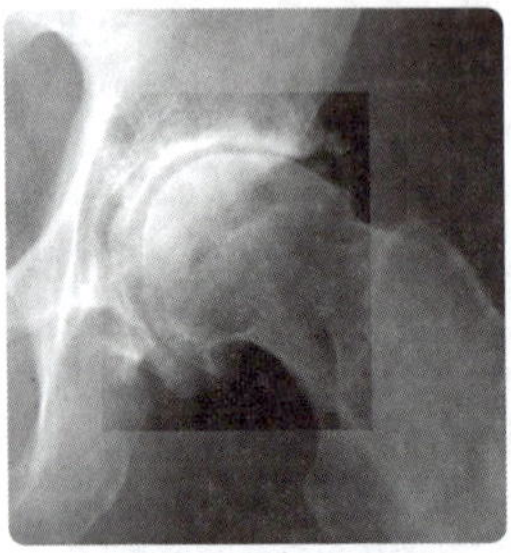

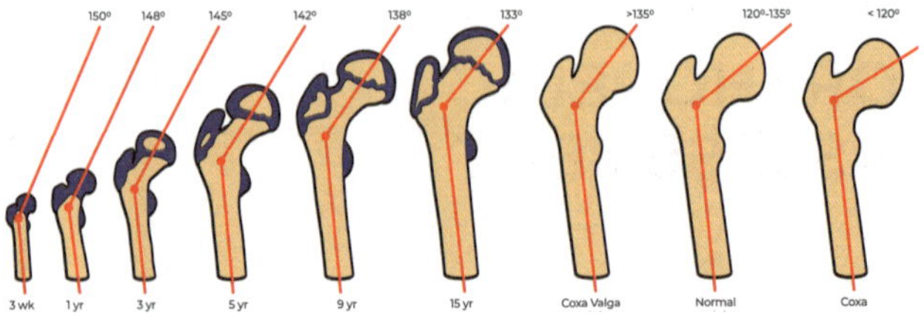

Hip & Thigh Rapid DDx

	Hx	SSx	Tx
Piriformis Syndrome 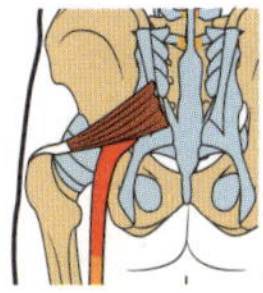	- Possible low back or buttock pain worsened by sitting - Possible sciatic compression	- **Tenderness on palpation** - Pain radiates down post. thigh - (+) SLR or Piriformis Test	- Stretching (piriformis, glutes) - Postural correction - METH for pain relief - Deep squats
Septic Arthritis 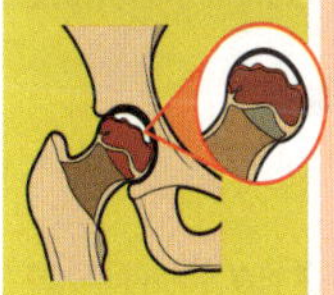	- **Rapid onset** of **severe hip pain** - Often follows respiratory or urinary tract infection	- **Severe pain** with joint movement - Swelling, redness, warmth - **Fever & fatigue**	- Emergency medical - Joint aspiration - Antibiotic therapy
SCFE (Slipped Capital Femoral Epiphysis) 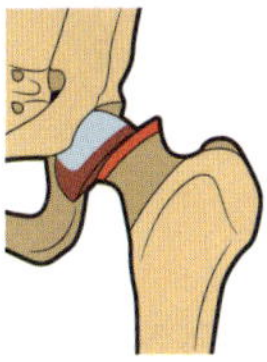	- Common in **adolescents** (ages 10–16) - Associated with obesity or rapid growth spurts	- **Groin, thigh, or knee pain** - Limp / altered gait - ↓ ROM in hip (especially internal rotation) - (+) Drehmann's Sign (hip externally rotates during flexion)	- Surgical treatment (pinning of femoral head) - Weight-bearing restrictions post-surgery - Gradual ExRx for mobility
Snapping Hip 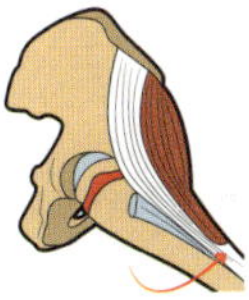	- **Repeated snapping** or popping during hip movements - Common in dancers & athletes	- Audible "pop" with ITB movement over greater trochanter - (+) Ober's Test	- Stretching (ITB, hip flexors) - Postural correction - METH - Rare surgery may be required
Trochanteric Bursitis 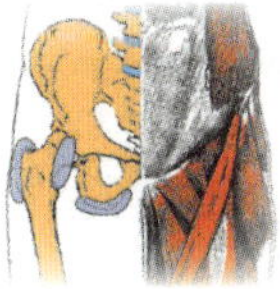	- **Overuse**, prolonged side-lying, or direct trauma to lateral hip	- Lateral hip pain - Pain ↑ with palpation over greater trochanter - (+) Palpation Tenderness	- Stretching (ITB & hip abductors) - Avoid prolonged side-lying - Activity mods

1. **Most common test for acetabular labral tear?**
   a) FABER test
   b) Trendelenburg test
   c) Craig's test
   d) Flexion-Adduction-Internal Rotation test

2. **Which condition is associated with sharp groin pain and often occurs in dancers or athletes?**
   a) Piriformis syndrome
   b) Snapping hip syndrome
   c) SCFE
   d) Trochanteric bursitis

3. **For patients with trochanteric bursitis, what is a recommended modification for activities?**
   a) Avoid crossing legs
   b) Gradual weight-bearing exercise
   c) Avoid side-lying on the affected side
   d) Increased resistance training

4. **Which test is used to confirm femoroacetabular impingement (FAI)?**
   a) FABER test
   b) Ober's test
   c) Scour (Quadrant) test
   d) Anterior Impingement test

5. **What is a key symptom of piriformis syndrome?**
   a) Pain with hip abduction
   b) Radiating pain down the leg
   c) Groin pain while walking
   d) Audible snapping sound

6. **Septic arthritis of hip is most often associated with?**
   a) Groin pain during activity
   b) Rapid onset of severe joint pain
   c) Audible hip click
   d) Pain relieved with rest

7. **A patient with SCFE is most likely to present with:**
   a) Pain localized to the iliac crest
   b) Limping and restricted internal hip rotation
   c) Shooting pain down the ITB
   d) Gradual onset of stiffness

8. **Contraindicated for patients with septic arthritis?**
   a) Joint mobilization
   b) Antibiotic therapy
   c) Rest
   d) Gentle ROM exercises post-recovery

9. **Primary finding in avascular necrosis of the hip?**
   a) Sudden locking of the hip
   b) Pain with weight-bearing and antalgic gait
   c) Pain relieved by sitting
   d) Audible snapping

10. **Trochanteric bursitis commonly presents with pain:**
    a) During hip abduction
    b) Localized to the greater trochanter
    c) While walking uphill
    d) Deep in the groin

11. **What is the typical treatment for snapping hip syndrome in athletes?**
    a) Surgery
    b) ITB stretching and hip flexor strengthening
    c) Rest with complete immobilization
    d) Manual therapy to the piriformis

12. **Which condition is linked to repetitive flexion movements in dancers and athletes?**
    a) SCFE
    b) Acetabular labral tear
    c) Snapping hip syndrome
    d) Femoroacetabular impingement

13. **A patient with hip DJD will likely benefit most from:**
    a) Surgery
    b) Weight control and ROM exercises
    c) Complete rest
    d) Strengthening only the glutes

14. **In inguinal hernia cases, what is a key clinical sign?**
    a) Visible bulge with increased intra-abdominal pressure
    b) Audible snapping of the hip
    c) Pain with hip abduction
    d) Tight ITB

15. **Common symptom of acetabular labral tear?**
    a) Groin pain with internal hip rotation
    b) Shooting pain down the lateral thigh
    c) Snapping or locking of the hip
    d) Radiating pain to the knee

16. **What is the initial management step for avascular necrosis?**
    a) Core decompression
    b) Manual therapy
    c) Gentle stretching
    d) Weight-bearing exercises

17. **A patient with piriformis syndrome may have a positive:**
    a) Trendelenburg test
    b) Ober's test
    c) FAIR test
    d) FABER test

18. **SCFE is most commonly seen in which age group?**
    a) 5–10 years
    b) 10–16 years
    c) 16–20 years
    d) 20–30 years

19. **Iliopsoas injury will cause weakness in what action?**
    a) Hip extension
    b) Hip external rotation
    c) Hip flexion
    d) Hip abduction

20. **Trochanteric bursitis is frequently managed by:**
    a) Stretching ITB & hip flexors
    b) Strengthening the adductors
    c) Complete immobilization
    d) Corticosteroid injections

PHS Certification

1: d	5: b	9: b	13: b	17: c
2: b	6: b	10: b	14: a	18: b
3: c	7: b	11: b	15: a	19: c
4: d	8: a	12: c	16: a	20: a

Case Study

Hip Osteoarthritis: A 68-yr-old reports chronic stiffness and pain in his hip, especially in the morning and after prolonged activity. He reports difficulty walking long distances and putting on socks. Examination reveals limited internal rotation and flexion of the hip joint, with crepitus on movement.

- What are the **key signs** of hip osteoarthritis?
- What **imaging findings** would confirm the diagnosis?
- What **conservative treatments** would you recommend?
- When would you consider **surgical intervention**, such as a hip replacement?

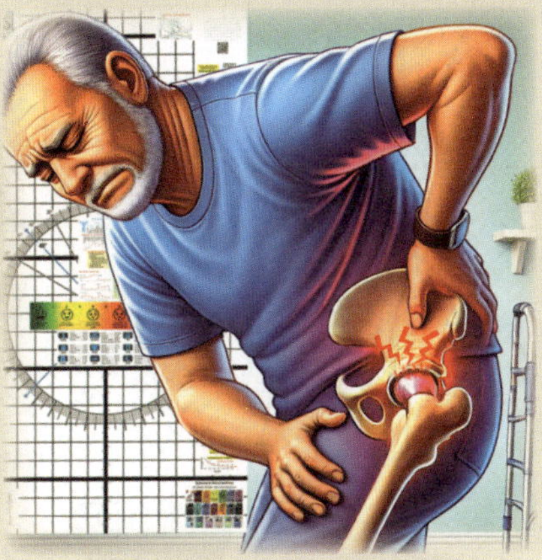

Case Study 2

A 35-yr-old office worker has developed a deep, aching pain in her buttocks and down her left leg over the past month. The pain increases when sitting for long periods and improves slightly with walking. She reports difficulty sleeping & concentrating during the day. Exam shows tenderness of the piriformis and pain with internal hip rotation. No prior trauma.

Questions:

- What is the most likely **differential diagnosis** for this patient?
- What **treatment options** should be explored to address the biomechanical and psychosocial aspects of her condition?
- How might **workplace ergonomic adjustments** play a role in her recovery?

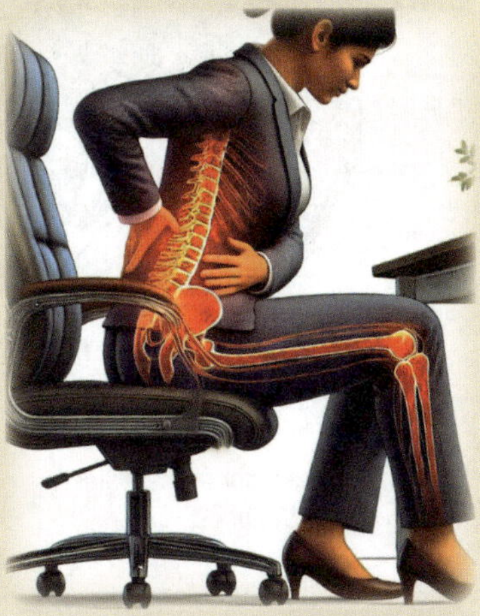

Case Study 3

A 45-year-old male presents with acute hip pain, fever, and difficulty walking. He describes the pain as severe, worsening over the past two days, and located deep in the left hip joint. He has a history of a recent upper respiratory infection but denies any direct trauma. Physical examination reveals restricted and painful hip motion, with warmth and swelling over the joint. Lab work shows an elevated white blood cell count and C-reactive protein levels. An X-ray is pending.

Questions:

- What is the most likely **differential diagnosis** for this patient?
- What **immediate interventions** are necessary to manage this condition?
- How might **delayed treatment** affect the patient's physical and psychological health?

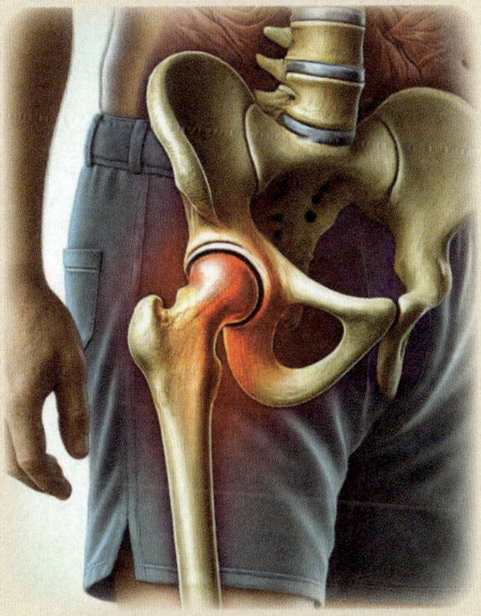

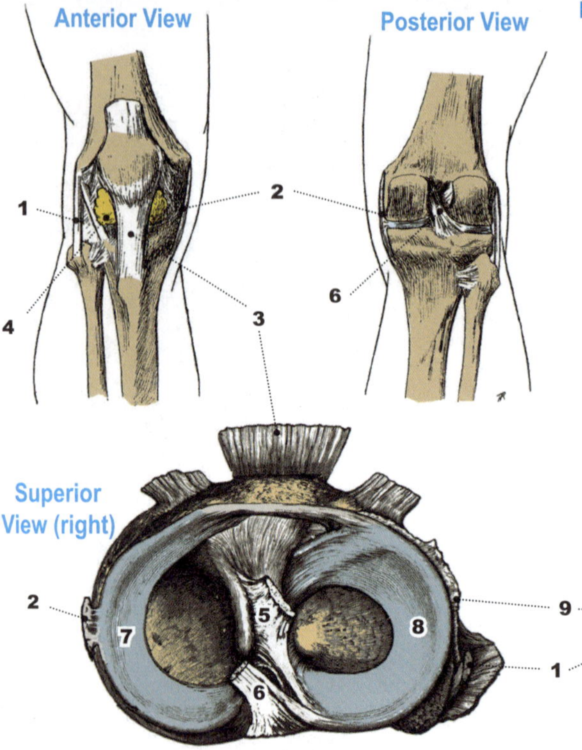

Knee ligaments

1. Lateral (fibular) collateral ligament
2. Medial (tibial) collateral ligament
3. Patellar ligament (infrapatellar tendon)
4. Infrapatellar fat pad
5. Anterior cruciate ligament
6. Posterior cruciate ligament
7. Medial meniscus
8. Lateral meniscus
9. Anterolateral Ligament (ALL)[1]

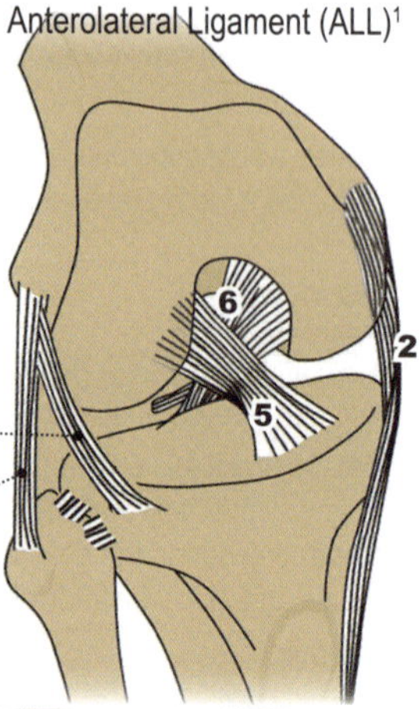

1. Tensor fasciae latae
2. Sartorius
3. Rectus femoris
4. Vastus lateralis
5. Vastus medialis
6. Iliotibial band
7. Iliopsoas
8. Pectineus
9. Adductor longus
10. Gracilis
11. Gluteus maximus
12. Semitendinosus
13. Biceps femoris
14. Semimembranosus
15. Gastrocnemius
16. Plantaris
17. Popliteus
18. Soleus

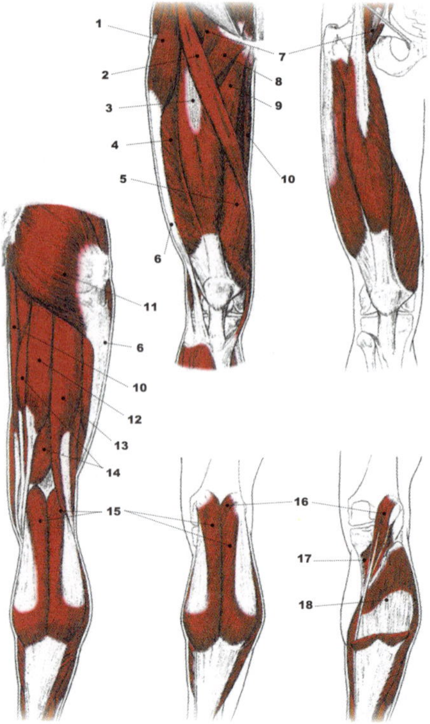

Knee/Thigh Regional Exam

☑ Check normal, circle & describe abnormal

Patient: ______________________ date: ________ (dd/mm/yr)
Insurance: ______________________
Date of birth: ______________________ M/F

CC & significant history: ______________________

Fracture screen (tuning fork, percussion, torsion test, 5-step test): □ WNL □ Refer for X-ray: ______________________

Observation: □ WNL

Development: □ good, □ fair, □ poor
□ Posture: ______________
□ Skin (bruising, scars): ______________
□ Swelling: ______________
□ Asymmetry: ______________

Observation □ WNL	L	R
Toe in / out		
Arch low / high		
Patella position (med, lat, ↑, ↓)		
Q-angle		
Genu varum / valgum		
Femur rotated int. / ext.		
Iliac crest height		
Lumbar hyper / hypolordosis		
Knee hyperextended		
Leg length		
Gait analysis		

Palpation: □ WNL, □ pain (circle), □ spasm (s), □ edema (e), □ fibrotic (f), □ MFTP (x), □ ache (a), □ tingling (t)

Palpation	L	R
Quadriceps		
Patella (facets, bursa)		
Patellar ligament		
Tibial tuberosity		
Retinaculum/plica		
Adductor canal		
Pes anserine		
Med. joint/meniscus		
Med. femoral condyle		
MCL & capsule		
Medial hamstrings		

Palpation	L	R
Saphenous vein		
Popliteal fossa		
Gastrocnemius heads		
Baker's cyst		
Lateral hamstrings		
Iliotibial band (ITB)		
Popliteus		
Lateral collateral lig.		
Lateral joint/meniscus		
Lat. femoral condyle		
Lat. tibial condyle		

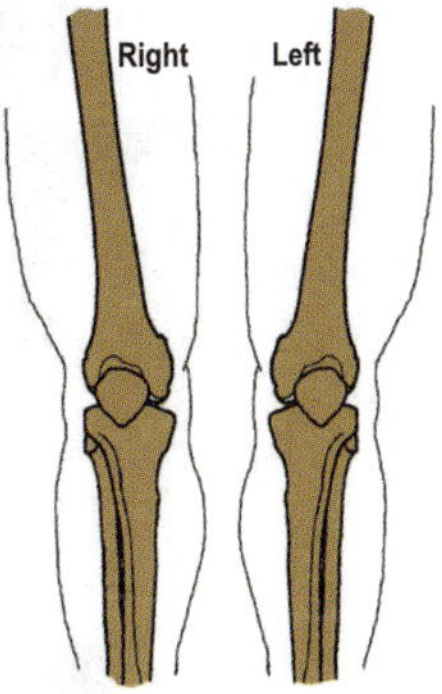

Vascular Screen: □ WNL

Pulses (0-4)	L	R
Popliteal pulse		
Tibial pulse		
Dorsal pedial		
Blanch test		

ROM & Joint Play: □ WNL

□ Pain at end ROM: ______________
□ Abnormal motion: ______________

ROM	Active L	Active R	Passive L	Passive R
Flexion (150°)				
Extension (0°)				
Internal rotation				
External rotation				

Joint Play	L	R	Comments
Anterior glide			
Posterior glide			
Medial tilt			
Lateral tilt			
Patella			
Internal rotation			
External rotation			
A↔P tibia/fibula			
Superior tib/fib			
Hamstring stretch			
Quadricep stretch			

Neurologic: □ WNL

Sensation, □ WNL	L	R
Light touch		
Sharp/dull		

Reflexes (0-5), □ WNL	L	R
Patellar (L4)		
Hamstring (L5)		
Patellar (S1)		
Babinski		

Motor (0-5), □ WNL	L	R
Med. hamstrings (L4-S1)(sciatic)		
Lat. hamstrings (L4-S2)(sciatic)		
Poplteus (L4-S1)(tibial)		
Hip adductors (L2-L4)(obturator)		
Sartorius (L2-L3)(femoral)		
TFL (L4-S1)(superior gluteal)		
Rectus femorus (L2-L4)(femoral)		
Vastus intermed. (L2-L4)(femoral)		
Vastus medialis (L2-L4)(femoral)		
Vastus lateralis (L2-L4)(femoral)		
other:		

Orthopedic: □ WNL

	L	R
Ballotment/ buldge		
Bounce home		
McMurray's		
Steinmann's		
Anterior drawer		
Posterior drawer		
Slocum's		
Lachman's		
Ober/Renne		
Valgus stress 0°		
Valgus stress 30°		

	L	R
Varus stress 0°		
Varus stress 30°		
Pivot shift		
Patellar apprehen.		
Plica tests		
Pat-femoral grind		
Clarke's test		
Genu recurvatum		
Apley compression		
Apley distraction		
Hyperflexion test		

Additional procedures: □ WNL

□ Hip exam: ______________
□ Ankle exam: ______________ □
Lumbosacral: ______________

DDx:

Signature: Date:

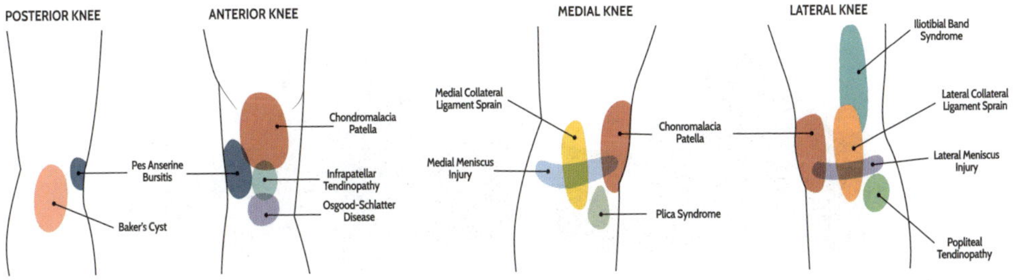

Compare bilaterally; prior to ROM the examiner makes an introduction statement:
"Try and move as far as possible, if any of the actions or movements are painful or uncomfortable please let me know, do not do any action you feel will cause you further injury."

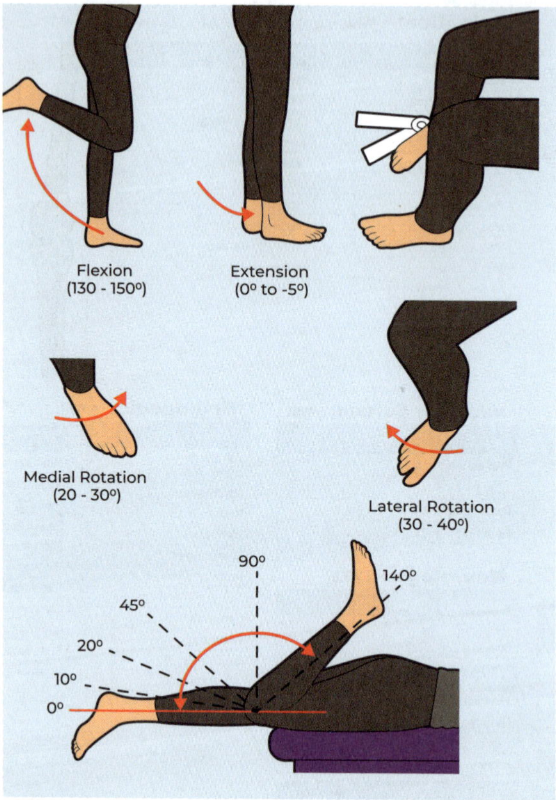

Which knee hurts?

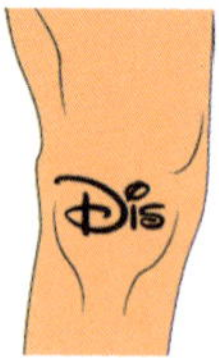

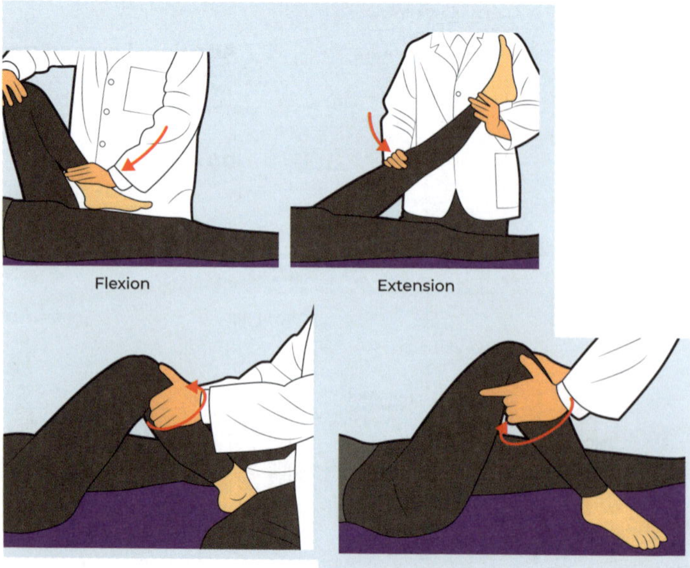

Knee

Prepared for: ______
Prepared by: ______
Purpose of program: ______

Knee Strengthen

Recover Faster & Prevent Injury - After an injury or surgery, exercise, stretch and strengthen speed recovery and reduce future risks. **Regular activity improves mood, healing times, and slows aging.**

Warm-Up - Start with 5–10 minutes of low-impact activity like walking or biking.

Ask Questions
If unsure about an exercise or routine, consult your doctor, therapist, or trainer.

Strengthen - To build & stabilize joints, relieve pain, and prevent further injuries.

Stretch - to restore motion, reduce soreness, and prevent injuries.

prohealthsys
PROFESSIONAL HEALTH SYSTEMS

Prescription (your doctor, therapist or trainer will circle desired exercises above and give appropriate directions on how to perform)
______ reps, ______ sets, ______ seconds to hold, ______ times/day or week

"We've got your back." By Dr. Nikita Vizniak. prohealthsys.com

Prepared for: ______
Prepared by: ______
Purpose of program: ______

Knee Stretches

Recover Faster & Prevent Injury - After an injury or surgery, exercise, stretch and strengthen speed recovery and reduce future risks. **Regular activity improves mood, healing times, and slows aging.**

Warm-Up - Start with 5–10 minutes of low-impact activity like walking or biking.

Ask Questions
If unsure about an exercise or routine, consult your doctor, therapist, or trainer.

Strengthen - To build & stabilize joints, relieve pain, and prevent further injuries.

Stretch - to restore motion, reduce soreness, and prevent injuries.

prohealthsys
PROFESSIONAL HEALTH SYSTEMS

Prescription (your doctor, therapist or trainer will circle desired exercises above and give appropriate directions on how to perform)
______ reps, ______ sets, ______ seconds to hold, ______ times/day or week

"We've got your back." By Dr. Nikita Vizniak. prohealthsys.com

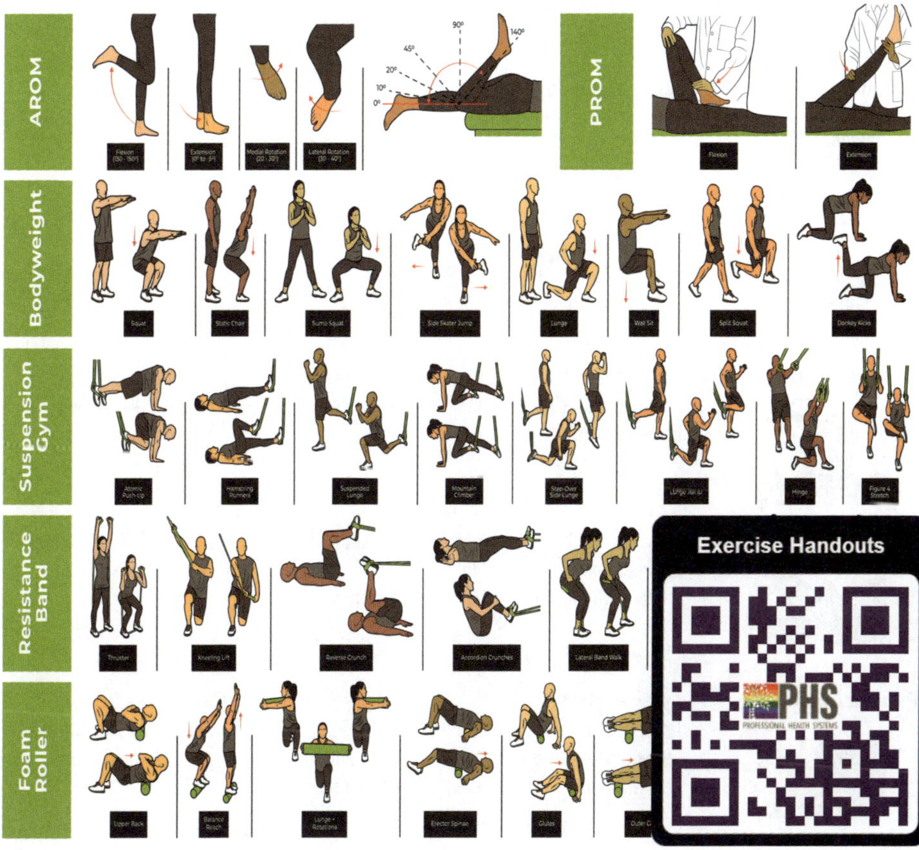

Exercise Handouts

Knee

Test	Procedure	Interpretation	Clinical Notes
Active Drawer Tests 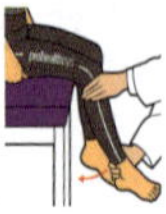	Pt seated, knee at 90°. Palpate joint line, stabilize foot, and ask pt to contract quads, then hams against resistance	(+) Tibia shifts anterior or posterior → PCL/ACL injury	Overactivation of hamstrings may mask findings
Apley's Compression 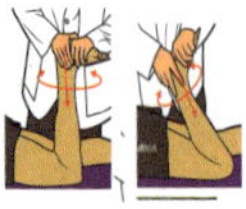	Pt prone, knee at 90°. Apply downward force while internally & externally rotating tibia	(+) Pain/clicking → Meniscal damage	Combine with other tests for increased diagnostic accuracy
Apley's Distraction 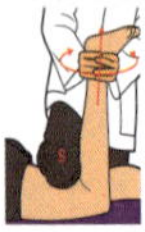	Pt prone, knee at 90°. Apply upward traction & rotate tibia	(+) Pain or laxity → Ligament injury	Pain localized to rotation direction indicates medial or lateral ligament involvement
Anterior Drawer Test 	Pt supine, knee at 90°. Stabilize foot, pull tibia forward	(+) Pain/excess motion → ACL injury	Overactive hamstrings may cause false negatives
Ballottement Test 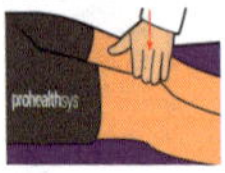	Pt supine, knee extended. Press patella downward	(+) Patella bounces back → Joint effusion	Use alongside clinical history for better joint assessment
Lachman Test 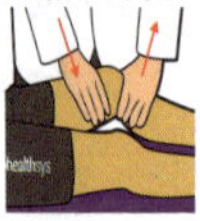	Pt supine, knee at 15–30°. Stabilize femur, pull tibia anterior, then push posterior	(+) Pain/motion → ACL or PCL injury	Gold standard for ACL evaluation
McMurray's Test 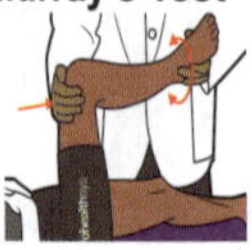	Pt supine, flex knee, apply valgus/varus stress with tibial rotation	(+) Pain/click → Meniscal tear	Pain during external rotation → Medial meniscus; internal rotation → Lateral meniscus
Noble Compression 	Pt supine, apply pressure to lateral femoral epicondyle while flexing/extending knee.	(+) Pain at 30° → IT Band syndrome.	Test simulates running-related pain
Patellar Apprehen. 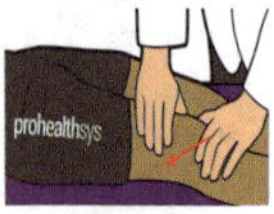	Pt supine, push patella laterally. Observe for signs of discomfort or apprehension.	(+) Apprehension → Patellar instability/ subluxation.	Can assess for sensitivity with inferior patellar movement

Test	Procedure	Interpretation	Clinical Notes
Patellar Grind Test 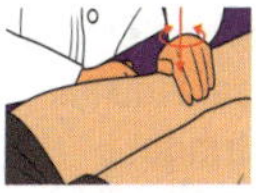	Pt supine, knee straight compress patella downward and move from side to side	(+) Pain or grinding → Patellofemoral dysfunction.	Useful for assessing cartilage integrity and patellar tracking issues
Posterior Drawer 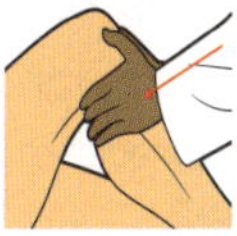	Pt supine, knee at 90°. Stabilize foot, push tibia posteriorly	(+) Pain/excess motion → PCL injury	Ensure pt relaxation to avoid false negatives
Thessaly's (Disco) 	Pt stands on one leg, knee flexed at 20°. Rotate body over knee	(+) Pain/click or knee buckles → Meniscal tear	Best for functional meniscus assessment. Be ready to support patient if they fall
Valgus Stress Test 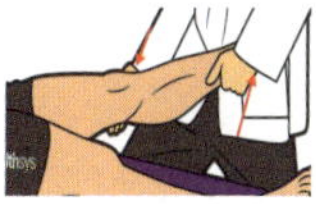	Pt supine, knee extended. Apply valgus force at knee	(+) Pain/laxity → MCL injury	Test with knee flexed to isolate MCL
Varus Stress Test 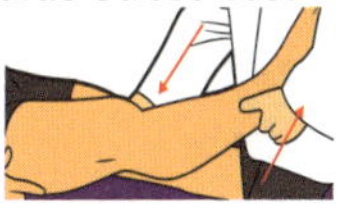	Pt supine, knee extended. Apply varus force at knee	(+) Pain/laxity → LCL injury	Test with knee flexed to isolate LCL

	Hx	SSx	Tx
ACL Tear 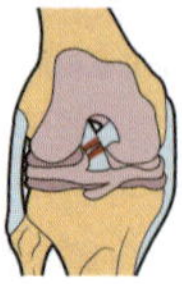	- Direct trauma with **valgus or hyperextension** - Audible "pop" during activity (soccer, basketball)	- **Swelling, knee instability** - (+) **Lachman's, Anterior Drawer Test, MRI** - ↓ ROM	- Surgical repair if severe - Physio for strengthening stabilizers (quads, **hamstrings**)
MCL Tear 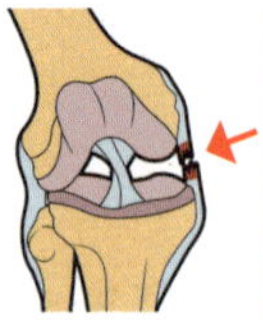	- Trauma with **valgus stress** (lateral blow to knee)	- Local tenderness over medial knee - (+) **Valgus Stress Test, MRI** - Instability with medial stress	- Brace for stabilization - ExRx for medial knee stabilizers
LCL Tear 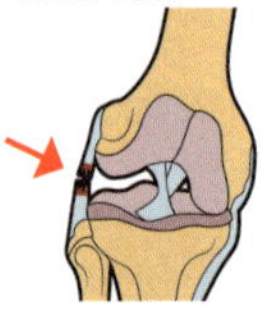	- Trauma with **varus stress** (medial blow to knee)	- Tenderness over lateral knee - (+) **Varus Stress Test, MRI** - Instability with lateral stress	- Brace stabilization - Physiotherapy for lateral knee stabilizers - Ice acute, METH
PCL Tear 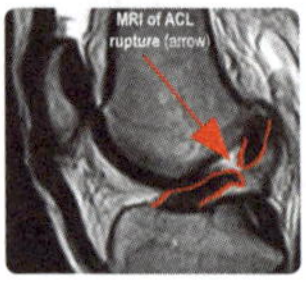	- Trauma with posterior-directed force (dashboard injury)	- Swelling, posterior knee pain - (+) **Posterior Drawer, Reverse Lachman's, MRI**	- Rehab for partial tears - Surgical repair for severe instability - **ExRx quads**
Chondromalacia Patellae 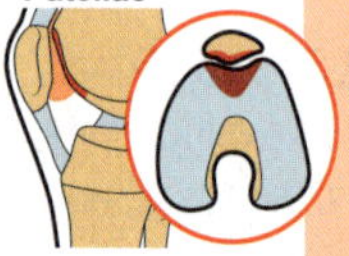	- Anterior knee pain worsened by **prolonged sitting or stairs** (Movie Theater Sign)	- Grinding sensation under patella - (+) **Patellar Grind Test**, Crepitus during flexion	- Patellar taping - Strengthening quads & glutes - Stretching IT band
Meniscus Tear 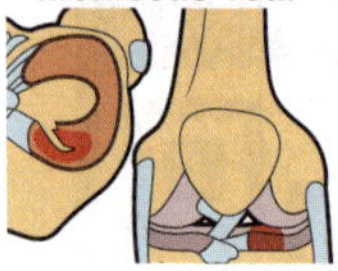	- **Twisting injury** or deep flexion trauma - **Painful clicking or locking**	- **Joint line tenderness** - (+) McMurray's, Thessaly Test - Swelling & ↓ ROM	- Conservative (rest, METH) - Arthroscopic repair if severe - Strengthening stabilizers
Osgood-Schlatter's 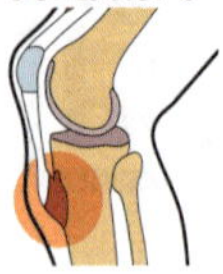	- **Pre-teens/teens** (active individuals) - Gradual onset of anterior knee pain with activity	- Tenderness over tibial tuberosity - Swelling, redness on **tibial tubercle** - Pain with kneeling or running	- Activity modification - Stretching (quads, hamstrings) - Ice post-activity

	Hx	SSx	Tx
ITB Friction Syndrome 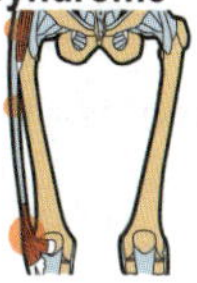	- **Overuse** injury (runners) - Lateral knee pain worsened with activity	- Tender lateral femoral epicondyle - (+) Ober's Test, Noble's Test	- Activity modification - Stretching IT band & lateral quads - METH for inflammation
Patellar Tendinitis (Jumper's Knee) 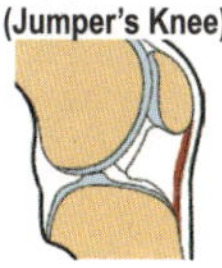	- Repetitive jumping or running - Athletes (volleyball, basketball)	- **Tender inf patella** - Pain ↑ w/ jumping or squatting - (+) Palpation Tenderness Test	- Ice, METH - Eccentric strengthening of quads - Patellar taping
Patellar Dislocation 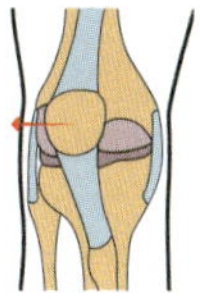	- **Trauma** or twisting force during knee extension - Often occurs in young athletes	- **Deformity with lateral patella displacement** - Pain & swelling - (+) Apprehension Test	- Immediate reduction (medical intervention) - Brace for stabilization - Physio strengthen stabilizers (VMO)
Knee Bursitis 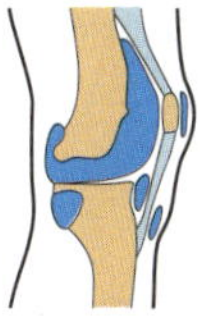	- **Repetitive kneeling** or direct trauma to knee ("housemaid's knee")	- Swelling & tender over patella or pes anserine - Pain with pressure or movement - (+) Palpation pain	- Ice, METH - Avoid aggravating activities - Gentle ROM exercises
Knee DJD (Osteoarthritis) 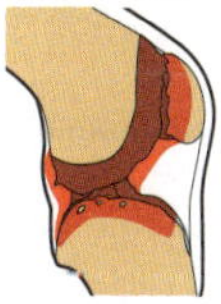	- **Gradual onset of pain & stiffness** - Common in older adults or post-trauma	- **Pain weight-bearing** - **Crepitus during movement** - ↓ ROM - (+) Scour Test	- Weight control - Strengthening quads & hams - Exercises, ROM, aquatherapy - METH

Knee

1. **Which condition is associated with anterior knee pain that worsens with prolonged sitting or stairs?**
   a) ITB Friction Syndrome
   b) Patellar Tendinitis
   c) Chondromalacia Patellae
   d) Meniscus Tear

2. **Which test is used to diagnose ACL tears?**
   a) McMurray's Test
   b) Anterior Drawer Test
   c) Ober's Test
   d) Patellar Grind Test

3. **Common symptom of ITB Friction Syndrome?**
   a) Medial knee pain
   b) Grinding under the kneecap
   c) Lateral knee pain during running
   d) Pain at the back of the knee

4. **Primary treatment for acute Meniscus Tear?**
   a) Weight control
   b) Patellar taping
   c) Rest, METH, and bracing
   d) Friction massage

5. **Which condition is typically seen in active pre-teens and involves anterior knee pain?**
   a) ITB Friction Syndrome
   b) Osgood-Schlatter's
   c) Patellar Dislocation
   d) PCL Tear

6. **Which test is most commonly associated with diagnosing Meniscus Tears?**
   a) Lachman's Test
   b) Valgus Stress Test
   c) McMurray's Test
   d) Posterior Drawer Test

7. **What is a key clinical feature of Patellar Tendinitis?**
   a) Pain with jumping and running
   b) Audible pop in the knee
   c) Lateral knee pain
   d) Medial joint line tenderness

8. **Which treatment option is most appropriate for Chondromalacia Patellae?**
   a) Arthroscopic surgery
   b) Patellar taping & strengthening quads
   c) Bracing lateral knee stabilizers
   d) Ice & METH

9. **Which structure is typically involved in PCL tears?**
   a) Medial collateral ligament
   b) Posterior cruciate ligament
   c) IT band
   d) Lateral meniscus

10. **What type of massage is recommended for ITB Friction Syndrome?**
   a) Effleurage around the quadriceps
   b) Friction massage over the IT band
   c) Trigger point therapy for hamstrings
   d) Petrissage of the lateral thigh

11. **Which condition is most commonly caused by trauma or twisting force?**
   a) Patellar Dislocation
   b) Patellar Tendinitis
   c) ITB Friction Syndrome
   d) Osgood-Schlatter's

12. **What is the hallmark test for diagnosing PCL tears?**
   a) McMurray's Test
   b) Posterior Drawer Test
   c) Ober's Test
   d) Patellar Grind Test

13. **What symptom is most commonly associated with Knee DJD?**
   a) Grinding during flexion
   b) Pain when weight-bearing
   c) Locking or clicking of the knee
   d) Lateral pain during running

14. **What is a common cause of Patellar Dislocation?**
   a) Repetitive jumping or running
   b) Trauma with a twisting force
   c) Poor footwear mechanics
   d) Weak quads

15. **Treatment is most effective for Osgood-Schlatter's?**
   a) Ice & METH
   b) Effleurage for quadriceps
   c) Strengthening exercises for lateral knee stabilizers
   d) Bracing for patellar alignment

16. **What is a common symptom of Knee Bursitis?**
   a) Tenderness over lateral epicondyle
   b) Swelling and pain over the patella
   c) Pain during flexion and extension
   d) Audible pop during activity

17. **Test is used to assess ITB Friction Syndrome?**
   a) Ober's Test
   b) Lachman's Test
   c) Posterior Drawer Test
   d) Patellar Grind Test

18. **Activity commonly exacerbates ITB Syndrome?**
   a) Jumping
   b) Prolonged sitting
   c) Running downhill
   d) Squatting

19. **Which condition is linked to medial joint line tenderness?**
   a) PCL Tear
   b) ACL Tear
   c) Meniscus Tear
   d) Chondromalacia Patellae

20. **What is the recommended massage treatment for Knee DJD?**
   a) MFR for IT band
   b) Effleurage for quadriceps
   c) Frictions for medial meniscal tissue
   d) Trigger point therapy for hamstrings

PHS Certification

1. c	5. b	9. b	13. b	17. a
2. b	6. c	10. b	14. b	18. c
3. c	7. a	11. a	15. a	19. c
4. c	8. b	12. b	16. b	20. b

Case Study 1

A 17-year-old soccer player complains of sharp pain and instability in her knee after twisting awkwardly during a match. She recalls hearing a "pop" and now has difficulty bearing weight. Examination reveals significant swelling, reduced ROM, and a positive **Lachman's Test.**

Questions:

- What is the **differential diagnosis** for this presentation?
- What **additional imaging or special tests** would confirm the condition?
- What **treatment options**, including rehabilitation and massage interventions, would you recommend?
- How might the player's **emotional response** to the injury (e.g., fear of re-injury or missing matches) affect her rehabilitation process?

Case Study 2

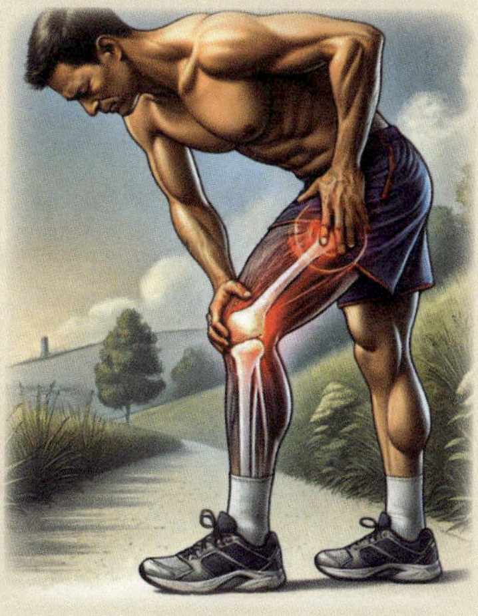

A 45-year-old marathon runner presents with gradual onset of lateral knee pain that intensifies during prolonged runs and downhill running. He denies any swelling but describes tightness and snapping along the outer thigh. Physical examination reveals tenderness along the iliotibial band and a positive **Ober's Test**.

Questions:

- What is the **differential diagnosis** for this condition?
- What **biomechanical or activity factors** could contribute to this presentation?
- What combination of **treatments**, including strengthening and manual therapy, would help resolve this condition?
- Could the runner's training habits, stress levels, or work-life balance contribute to the persistence of his pain?

Case Study 3

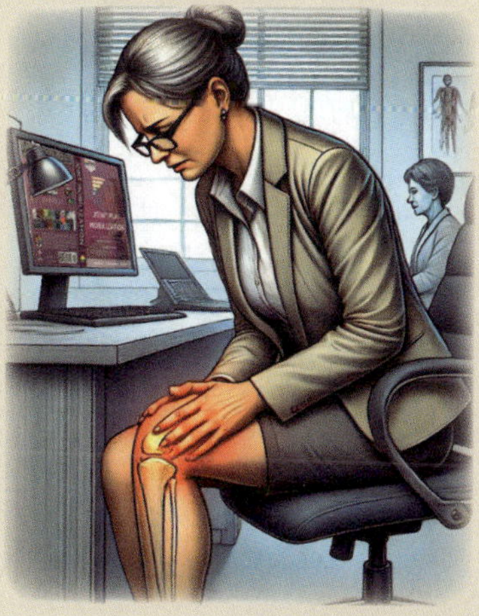

A 55-year-old office worker reports chronic anterior knee pain that worsens after prolonged sitting, climbing stairs, or descending inclines. She reports occasional grinding sensations but no history of trauma. Exam reveals tenderness under the patella, crepitus during movement, and a positive **Patellar Grind Test**.

Questions:

- What is the **differential diagnosis** for these symptoms?
- What **therapeutic exercises** could improve condition?
- How might **workplace ergonomics, physical activity levels, or psychosocial stressors** influence the progression or recovery of her condition?
- How could **massage and soft tissue techniques** complement the treatment plan?

Lateral ankle

1. Posterior tibiofibular ligament
2. Anterior tibiofibular ligament
3. Posterior talofibular ligament
4. Calcaneofibular ligament
5. Anterior talofibular ligament

Medial ankle

6. Deltoid (medial collateral) ligament

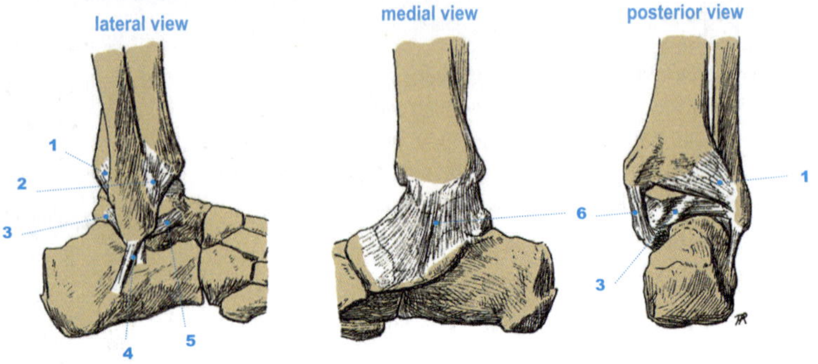

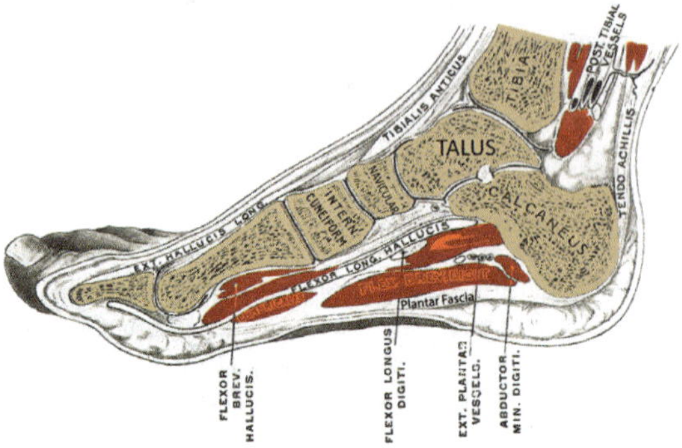

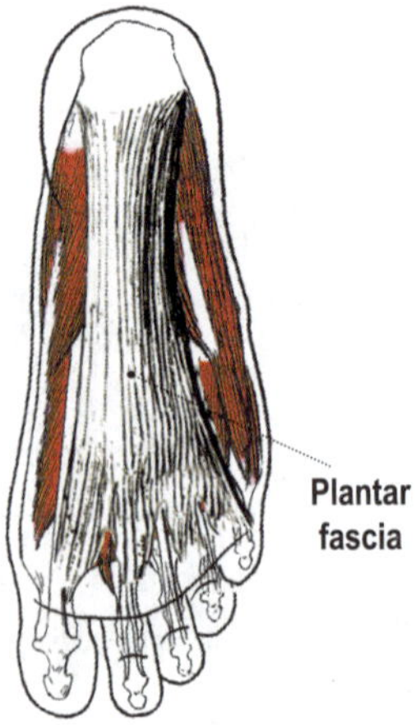

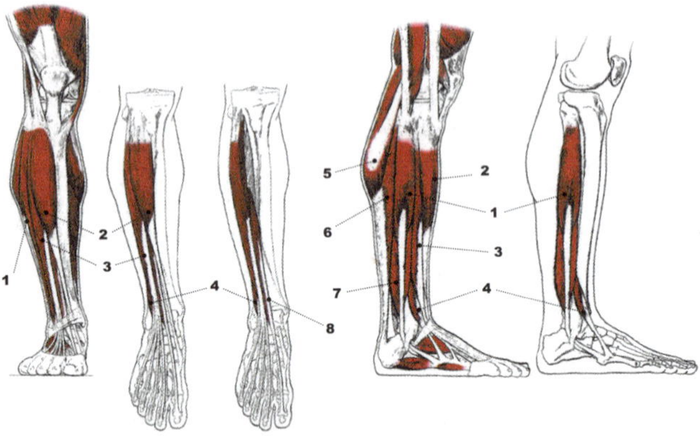

1. Fibularis (peroneus) longus
2. Tibialis anterior
3. Extensor digitorum longus
4. Fibularis (peroneus) tertius
5. Gastrocnemius
6. Soleus
7. Fibularis (peroneus) brevis
8. Extensor hallucis longus
9. Plantaris
10. Popliteus
11. Tibialis posterior
12. Flexor hallucis longus
13. Flexor digitorum longus
14. Achilles tendon

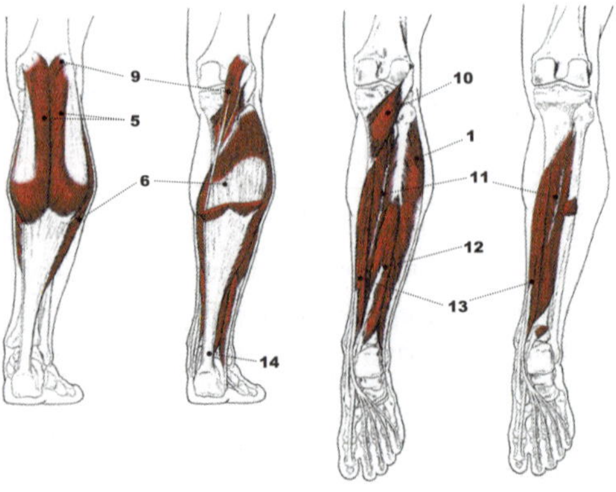

Ankle/Leg Regional Exam

☑ Check normal, circle & describe abnormal

Patient:__________________________ date: ______ (dd/mm/yr)
Insurance: __________________________
Date of birth: __________________________ M/F

CC & significant history: ____

Fracture screen (tuning fork, percussion, torsion test, 5-step test): □ WNL □ Refer for X-ray: ____________________

Observation: □ WNL

Development: □ good, □ fair, □ poor
□ Posture: ____________________
□ Skin (bruising, scars): ____________________
□ Swelling: ____________________
□ Asymmetry: ____________________

Observation □ WNL	L	R
Toe in / out		
Arch low / high		
Patella position (med, lat, ↑, ↓)		
Q-angle		
Genu varum / valgum		
Femur rotated int. / ext.		
Iliac crest height		
Lumbar hyper / hypolordosis		
Knee hyperextended		
Leg length		
Gait analysis		

Palpation: □ WNL, □ pain (circle), □ spasm (s), □ edema (e), □ fibrotic (f), □ MFTP (x), □ ache (a), □ tingling

Palpation	L	R
Tibial tub./fibular head		
Tibial crest		
Lateral malleolus		
Medial malleolus		
Navicular		
Cuboid		
Cuneiforms		
Talus (head, neck, trochlea)		
Calcaneus		
Sustentaculum tali		
Metatarsals		
Phalanges		
Sinus tarsi		
Ant. talofibular lig.		
Calcaneofibular lig.		
Post. talofibular lig.		
Spring ligament		
Deltoid ligament		

	L	R
Subtalar joint		
Midtarsal joint		
Tarsometatarsal joints		
MP joints		
PIP joints		
DIP joints		
Gastroc/soleus		
Lateral leg muscles		
Anterior leg muscles		
Achilles tendon		
Fibularis tendons		
TDH muscles		
Tarsal tunnel		
Tib. anterior/posterior		
Calcaneal bursa		
Plantar fascia		
Plantar muscles		
Saphenous vein		

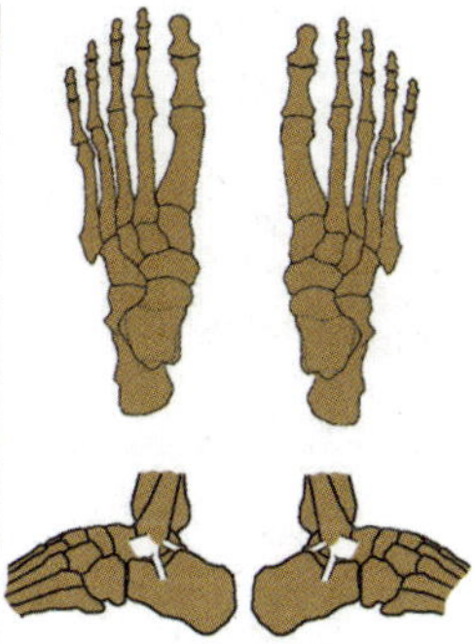

ROM & Joint Play: □ WNL

□ Pain at end ROM: ____________________
□ Abnormal motion: ____________________

ROM	Active		Passive	
	L	R	L	R
Plantarflexion (40°)				
Dorsiflexion (20°)				
Inversion (20°)				
Eversion (10°)				

Joint Play	L	R	Comments
Inferior tib-fib			
Ankle joint			
Subtalar joint			
Midtarsal joint			
Navicular-cuneif.			
Cuneiform-meta			
Intermetatarsal			
Hallux-metatarsal			
Metatarsophalang.			
PIP			
DIP			

Vascular Screen: □ WNL

Pulses (0-4)	L	R
Popliteal pulse		
Tibial pulse		
Dorsal pedial		
Blanch test		

Neurologic: □ WNL

Sensation, □ WNL	L	R
Light touch		
Sharp/dull		

Reflexes (0-5), □ WNL	L	R
Patellar (L4)		
Hamstring (L5)		
Achilles (S1)		
Babinski		

Motor (0-5), □ WNL	L	R
Plantarflexion (L4-S2)(tibial)		
Dorsiflexion (L4-S1)(deep fibular)		
Inversion (L4-L5)(deep fibular)		
Eversion (L4-S1)(superficial fib.)		
Toe flexion (L5-S2)(tibial)		
Toe extension (L4-S1)(deep fib.)		
Toe abd./add. (S1-S2)(tibial)		
other:		

Orthopedic: □ WNL

	L	R
Anterior drawer plantarflexed		
Anterior drawer neutral		
Inversion talar tilt plantarflexed		
Inversion talar tilt neutral		
Eversion talar tilt		
Rotational stress (Kleiger)		
Hoffa's sign		
Thompson/Simmond's test		
Achilles squeeze		
Calcaneal squeeze x 3		
Homan's sign/calf squeeze		
Buerger's claudication test		
Morton's foot squeeze		
Tinel's test at ankle		

Additional procedures: □ WNL

□ Hip exam: ____________________
□ Knee exam: ____________________
□ Lumbosacral: ____________________

DDx:

Signature: Date:

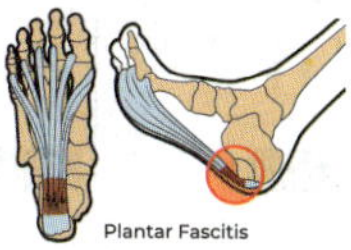

Plantar Fascitis

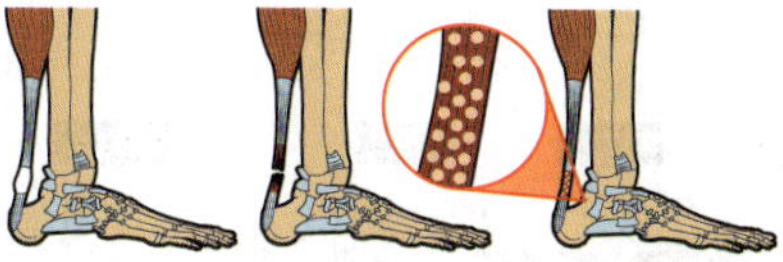

Achilles Tendonitis

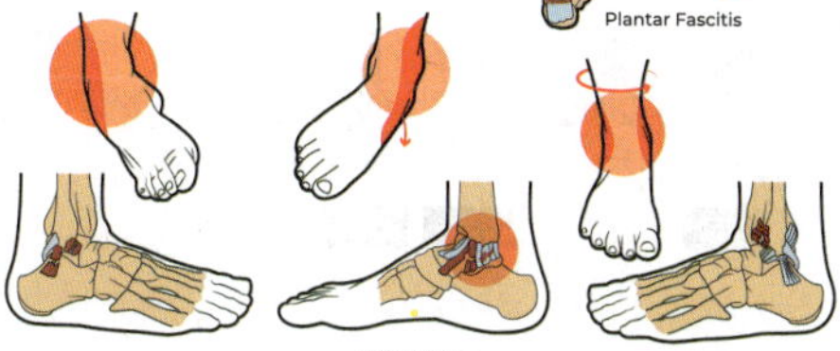

Ankle Sprain

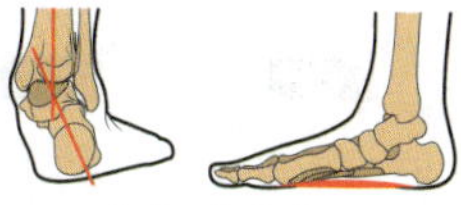

Over Pronation Syndrome

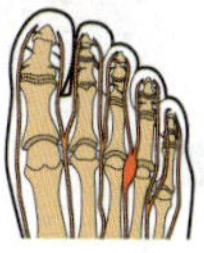

Morton's Neuroma

Compare bilaterally; prior to ROM the examiner makes an introduction statement:
"Try and move as far as possible, if any of the actions or movements are painful or uncomfortable please let me know, do not do any action you feel will cause you further injury."

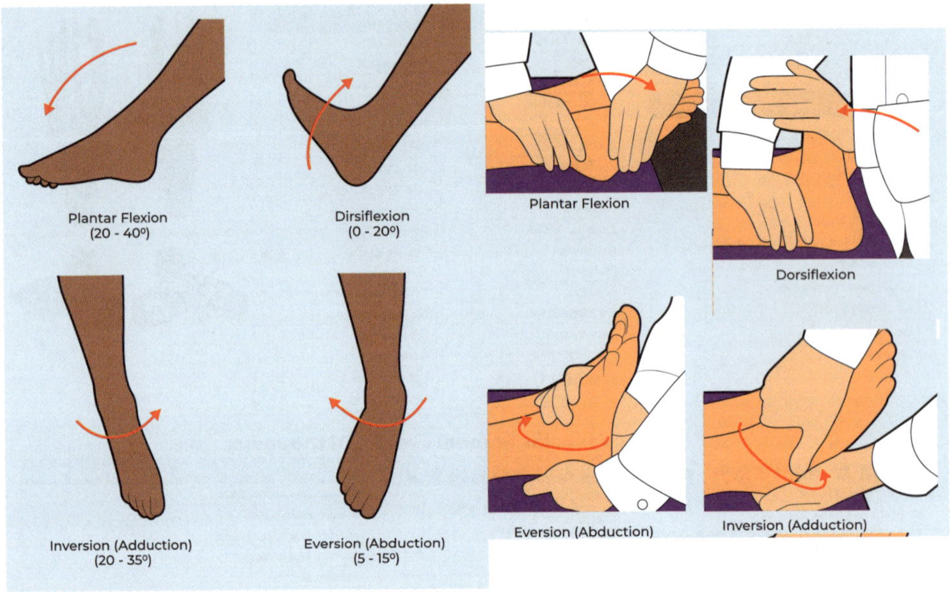

Muscle Testing

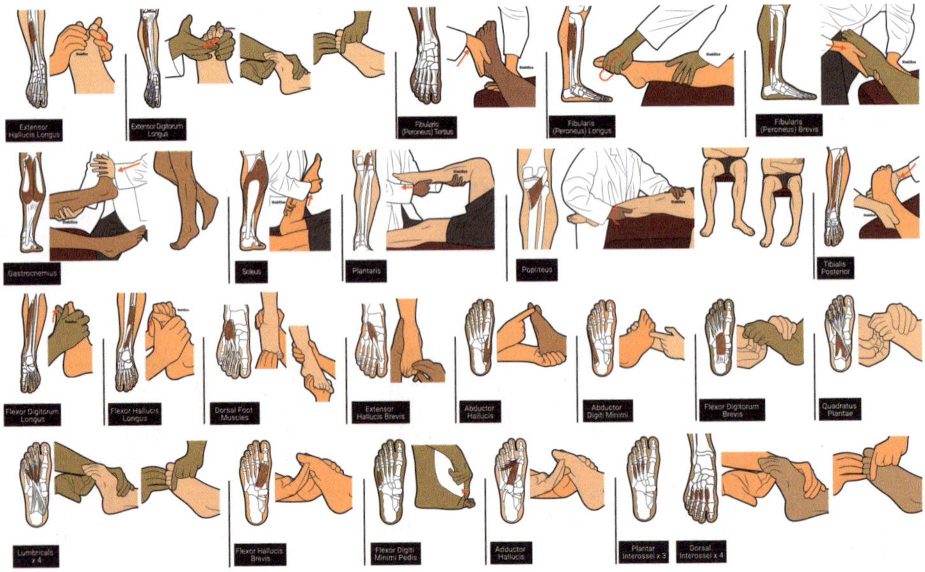

Leg Ankle Foot

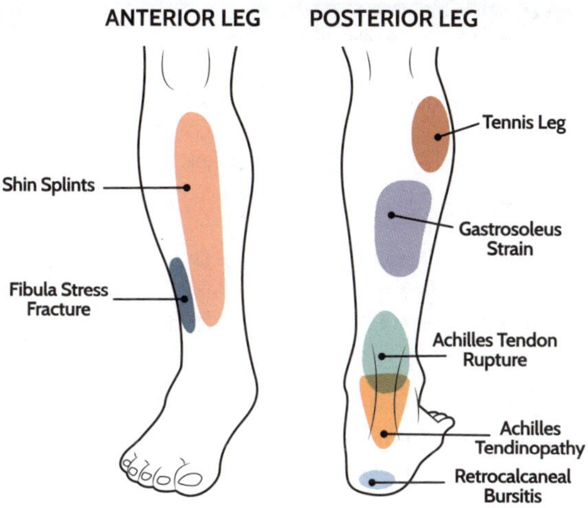
ANTERIOR LEG
POSTERIOR LEG
Shin Splints
Fibula Stress Fracture
Tennis Leg
Gastrosoleus Strain
Achilles Tendon Rupture
Achilles Tendinopathy
Retrocalcaneal Bursitis

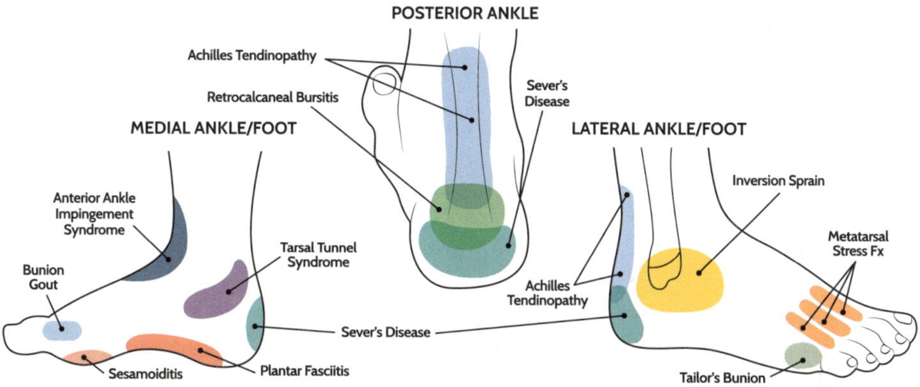
POSTERIOR ANKLE
Achilles Tendinopathy
Retrocalcaneal Bursitis
Sever's Disease
MEDIAL ANKLE/FOOT
Anterior Ankle Impingement Syndrome
Bunion
Gout
Tarsal Tunnel Syndrome
Sever's Disease
Sesamoiditis
Plantar Fasciitis
LATERAL ANKLE/FOOT
Inversion Sprain
Metatarsal Stress Fx
Achilles Tendinopathy
Tailor's Bunion

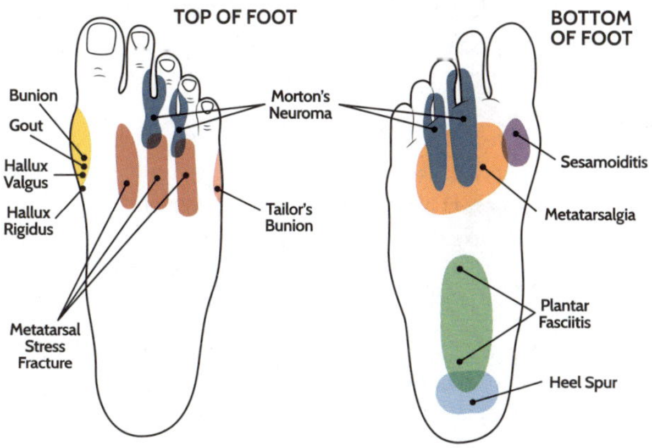
TOP OF FOOT
Bunion
Gout
Hallux Valgus
Hallux Rigidus
Metatarsal Stress Fracture
Morton's Neuroma
Tailor's Bunion
BOTTOM OF FOOT
Sesamoiditis
Metatarsalgia
Plantar Fasciitis
Heel Spur

Ankle-Foot Special Tests

Test	Procedure	Interpretation	Clinical Notes
Achilles Squeeze 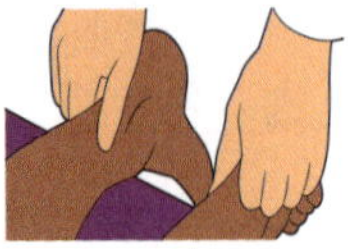	Squeeze the Achilles tendon along its length	(+) Pain → Peritendinitis or Achilles pathology	Pain may indicate inflammation or injury at the tendon insertion
Achilles Tap Test 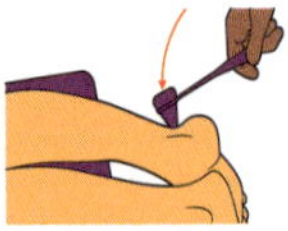	Gently tap the Achilles tendon with fingers or a reflex hammer.	(+) Pain or lack of reflex → Achilles tendinitis or rupture.	Lack of reflex may indicate a complete tendon rupture
Ankle Drawer Test 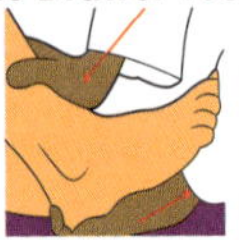	Stabilize tibia; pull or push the foot to assess talar motion	(+) Excess motion → ATFL/PTFL ligament injury	Test in both neutral and plantar flexed positions for specificity
Buerger's Test 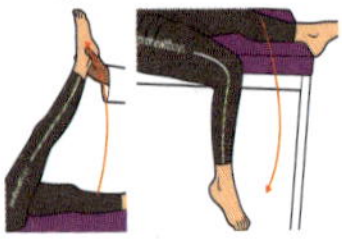	Raise straight leg to 45° for 3 minutes, then lower and observe foot color	(+) Delayed color return → Vascular insufficiency	Useful for assessing arterial circulation and chronic compartment syndrome
Calcaneal Squeeze 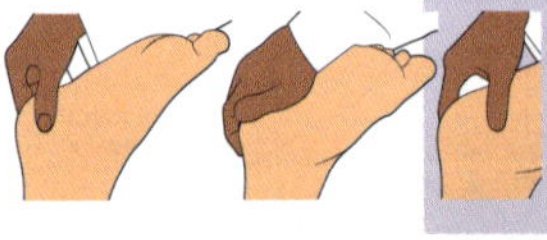	Squeeze calcaneus medially, laterally, & posteriorly	(+) Pain → Calcaneal fracture, plantar fasciitis, or bursitis	Effective as a quick diagnostic test for calcaneal pathology
Calf Squeeze (Thompson) 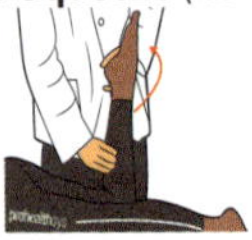	Squeeze the calf while the patient is prone with feet over the edge.	(+) Lack of plantar flexion → Achilles tendon rupture.	A simple and highly sensitive test for Achilles rupture
Flatfoot Tests 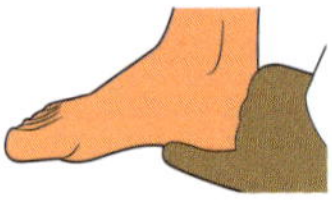	Use Feiss Line or palpate arch during weight-bearing 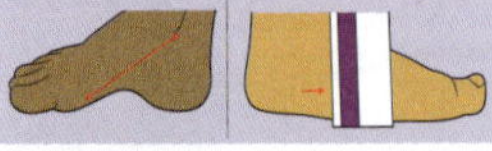	(+) Fallen arch → Pes planus or plantar fasciitis	Check for associated pronation or overuse injuries
Hoffa's Test 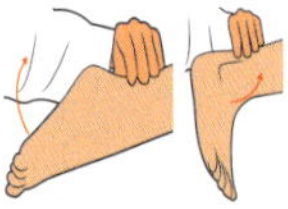	Palpate Achilles tendon while the patient plantar flexes/ dorsiflexes	(+) Pain or abnormal movement → Achilles strain or rupture	May indicate calcaneal fracture or tendon pathology
Homan's Test 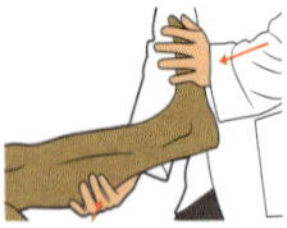	Passively dorsiflex the foot while squeezing the calf	(+) Pain → Deep vein thrombosis (DVT)	Limited sensitivity; combine with clinical symptoms for DVT diagnosis

Test	Procedure	Interpretation	Clinical Notes
Morton's Test 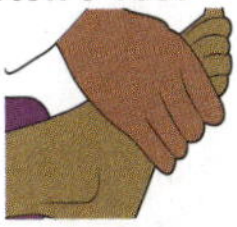	Squeeze the forefoot while palpating between metatarsal heads	(+) Pain → Morton's neuroma or metatarsalgia	Differentiates between neuroma and stress fractures based on pain location
Rotational Stress 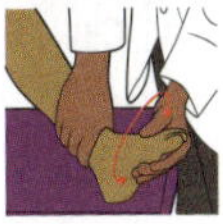	Rotate the foot medially and laterally to stress the syndesmosis	(+) Pain → Syndesmotic injury	Assess for ankle stability in cases of high ankle sprain
Talar Tilt Test 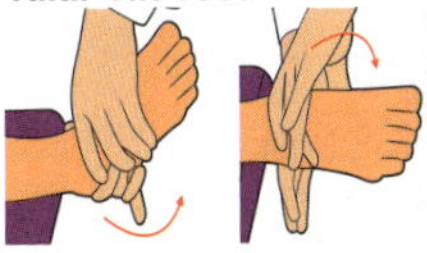	Apply inversion and eversion stress to the ankle	(+) Pain or laxity → Medial or lateral ligament injury	Useful for assessing chronic ankle instability
Tinel's Foot Test 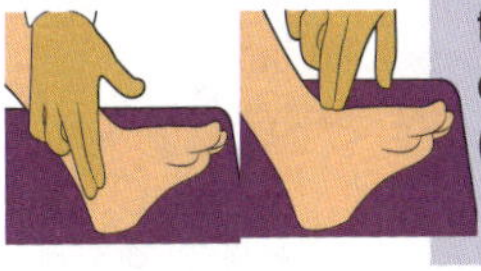	Tap over the tarsal tunnel (tibial nerve), dorsum of foot (peroneal nerve)	(+) Tingling → Tarsal tunnel syndrome	A positive test may indicate nerve compression or irritation
Windlass Test 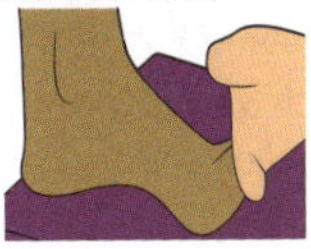	Passively dorsiflex the great toe while palpating the plantar fascia	(+) Pain → Plantar fasciitis	Highlights the functional role of the plantar fascia in gait

	Hx	SSx	Tx
Achilles Rupture 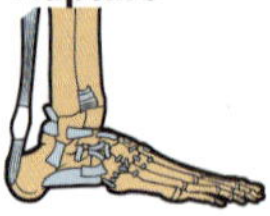	- Sudden forceful plantarflexion (jumping, running).	- **Audible "pop" w/ immediate pain** - (+) Thompson Test - Inability to plantarflex	- Surgical consult - Short term immobilization in plantarflexion - Gradual ExRx
Achilles Tendinitis 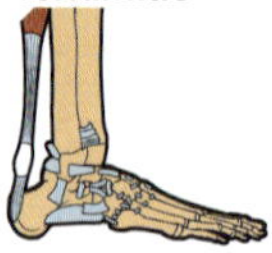	- Painful tendon, worsened by running, jumping, & stairs - Improves with rest	- **Tender palpation** - (+) Thompson Test, Achilles Squeeze Test - Swelling over tendon	- Ice, rest, METH - Stretching & strengthening calf muscles - Heel lifts for offloading
Ankle Sprain 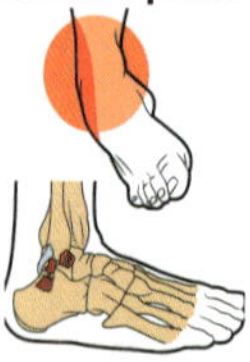	- **Trauma** with inversion, eversion, or twisting of ankle - Common in athletes	- **Swelling, pain over ligaments** - (+) Anterior Drawer Test, Talar Tilt Test - Difficulty bearing weight	- RICE (rest, ice, compression, elevation) - Strengthening ankle stabilizers - Bracing/Tape if necessary
Compartment Syndrome 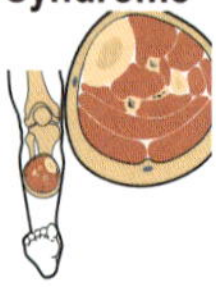	- Exercise-induced pain in lower leg - Better with rest	- **Tightness & swelling in leg** - (+) Calf Circumference - Weak dorsiflexion - **Hard on palp.**	- Immediate medical eval (acute) - Fasciotomy if severe - Stretch & activity mods prevention
Deep Vein (DVT) **Thrombosis** 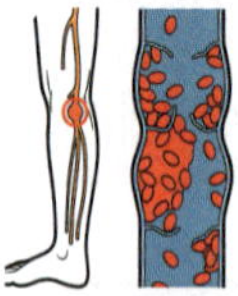	- Long **immobility** (travel, bedrest) - Recent surgery or trauma - Risks: obesity, smoking, oral contraceptives	- Calf pain, swelling, warmth, & redness - (+) Homan's Sign (pain on dorsiflexion) - Tender along vein	- Immediate medical referral - Anticoagulant therapy - Compression stockings post-treatment
Hallux Valgus (Bunion) 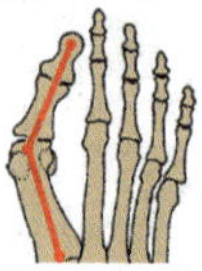	- **Deformity at base of great toe** - Often due to tight footwear or genetics	- Medial foot pain - Visible deformity - Difficulty finding comfortable footwear	- Shoe modifications - Toe spacers - Surgical correction if severe

	Hx	SSx	Tx
Morton's Neuroma 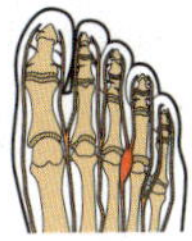	- **Burning pain between metatarsals** - Women with narrow footwear	- Local tenderness - **(+) Metatarsal Squeeze Test** - Numbness in toes	- **Orthotics for off-loading** - Avoid tight footwear - Steroid injections
Over-Pronation 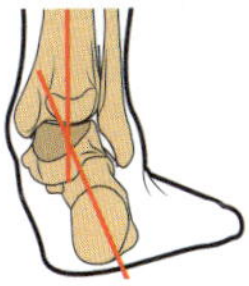	- Flat feet or poor footwear - Associated with prolonged standing, running, or walking	- Medial foot pain - **Flat arch on weight-bearing** - **↑ wear on inner edge of shoes** - Possible knee or hip discomfort	- **Orthotics for arch support** - Strengthen foot intrinsics & tibialis posterior - Stretch calf - **Barefoot walking**
Plantar Fasciitis 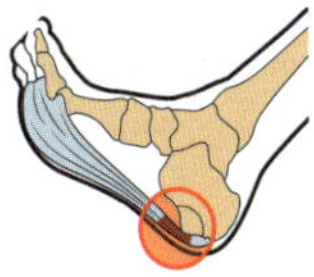	- **Pain worse in morning** with first steps - Common in runners or prolonged standing	- Tender at heel or medial arch - (+) **Calcaneal Squeeze** Test - Pain with dorsiflexion	- Stretching plantar fascia & calves - Orthotics for arch support - Night splints for positioning
Stress Fracture 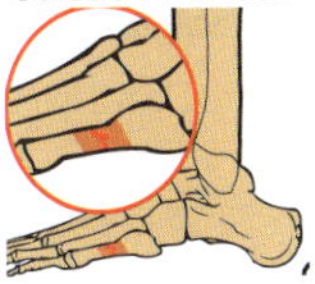	- **Overuse or repetitive loading** (running, jumping)	- Tenderness over tibia, metatarsals, or calcaneus - **Pain ↑ w/ activity** - (+) Tuning Fork or fracture screen	- Rest & activity modification - Gradual return to activity - Calcium & Vit D supplementation
Tarsal Tunnel Syndrome 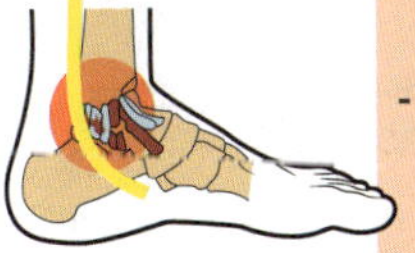	- Plantar foot pain or paresthesia (tibial nerve) - Often caused by overuse or trauma	- Pain worsened with prolonged standing or walking - **(+) Tinel's Sign at tarsal tunnel** - Numbness in sole	- Orthotics for arch support - METH for inflammation - ROM & nerve gliding exercises

1. Which test is used to confirm Achilles Tendinitis?
a) Thompson Test
b) Talar Tilt Test
c) McMurray's Test
d) Tinel's Sign

2. What is a common symptom of Plantar Fasciitis?
a) Pain over lateral malleolus
b) Morning heel pain with first steps
c) Burning pain in the toes
d) Swelling over the Achilles tendon

3. Best initial treatment for Stress Fractures?
a) Surgery
b) Compression stockings
c) Rest & activity modification
d) Corticosteroid injections

4. Which condition is associated with burning pain between metatarsals?
a) Tarsal Tunnel Syndrome
b) Morton's Neuroma
c) Compartment Syndrome
d) Hallux Valgus

5. Which orthopedic test is used to assess Tarsal Tunnel Syndrome?
a) Tinel's Sign
b) Ober's Test
c) Lachman's Test
d) Homan's Sign

6. Overuse or repetitive loading is a common cause of which condition?
a) Hallux Valgus
b) Deep Vein Thrombosis
c) Stress Fractures
d) Plantar Fasciitis

7. Primary symptom of Deep Vein Thrombosis?
a) Burning pain in the heel
b) Calf pain with swelling & redness
c) Numbness in the toes
d) Instability of the ankle

8. Which condition is commonly associated with poorly fitting footwear?
a) Tarsal Tunnel Syndrome
b) Hallux Valgus
c) Achilles Tendinitis
d) Ankle Sprain

9. Which test confirms Compartment Syndrome?
a) Talar Tilt Test
b) Calf Circumference Test
c) Patellar Grind Test
d) Anterior Drawer Test

10. Which intervention is contraindicated during the acute phase of Deep Vein Thrombosis?
a) Anticoagulant therapy
b) Compression stockings
c) Effleurage massage
d) Medical evaluation

11. Common aggravating factor for Over-Pronation?
a) Standing or walking for prolonged periods
b) High-impact jumping activities
c) Medial foot pain during dorsiflexion
d) Swelling at the Achilles tendon

12. Which structure is compressed in Tarsal Tunnel Syndrome?
a) Peroneal nerve
b) Tibial nerve
c) Achilles tendon
d) Plantar fascia

13. What is a typical cause of Morton's Neuroma?
a) Trauma to the lateral foot
b) Repetitive high-impact loading
c) Wearing narrow footwear
d) Overuse of the Achilles tendon

14. Which condition involves pain along the medial tibia during activity?
a) Hallux Valgus
b) Shin Splints
c) Morton's Neuroma
d) Stress Fractures

15. What is the recommended initial management for an ankle sprain?
a) Arthroscopic surgery
b) Weight-bearing exercises
c) RICE or METH
d) Corticosteroid injections

16. What orthopedic test confirms Hallux Valgus?
a) Anterior Drawer Test
b) Patellar Grind Test
c) No specific test; visual inspection
d) Talar Tilt Test

17. Test is commonly used to identify Achilles Rupture?
a) Thompson Test
b) McMurray's Test
c) Tinel's Sign
d) Windlass Test

18. Which intervention is most effective for reducing tension in the Achilles tendon?
a) Strengthening glutes
b) Stretching plantar fascia
c) Myofascial release for gastrocnemius
d) Weight-bearing exercises

19. Which symptom differentiates Plantar Fasciitis from a calcaneal stress fracture?
a) Pain localized to the arch of the foot
b) Heel pain worse with first steps in the morning
c) Tenderness along the Achilles insertion
d) Pain relieved with ice

20. What is a key characteristic of Stress Fractures?
a) Pain worsened by plantarflexion
b) Audible "pop" during injury
c) Pain improves with rest & worsens with activity
d) Numbness over the lateral foot

1. a 2. b 3. c 4. b
5. a 6. c 7. b 8. b
9. b 10. c 11. a 12. b
13. c 14. b 15. c 16. c
17. a 18. c 19. b 20. c

Case Study 1

Achilles Tendinitis: A 35-year-old recreational runner presents with pain along the back of their heel that worsens with running and stairs but improves with rest. On examination, there is tenderness over the Achilles tendon, and the Thompson Test is negative. The patient reports recently increasing their running mileage.

Questions:

- What **initial treatment plan** would you recommend to reduce the patient's symptoms and promote recovery?
- How would you address **biomechanical factors**, such as overpronation, that could contribute to tendinitis?
- How might the patient's **stress levels or lifestyle choices**, such as their running schedule and rest habits, influence the onset and recovery of Achilles Tendinitis?

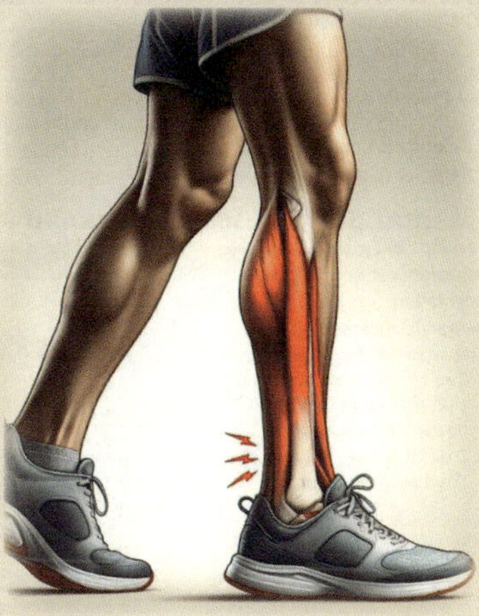

Case Study 2

Plantar Fasciitis: A 42-yr-old office worker complains of pain in their right heel that is most severe during the first few steps in the morning and improves throughout the day. The Calcaneal Squeeze is negative, but there is tenderness along the medial plantar fascia. She spends long hours standing.

Questions:

- What **modifications to daily activities** or footwear would you suggest to alleviate the patient's symptoms?
- What role would **stretching and strengthening** exercises play in managing this condition, and which muscle groups would you target?
- What **psychosocial factors**, like workplace stress or standing demands, could impact the patient's adherence to treatment recommendations for plantar fasciitis?

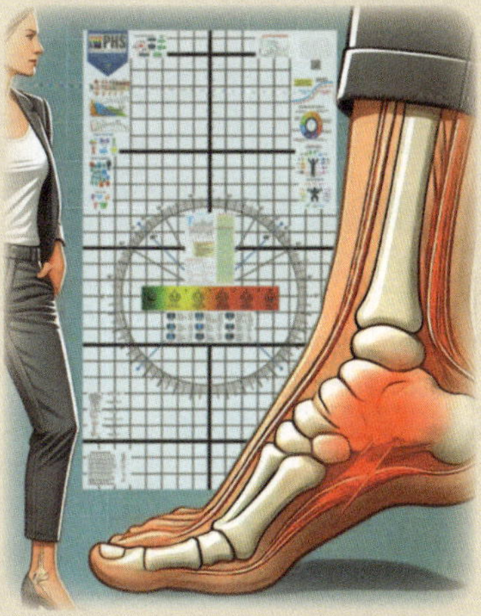

Case Study 3

Tarsal Tunnel Syndrome: A 50-year-old nurse reports burning pain and tingling in the sole of their foot, which worsens with prolonged standing and walking. The Tinel's Sign is positive over the tarsal tunnel. They have a history of flat feet and wear unsupportive footwear.

Questions:

- What **interventions**, including orthotics and exercises, would you implement to manage symptoms?
- How could this **condition progress** if left untreated, and what signs would indicate the need for surgical referral?
- How might the patient's footwear choices or work-related responsibilities affect their **long-term management** of Tarsal Tunnel Syndrome, both physically and emotionally?

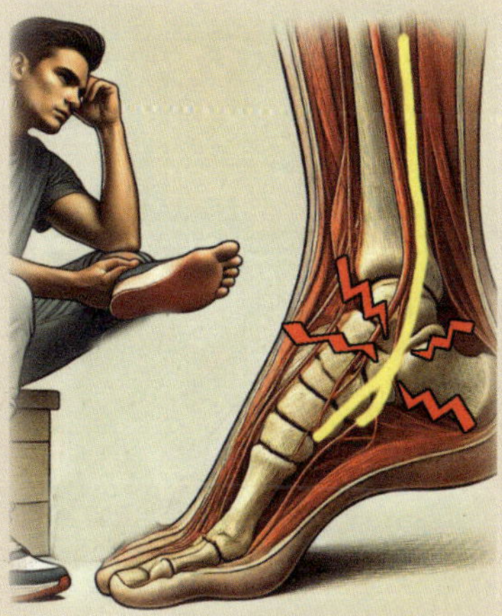

PHS
PROFESSIONAL HEALTH SYSTEMS

Neurologic Examination

☑ Check normal, circle & describe abnormal

Patient: ______ date: ______ (dd/mm/yr)
Insurance: ______
Date of birth: ______

CC & significant history: ______

Key considerations: □ headache, □ head injury, □ dizziness/vertigo, □ seizures, □ tremors, □ weakness, □ incoordination, □ numbness/tingling, □ difficulty swallowing, □ difficulty speaking, □ significant past history, □ environmental hazards, □ other: ______

□ Refer for secondary consultation: ______
□ Refer for diagnostic imaging: ______

Mental Status □ WNL

Development (□ good, □ fair, □ poor)
Behavior (Alert, lethargic, confusion, speech)
Orientation (Time, person, place & situation)
Memory/Concentration

- □ Name president/recent newsworthy events
- □ 3 word or place recall at 0 and 5 minutes
- □ (100) - (7) up to five times (93, 86, 79...)
- □ Spell word backwards
- □ Draw a clock (make the time 12:30)
- □ Draw overlapping pentagons

Reflexes □ WNL

DTR (0-5)	R	L
Biceps (C5)		
Brachioradialis (C6)		
Triceps (C7)		
Patella (L4)		
Hamstring (L5)		
Achilles (S1)		

Pathologic	R	L
Babinski		
Abdominal		
Hoffman's		

*Note presence of clonus

Motor Function □ WNL

Motor (0-5)	R	L
Deltoid (C5, C6) (axillary)		
Brachioradialis (C5, C6) (radial)		
Biceps (C5, C6) (musculocut.)		
Triceps (C6, C7, C8, T1) (radial)		
Wrist flexors (C6, C7) (med./ulnar)		
Wrist extensors (C6, C7, C8) (rad.)		
Interossei (C7, C8, T1) (ulnar)		
Tib. anterior (L4, L5) (deep per.)		
Extensor hallicus longus (L4, L5, S1) (deep peroneal)		
Fibularis (peroneus) longus (L5, S1) (superficial peroneal)		

Cranial Nerves □ WNL

I - Olfactory	R	L
Scent #1		
Scent #2		
II - Optic		
Visual acuity		
Visual fields		
Fundiscopic exam		
III, IV, VI - Oculomotor, trochlear, abducens		
'H' pattern		
Convergence		
Nystagmus		
Consensual light reflex		
V - Trigeminal		
Lateral jaw deviation		
Masseter contraction		
Face sensation		
Corneal touch reflex		

VII - Facial	R	L
Facial expressions		
Facial expression #2		
Normal eye moisture		
VIII - Vestibulocochlear		
Rhomberg's test		
Auditory acuity		
Weber		
Rinne		
IX, X - Glossopharyngeal & Vagus		
Gag reflex		
Elevation of palate		
XI - Spinal accessory		
Trapezius muscle test		
SCM muscle test		
XII - Hypoglossal		
Stick out tongue		

Cerebellar □ WNL

	R	L
Rapid finger movement		
Rapid pro/supination		
Finger-to-nose/finger		
Heel down shin		
Holme's rebound sign		
Gait/heel-toe walk		

Nerve Tension □ WNL

	R	L
Straight Leg Raise		
Maximal SLR		
Bragard's		
Femoral nerve traction		
Median nerve traction		
Radial nerve traction		
Ulnar nerve traction		
Tinel's		

Sensory □ WNL

	R	L
Light touch		
Vibration		
Stereognosis		
Graphesthesia		
2-point discrim		
Position sense		
Proprioception		
Romberg		
Sharp/dull		
Hot/cold		

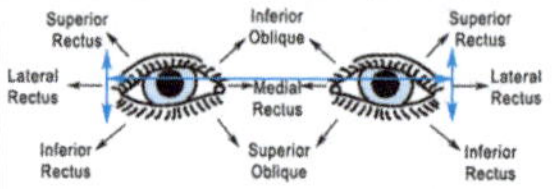

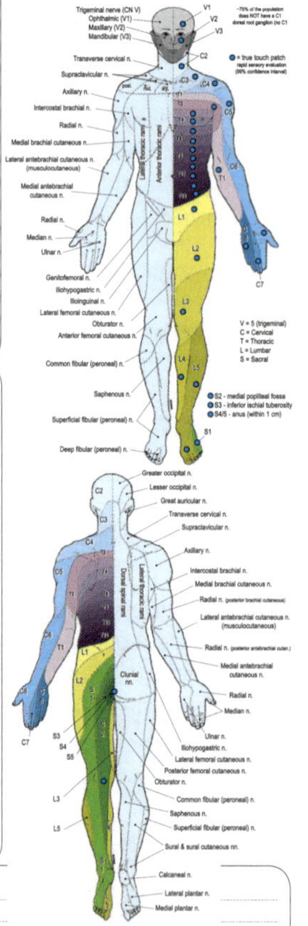

DDx:

Signature: ______ Date: ______

Types of Nerve Injuries

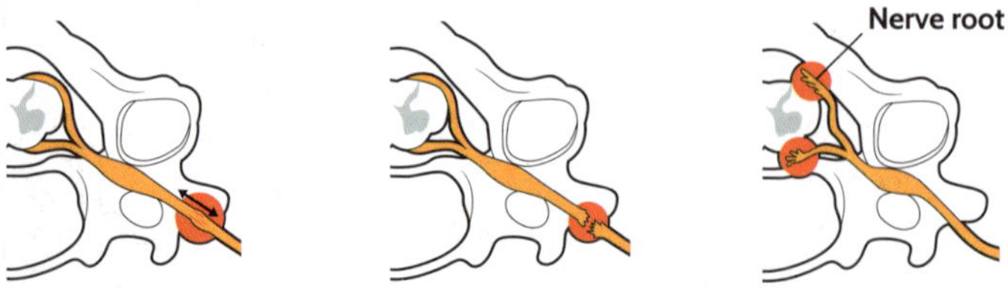

Neuro

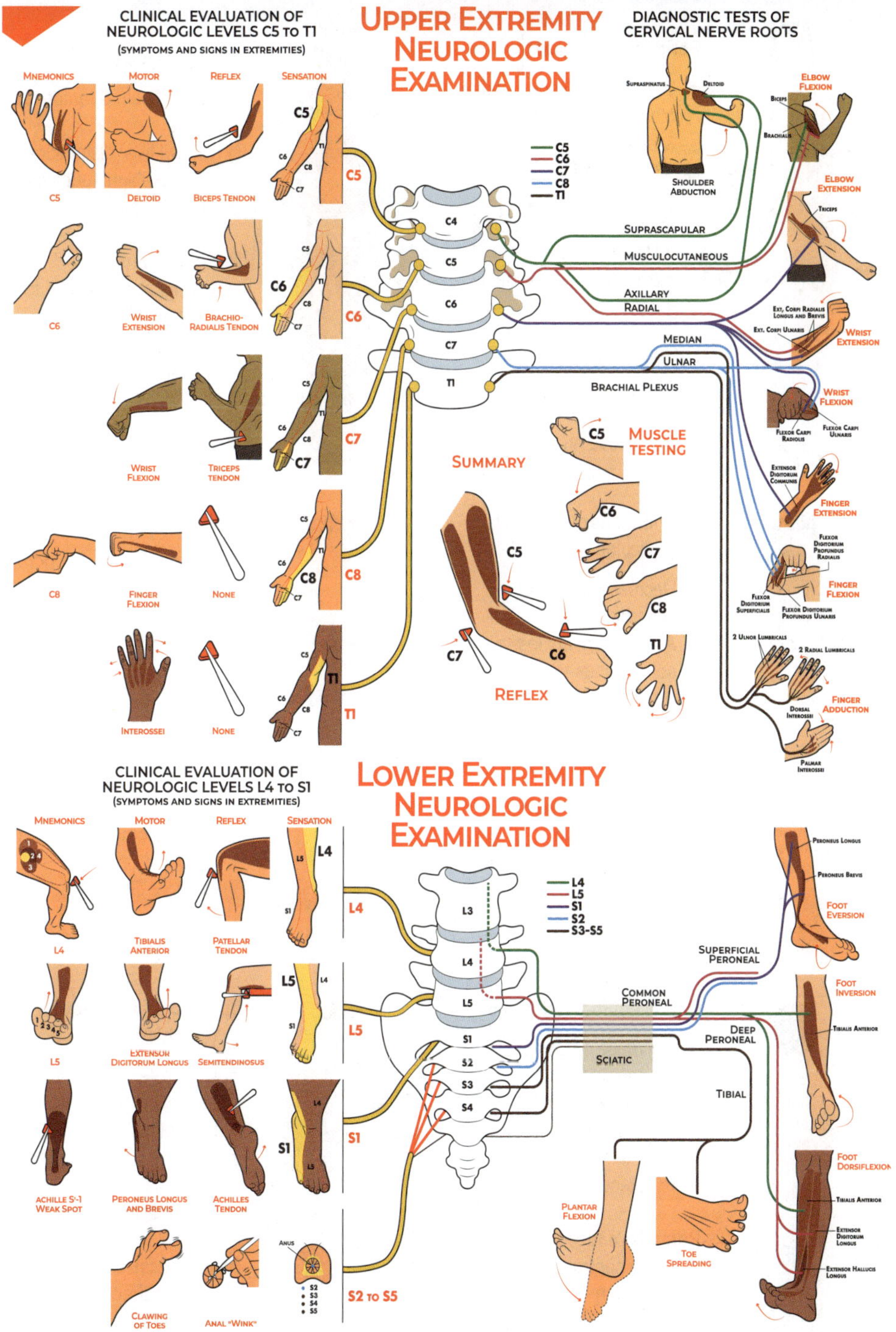

Remember there is overlap and anatomical variation in specific nerve innervation look for multiple levels of evidence to support findings (DTRs, motor pathways, dermatomes, myotomes and scleratomes).

PMID: 30571022, 21628826, 18470936, 23824984, 31087420, 31227260, 35561698, 36597659, 32965909, 30285397

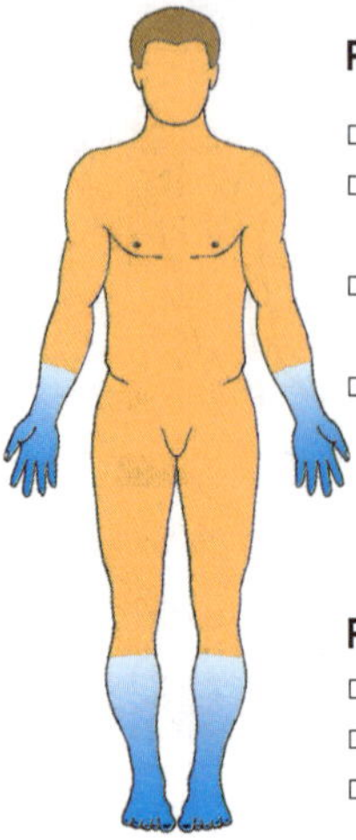

Peripheral neuropathy

- □ Loss of all sensory modes
- □ More severe distally (feet & hands)
- □ "Glove & stocking" anesthesia
- □ Improved sensation proximally; anesthesia zone moves into hypoesthesia then to normal

Potential causes
- □ Diabetes, metabolic Dz
- □ Nutritional deficiency
- □ Pernicious anemia

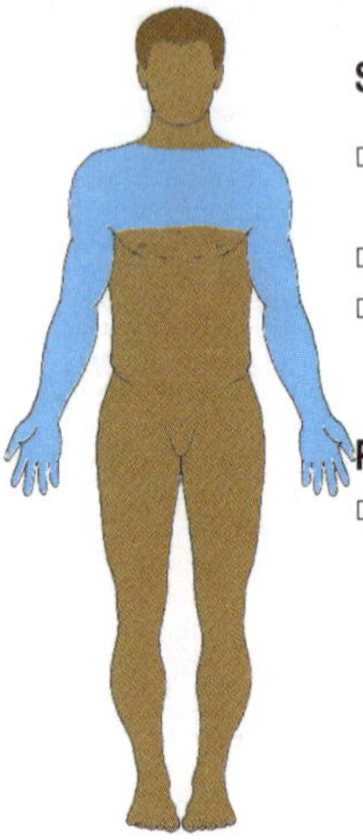

Syringomyelia

- □ Loss of pain & temperature sense
- □ "Shawl-like" distribution
- □ Normal – light touch & proprioception

Potential cause
- □ Syringomyelia = fluid filled cavitation in spinal canal that causes pressure on spinothalamic tract

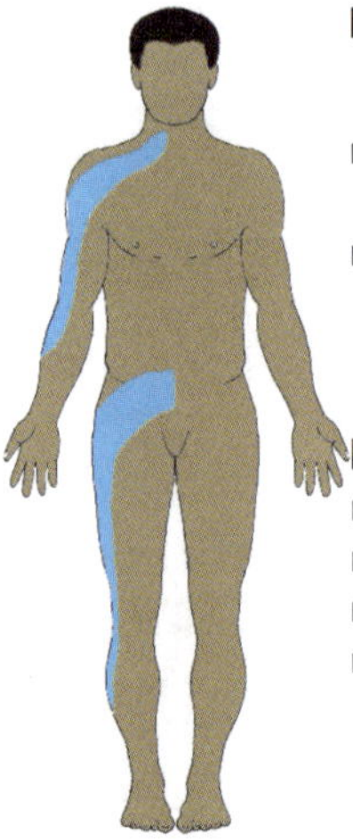

Individual nerve or roots (radicular syn.)

- □ Decrease or loss of all sensory modes
- □ Area of sensory loss corresponds to anatomical distribution of nerves

Potential causes
- □ Trauma
- □ Vascular occlusion
- □ Disc herniation
- □ Impingement syndrome

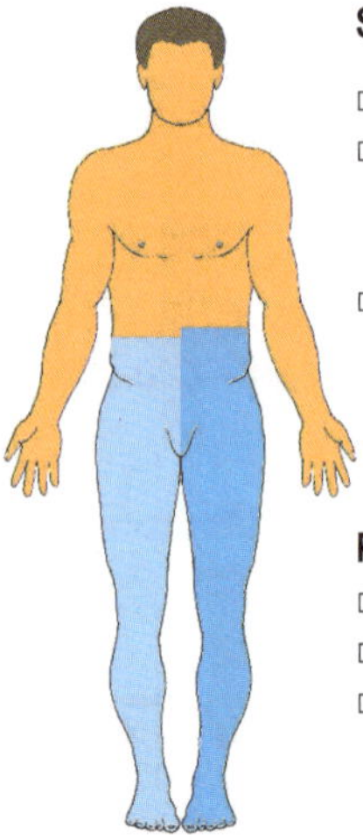

Spinal cord hemisection

- □ "Brown-Séquard syndrome"
- □ Loss of pain & temperature, contralateral side starting two levels below lesion
- □ Loss of vibration & position sense, spastic paralysis & hyperreflexia on ipsilateral side, below level of lesion

Potential causes
- □ Meningioma, neuro-fibroma
- □ Cervical Spondylosis
- □ Multiple Sclerosis

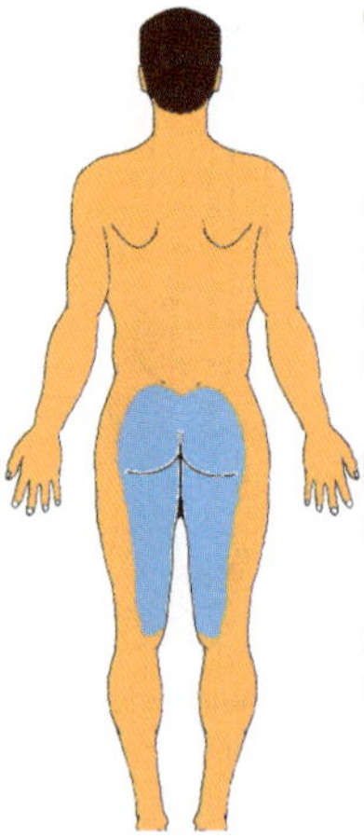

Cauda equina syndrome

- □ Decrease or loss of all sensory modes
- □ Saddle anesthesia
- □ Urinary retention
- □ Incontinence
- □ Impotence

Potential causes
- □ Large central disc herniation
- □ Tumor
- □ Trauma (fracture)

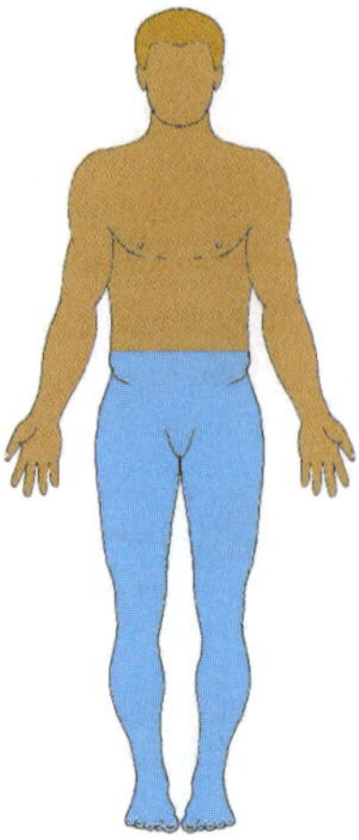

Spinal cord transection (complete)

- □ Complete loss of all sensory modes below level of lesion
- □ Associated with spastic paralysis, hyperreflexia & loss of sphincter control

Potential causes
- □ Trauma (fracture)
- □ Demyelinating disorders
- □ Tumor

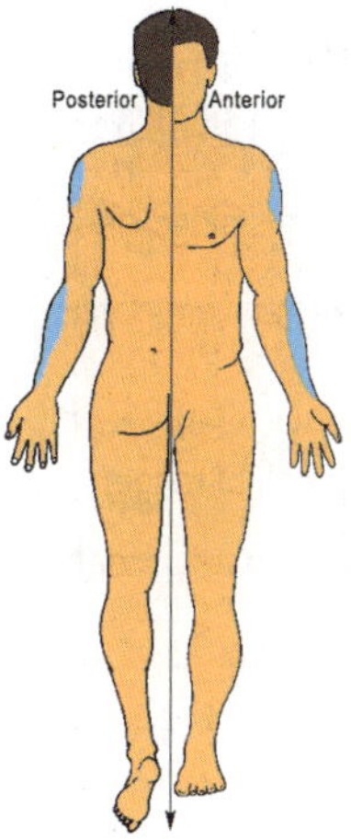

Axillary & musculocut. injury

- Axillary - lateral shoulder sensory loss, deltoid atrophy
- Musculocutaneous - lateral forearm sensory loss, muscle weakness in elbow flexion

Potential causes
- Humeral head fracture
- Surgical error

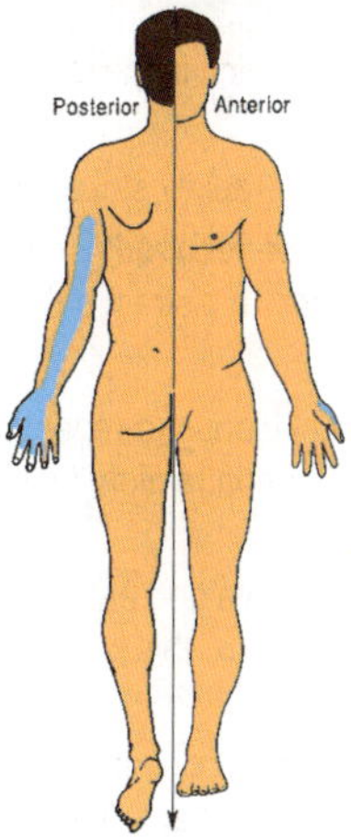

Radial nerve injury

- Decrease or loss of all sensory modes over posterior arm, forearm, wrist & lateral posterior hand
- "Wrist drop"
- Wrist extensor atrophy

Potential cause
- Brachial plexus injury
- Shoulder dislocation
- Direct trauma

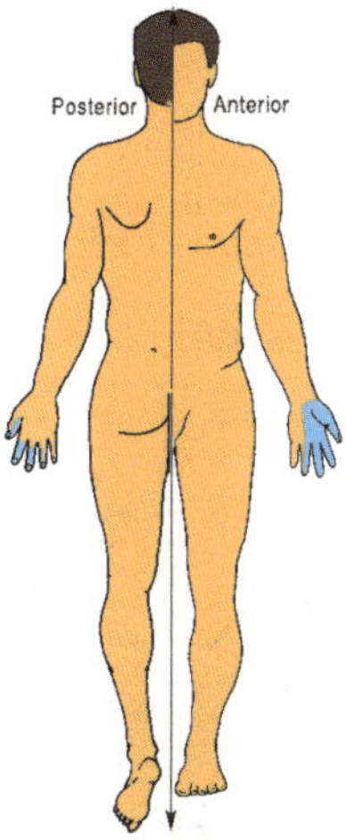

Median nerve injury

- Decrease or loss of all sensory modes on lateral hand
- "Ape hand"
- Thenar atrophy

Potential cause
- Brachial plexus injury
- Elbow dislocation
- Direct trauma
- Carpal tunnel syndrome

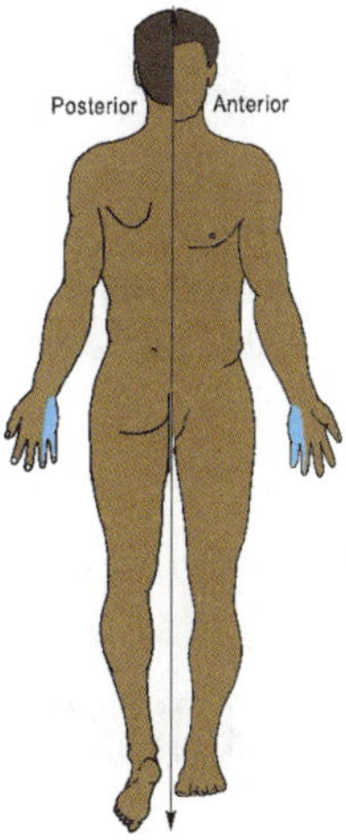

Ulnar nerve injury

- Decrease or loss of all sensory modes on medial hand
- "Claw hand" (unopposed action of extensor digitorum)
- Interosseus atrophy
- (+) Froment's Sign

Potential cause
- Brachial plexus injury
- Humeral head fracture
- Elbow dislocation
- Direct trauma

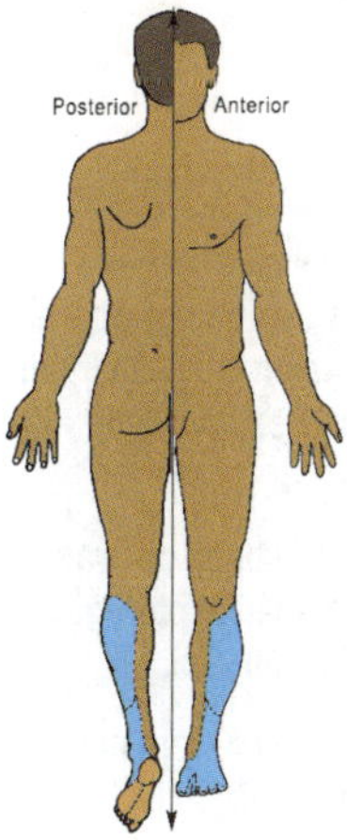

Common fibular nerve injury

- Decrease or loss of all sensory modes on lateral shin & foot dorsum
- "Foot drop"
- Steppage gait

Potential cause
- Prolonged sitting with crossed knees
- Direct trauma to fibular head
- Fibular head fracture
- Compression from high boots

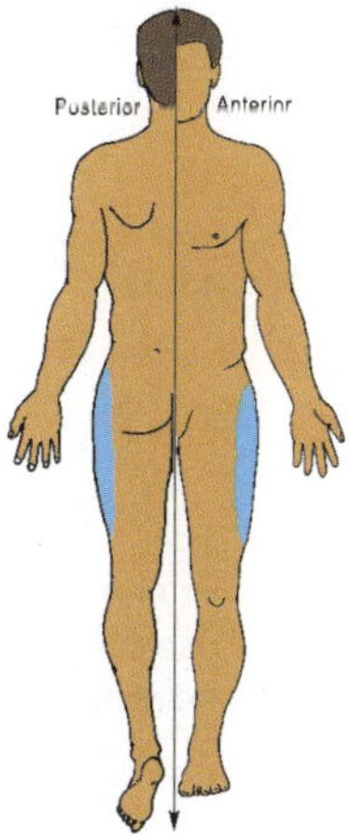

Meralgia paresthetica

- Paresthesia over anterior lateral thigh
- Decreased light touch sensation
- No motor loss

Potential cause
- Direct trauma
- Pelvic mass or pregnancy
- Tight belts/tool belts
- Obesity

Procedure

1. Patient is relaxed, with mild stretch in muscle to be tested
2. Use a quick, precise stimulus (rapidly strike tendon)
3. ***Jendrassik maneuver*** may be required (isometric contraction at another location to distract patient)
4. Compare results bilaterally
5. Note presence or absence of clonus (a repeating reflex with alternate muscular contraction & relaxation in rapid succession)

Note: many elderly patients will have decreased or complete lack of an Achilles reflex; this is usually a normal finding

When possible the examiner may choose to palpate muscle being tested when reflexes are difficult to visually observe

Reflex Grading Scale

Grade	Description
5+	Hyperreflexia - sustained clonus
4+	Hyperreflexia - transient clonus
3+	Hyperreflexia
2+	Normal (lower half of range)
1+	Hyporeflexia (trace response)
0	Absent/no response

Chart reflexes out of 5, e.g.: *2+/5 biceps DTR*

Hyporeflexia

Diminished to absent DTRs
Potential causes:
1. **Technique error** (most common)
2. **LMNL** (Lower Motor Neuron Lesion)
3. **Peripheral neuropathy** (common)
4. **Radiculopathy** (nerve root - disc lesions)

Hyperreflexia

Increased or hyperactive DTRs
Potential causes:
1. **UMNL** (Upper Motor Neuron Lesion), secondary to brain, brainstem / spinal cord lesion or compression
2. Clonus is often associated with UMNL

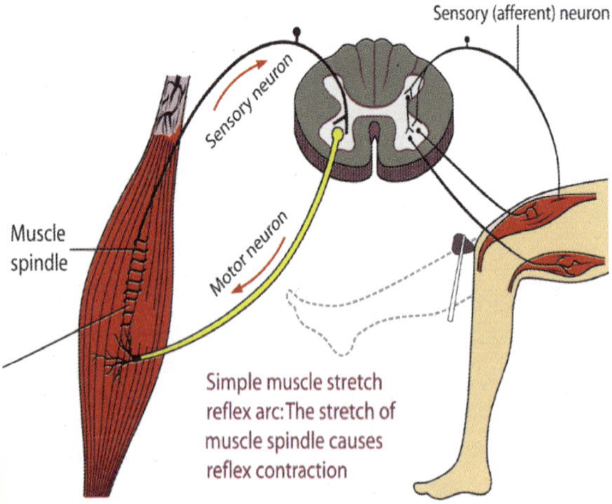

Simple muscle stretch reflex arc: The stretch of muscle spindle causes reflex contraction

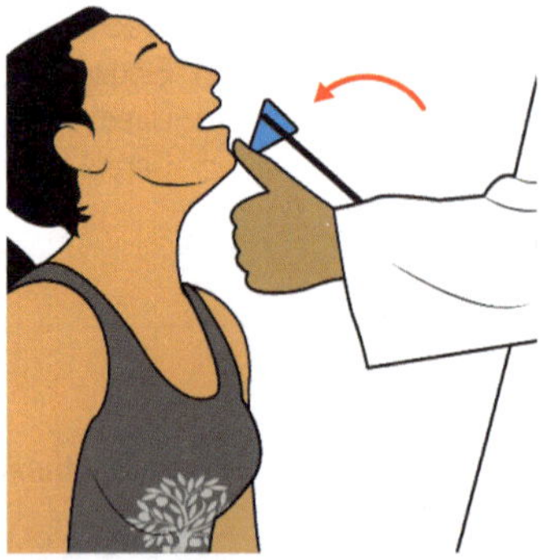

DTR Jaw Reflex (V)

Procedure: Patient relaxed with jaw open about 10°-15°, examiner applies gentle over pressure on jaw with thumb & proceeds to briskly strike thumb with reflex hammer

Interpretation: Normal: brisk contraction of masseter & medial pterygoid muscles & closure of the mouth

Clinical notes: Afferent/efferent nerve: Trigeminal nerve Level: Pons

Nerve level - DTR

C5 - Biceps	L4 - Patellar
C6 - Brachioradialis	L5 - Semitendinosus
C7 - Triceps	S1 - Achilles

Neuro

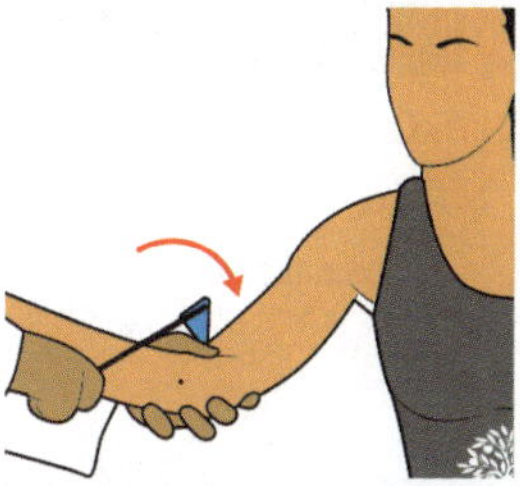

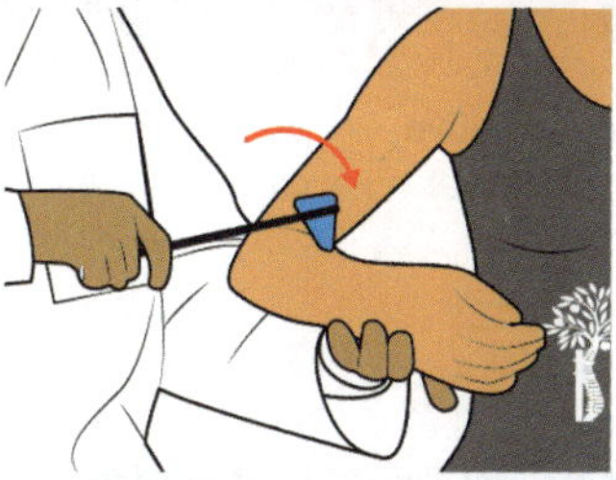

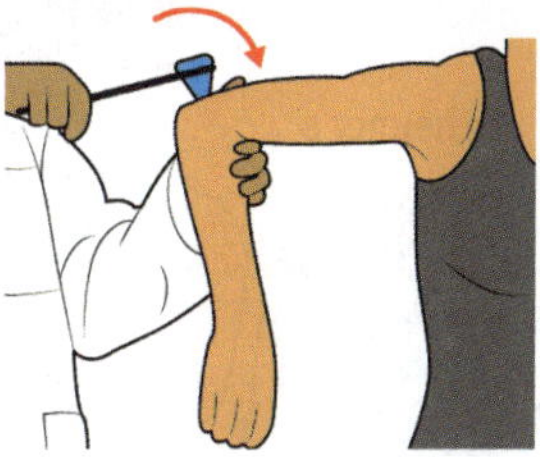

Biceps (C5)	Brachioradialis (C6)	Triceps (C7)
Apply downward traction on **biceps tendon** with thumb. Strike with reflex hammer while palpating contraction.	Strike midpoint of **brachioradialis tendon.** Observe contraction and forearm supination.	Strike **triceps tendon** near olecranon. Observe contraction and elbow extension.
Normal: Brisk biceps contraction and elbow flexion.	Normal: Brisk brachioradialis contraction and forearm supination.	Normal: Brisk triceps contraction and elbow extension.
Nerve: Musculocutaneous, Level: C5-C6.	**Nerve: Radial, Level: C5-C6.**	**Nerve: Radial, Level: C6-C7.**

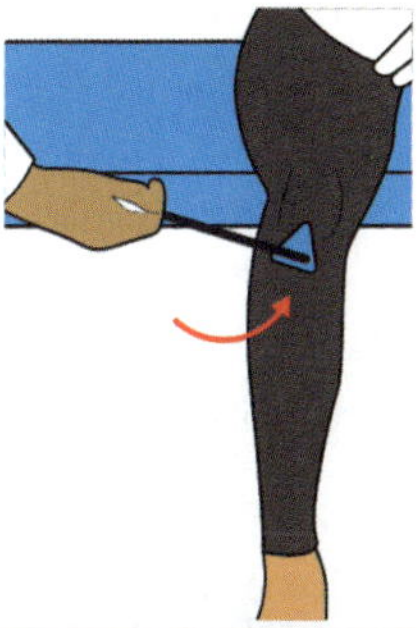

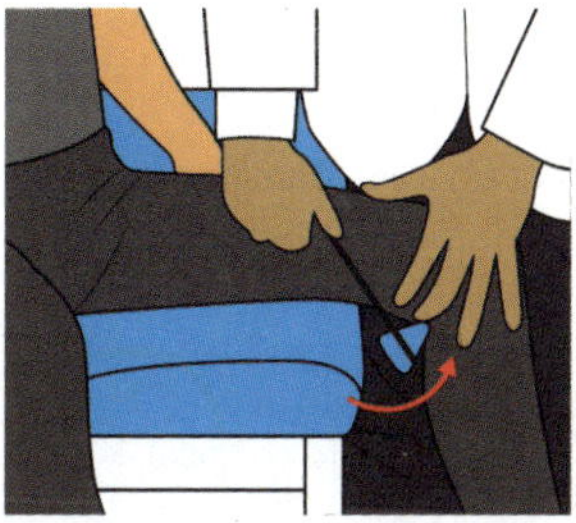

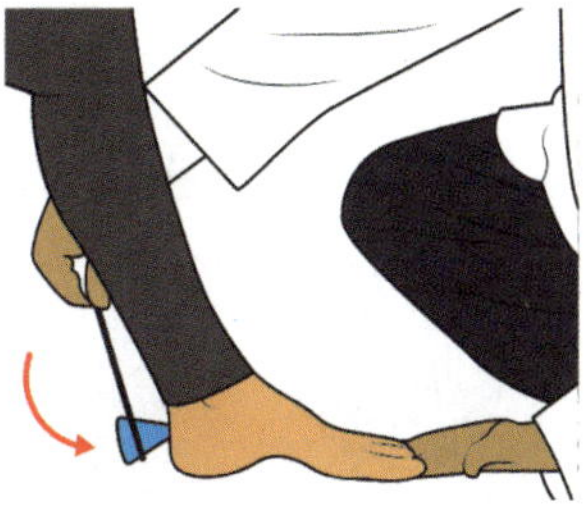

Patella (L3-L4)	Medial Hamstring (L5)	Achilles (S1)
Strike **patellar tendon** with reflex hammer. Observe quadriceps contraction and knee extension.	Apply tension with fingers to **semitendinosus**, strike, and palpate hamstring contraction.	Apply dorsiflexion tension, strike **Achilles tendon**, and observe calf contraction.
Normal: Brisk quadriceps contraction and knee extension.	Normal: Brisk contraction of hamstring muscles.	Normal: Brisk contraction of gastrocnemius and soleus; plantar flexion of ankle.
Nerve: Femoral, Level: L3-L4.	**Nerve: Sciatic, Level: L5-S1.**	**Nerve: Tibial, Level: L5-S1.**

PMID: 29083617, 32965909, 30285397

	Hx	SSx	Tx
Alzheimer's 	- **Progressive cognitive decline**, typically over many years	- Memory loss, confusion, changes in behavior.	- Cognitive therapy - Exercise - Medications (acetylcholinesterase inhibitors)
Bell's Palsy 	- Sudden onset facial weakness or paralysis - Stroke must be ruled out	- Unilateral facial drooping, difficulty closing eyelid - Loss of taste on one side	- Corticosteroids - Physical therapy for facial muscles
Cerebral Palsy 	- Congenital disorder affecting motor skills and muscle tone	- Spasticity, limited movement - Coordination issues	- Physiotherapy - Orthopedic intervention - Medications
Chronic Fatigue Syndrome 	- History of prolonged, unexplained fatigue	- Severe tiredness, difficulty sleeping, muscle pain.	**- Sleep hygiene** **- Pain relief** **- Cognitive behavior therapy** **- Exercise**
Fibromyalgia 	- Widespread MSK pain	- Chronic pain, fatigue, sleep disturbances - 11^+ of 18 tender points on body	- Pain management (medications) - Exercise - Cognitive therapy
Guillain-Barré Syndrome 	- Autoimmune disorder affects the peripheral nervous system	- Muscle weakness - Tingling, or paralysis	- Immunotherapy (plasma exchange, IVIG) - Physical therapy
Multiple Sclerosis 	- Chronic condition affecting the central nervous system	- Fatigue, muscle weakness, numbness, difficulty walking	- Disease-modifying therapies, symptom management (medications)

	Hx	SSx	Tx
Muscular Dystrophy 	- Genetic - Family history of progressive muscle weakness.	- Progressive muscle weakness, difficulty walking, muscle wasting, scoliosis, and respiratory issues	- No cure - Manage SSx with physical therapy, orthopedic interventions, and breathing support
Myasthenia Gravis 	- Autoimmune neuromuscular disorder affecting voluntary muscles	- Weakness that worsens with activity - Improves with rest, ptosis, and double vision	- Anticholinesterase meds - Immuno-suppressants - Thymectomy.
Parkinson's 	- Progressive neuro-degenerative disorder	- Tremors (pill rolling) - Rigidity - Bradykinesia (slowness of movement)↓	- Dopamine replacements - Physical & occupational therapy
Peripheral Neuropathy 	- Nerve damage due to diabetes, alcohol, or other factors (inflammation, infection, compression)	- Numbness, tingling, and weakness, often in the feet and hands.	- Control underlying causes (diabetes) - Pain relief
Spinal Cord Injury (SCI) 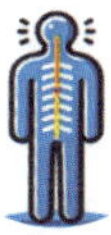	- Acute injury due to trauma, often from accidents, falls, or violence	- Paralysis, loss of sensation - Bowel and bladder dysfunction - Spasticity, hyper reflexia on DTRs	- Stabilization - Surgery - Meds (corticosteroids) - Rehabilitation
Stroke Recovery 	- History of ischemic or hemorrhagic stroke	- Hemiparesis - Speech difficulties - Poor coordination	- Rehabilitation - Physiotherapy - Speech therapy

Arthritides

	Hx	SSx	Tx
Ankylosing Spondylitis 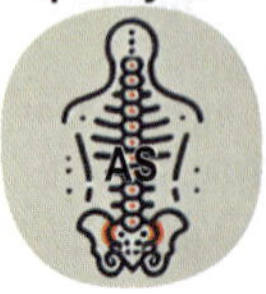	- Genetic predisposition (HLA-B27), more common in young men	- Chronic back pain, stiffness, particularly in low back and hips - (+) Schober's Test	- NSAIDs, biologics, physical therapy for posture and mobility
Enteropathic Arthritis 	- Associated with **inflammatory bowel disease (IBD), Crohn's or ulcerative colitis**	- Joint pain, stiffness, often in the lower limbs, flare-ups coincide with IBD flare-ups	- NSAIDs - Disease-modifying drugs - Biologics
Gout 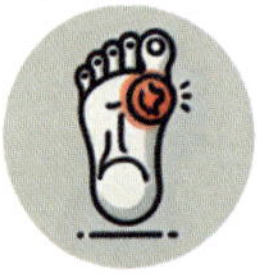	- History of uric acid buildup, alcohol consumption, certain meds	- Sudden and severe joint pain, redness, swelling, often in the **big toe**	- NSAIDs, corticosteroids, colchicine - Diet modification (lower uric acid)
Lupus (SLE) 	- Autoimmune disease, family history, more common in women	- Joint pain - Butterfly-shaped rash - Fatigue, light sensitive	- Immuno-suppressive drugs, NSAIDs, corticosteroids - Physical therapy ROM
Lyme Disease 	- Caused by tick-borne bacteria (Borrelia burgdorferi) - Tick exposure	- Joint pain (often in large joints like knees), fever, fatigue - Bullseye rash (erythema migrans)	- Antibiotics, pain management - Anti-inflammatory drugs
Osteoarthritis (OA or DJD) 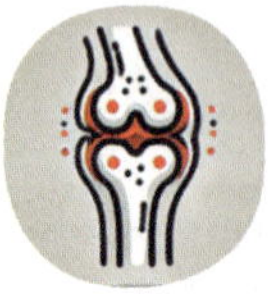	- Degenerative joint disease, often associated with aging or joint wear	- Joint pain, stiffness, especially after activity or rest, limited ROM	- Pain management (acetaminophen), joint replacement (severe cases) - Physical therapy.

	Hx	SSx	Tx
Polymyalgia Rheumatica 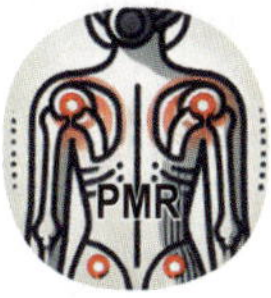	- Associated with age, more common in women, temporal arteritis may coexist	- Muscle pain and stiffness, especially in the shoulders and hips	- Corticosteroids (high doses initially) - Physical therapy
Psoriatic Arthritis 	- Associated with psoriasis - Genetic factors, family history.	- Joint pain, swell - Skin lesions (psoriasis) - Dactylitis (sausage fingers) - Nail pitting	- DMARDs, biologics - Pain management - Physical therapy
Reactive Arthritis 	- Follows an infection (genitourinary or gastrointestinal)	- Joint pain & swell (knees, ankles, and feet) - Cconjunctivitis - Urinary issues	- Antibiotics (if infection persists) - NSAIDs - Physical therapy
Rheumatoid Arthritis 	- Autoimmune disorder, family history - More common in women	- Symmetrical joint pain, swelling, stiffness - Fatigue - Morning stiffness	- Disease-modifying antirheumatic drugs (DMARDs) - Biologics, pain management - Physical therapy

Case Study

Rheumatoid Arthritis: A 55-year-old male presents with morning stiffness, joint pain, and swelling in wrists, knees, and fingers for the past two months. His symptoms worsen in the morning but improve with movement. Blood tests show elevated rheumatoid factor and anti-CCP antibodies.

- What **other conditions should be ruled out** before confirming a diagnosis of rheumatoid arthritis, and how can these conditions be differentiated?
- What are the **long-term implications** of untreated rheumatoid arthritis, and how can early intervention help prevent joint damage?
- How might **lifestyle changes**, such as exercise or diet, play a role in managing rheumatoid arthritis, alongside pharmacological treatments?

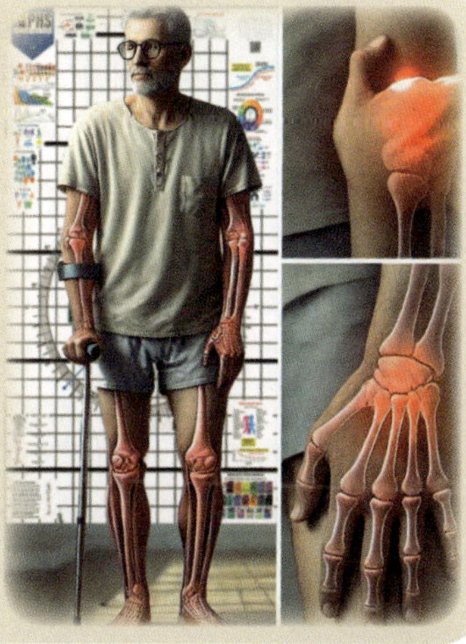

	Hx	SSx	Tx
ADHD 	- Childhood onset, often hereditary - More common in males	- Inattention, hyperactivitive, impulsive, poor concentrating - Hypermobililty	- Stimulants (methylphenidate) - Behavior therapy - Physical activity & ExRx
Bipolar Disorder 	- History of extreme mood fluctuations - Family history	- Manic episodes (high energy, impulsiveness) - Depressive episodes	- Mood stabilizers (lithium) - Aantipsychotics - Psychotherapy - Physical activity
Complex Region Pain Syndrome 	- Often follows an injury (particularly in limbs) - More common after trauma	- Severe, burning pain, swelling, and changes in skin color and temperature in the affected limb	- Pain management (analgesics, nerve blocks), - Physical therapy - Psychotherapy
Depression 	- Family history, history of trauma or major life stressors - Lack of exercise - Poor diet	- Persistent sadness, fatigue, loss of interest, changes in sleep and appetite.	- Antidepressants - Psychotherapy - Lifestyle changes (diet & exercise) - Social connection
Diabetes Mellitus 	- Family history, obesity, poor diet, sedentary lifestyle.	- Increased thirst, frequent urination, fatigue, blurred vision, slow-healing wounds.	- Insulin therapy - Oral medications **- Lifestyle changes (diet, exercise)**
Dyslipidemia 	- Family history, obesity - Sedentary lifestyle - Poor diet	- Typically asymptomatic -Will result in heart disease or stroke over time	- Statins - Lifestyle changes (diet, exercise) - Blood pressure control
Hypertension 	- Family history - Obesity - Stress - High salt intake	- Often no symptoms, may cause headaches, dizziness, or shortness of breath if severe	- Antihypertensive medications (ACE inhibitors, diuretics) **- Regular exercise** **- Diet (DASH)**

	Hx	SSx	Tx
Osteoporosis 	- Age, family history - Menopause - Low calcium intake	- Bone pain - Fractures with minimal trauma - Stooped posture	- Calcium & Vit D supplementation - Weight-bearing exercises - Bisphosphonates
Post Traumatic Stress Disorder 	- History of trauma, often from combat, accidents, or abuse.	- Flashbacks, hypervigilance, emotional numbness, difficulty sleeping.	- Trauma-focused therapy (CBT, EMDR), antidepressants, lifestyle changes.
Sarcopenia 	- Aging - Inactivity - Poor nutrition	- Muscle weakness, frailty - Difficulty with daily activities	**- Resistance training** **- Protein intake** - Vitamin D
Schizophrenia 	- Family history, often appears in late teens to early 30s	- Hallucinations, delusions - Disorganized thinking - Social withdrawal	- Antipsychotics - Psychotherapy - Social skills training - Physical activity

Case Study

Depression Case: A 45-year-old female presents with persistent sadness, fatigue, loss of interest in daily activities, and difficulty concentrating. She has a history of stress and poor diet. She reports that her symptoms have worsened over the past three months and she has trouble sleeping.

- What treatment options, including **manual therapy, exercise, and dietary changes**, would you recommend to manage her symptoms?
- How might untreated depression affect her physical health, and when would you **consider referring** her to a mental health professional?
- How can the patient's lifestyle factors, such as **stress management, physical activity, screen time,** and diet, impact her recovery from depression, and what strategies could be implemented for long-term improvement?

	Hx	SSx	Tx
Addison's Dz 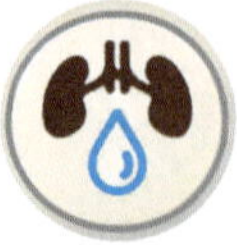	- **Adrenal insufficiency** - Chronic fatigue, weakness, weight loss	- Low blood pressure, darkening of skin, salt cravings	- Corticosteroid therapy (Hydrocortisone, Fludrocortisone)
Cushing's Synd. 	- ↑ **cortisol** (adrenal or overuse issue)	- **Weight gain**, fatigue, high blood pressure, - **Moon face, buffalo hump**	- Medications to reduce cortisol levels, surgery, radiation
Diabetes Insip. 	- ↓ **antidiuretic hormone (ADH)** = ↓ kidney water resorption	- Excessive thirst - Frequent urination	- Hormone replacement therapy (ADH) - Managing fluid balance
Diabetes Mel. T1 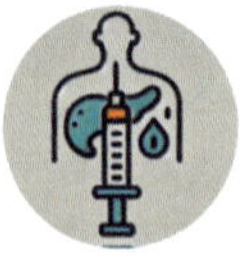	- Autoimmune destruction of insulin-producing beta cells in pancreas	- Hyperglycemia, increased thirst, urination, fatigue	- Insulin therapy - Diet - Exercise
Diabetes Mel. T2 	- **Insulin resistance, reduced insulin secretion** (linked to obesity)	- Hyperglycemia, increased thirst, urination, fatigue - Later neuropathy, stroke, heart attack	- **Lifestyle (diet, exercise)** - **Oral med** - **Insulin therapy**
Hyperpara-thyroidism 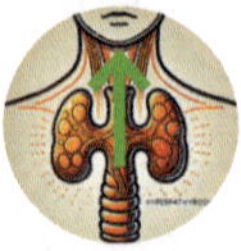	- Overactive parathyroid glands	- **Osteoporosis** - Kidney stones - Fatigue - Bone pain	- Surgery, - Medication to control calcium levels
Hypopara-thyroidism 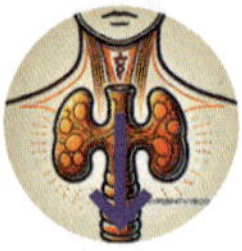	- Underactive parathyroid glands	- Muscle cramps - Fatigue - Dry skin - Hair loss	- Calcium and vitamin D supplements - Meds to regulate calcium levels

	Hx	SSx	Tx
Hyper-thyroidism 	- Overactive thyroid, excess thyroid hormone production - **Graves'** disease	- **Weight loss** - **Heat intolerance,** - **Tremors** - **Bulging eyes**	- Antithyroid medications - Radioactive iodine therapy - Surgery
Hypo-thyroidism 	- Underactive thyroid, reduced thyroid hormone production - **Hashimoto's** (autoimmune)	- **Fatigue** - **Weight gain** - **Cold intolerance** - **Hair loss** - **Dry skin**	- Thyroid hormone replacement therapy
Pheochromo-cytoma 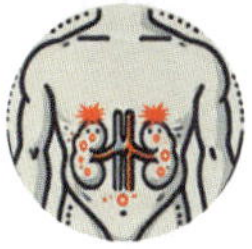	- High blood pressure - Headaches - Sweating - Palpitations	- Rapid heartbeat - Anxiety - Weight loss - Flushing	- Surgery (tumor removal) - Meds (Alpha and beta blockers)
Polycystic Ovary Synd. (PCOS) 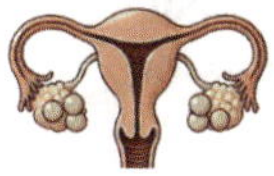	- Hormonal imbalance, often related to insulin resistance	- Irregular periods - Weight gain - Excess hair growth	- Birth control, medications for insulin resistance - Lifestyle changes

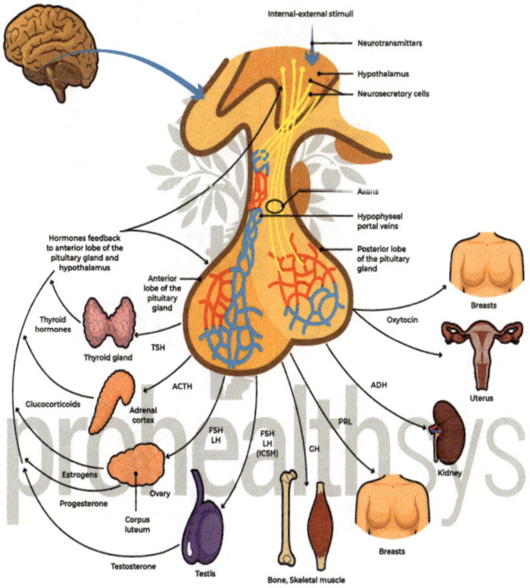

Case Study

Diabetes Mellitus Type 2 (T2D): A 55-yr-old female presents with increasing fatigue, frequent urination, and difficulty controlling her blood sugar despite dietary changes. She has a history of hypertension and obesity. Her blood sugar levels are elevated, and she has been prescribed metformin.

What **manual therapy & exercise interventions** would support her?

What **complications can arise from unmanaged Type 2 Diabetes**, and when should you refer to a specialist?

How do lifestyle factors like diet and activity impact her condition, and what strategies could help manage it better?

Health is a state of complete physical, mental and social well-being

World Health Organiation (WHO)

Scientists generally recognize five determinants of health:

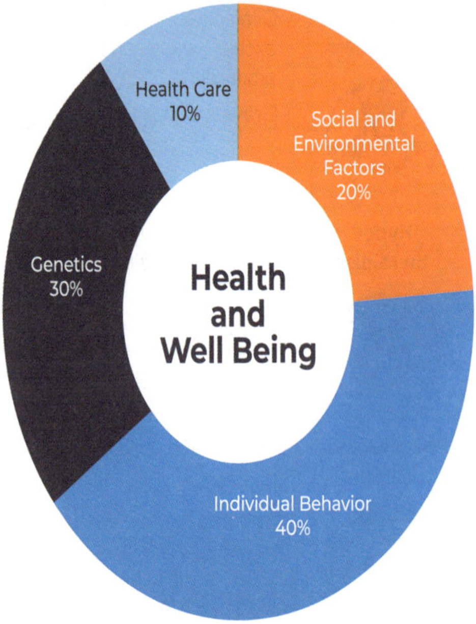

Individual behavior - Yours to Control!

- **Diet** (eat whole, unprocessed foods)
- **Physical activity** (just do it!) - According to the world health organization Physical Inactivity is the 4th leading cause of global mortality
- **Sleep** (this is where you recover)
- Poor 'foods,' alcohol, cigarette & drugs

Genetics and biology

- **Age** (you can be physiologically younger by the choices you make)
- Gender & Inherited conditions (genetics)

Social determinants

- Availability of resources to meet daily needs (education, jobs, real foods)
- Exposure to crime, violence, and social disorder (eg. trash or discrimination)
- Transportation options & public safety

Environment determinants

- Natural environment (plants, forests, weather, climate, light and pets)
- Built environment (buildings, workstation ergonomics, transportation)
- Toxic substances, physical hazards and barriers (esp. for disabled individuals)

Health services determinants

- Both **access and quality are key**
- Lack of **good quality** availability
- Limited language access, high cost

You can control behavior, healthcare and many social/ environmental factors that influence genetic expression.

Things You Can Control

PMID: 33515188, 34083223, 32910100

High Quality MSK Treatments

(systematic reviews - PMID 12221356 - 11880847 - 32150934 - 32749874 - Corpus ID: 73494417)

Manual Therapies with other evidence-based treatments

Motivational person-centered care. Screen for red flags

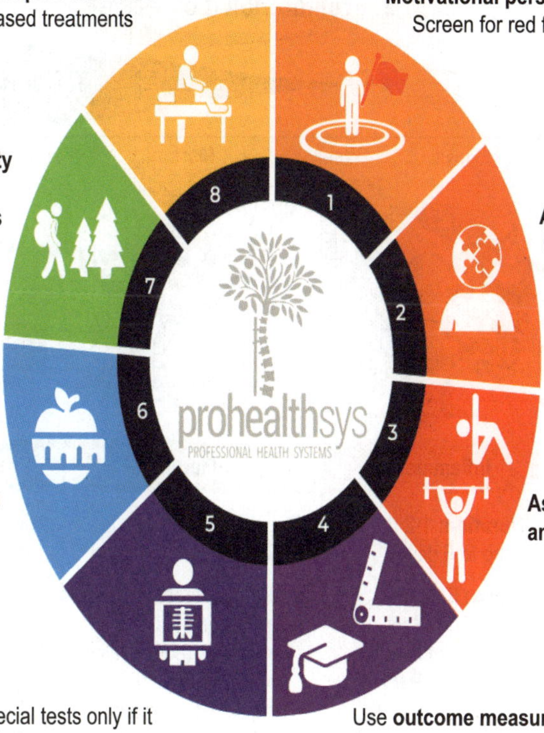

Graded Activity Exposure that facilitates ADLs

Assess Biopsychosocial fears, beliefs and goals
Evaluate **sleep hygiene**

Nutrition Assessment, Education & Modification

Assess mobility, strength and neurologic function

Use **imaging** & special tests only if it changes differential diagnosis or treatment
(rule pathology in or out)

Use **outcome measures**,
Provide **education** on condition(s)

6 BEST DOCTORS

(systematic reviews - PMID 12221356, 11880847, 32150934, 32749874, ID: 73494417)

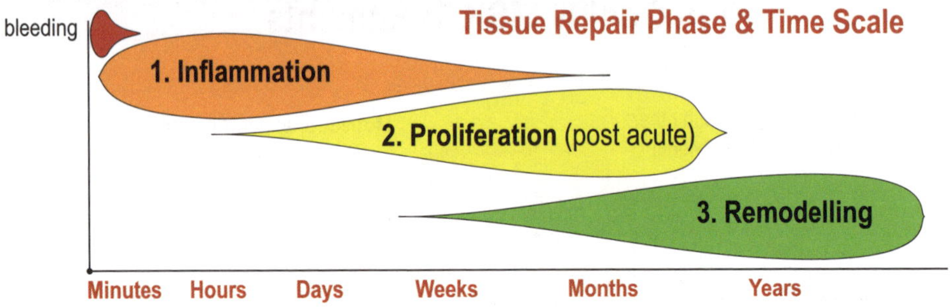

Bleeding	Inflammation	Proliferation	Remodeling
Duration: Seconds to minutes (wound homeostasis) Promote clotting, avoid clot-disruptive agents.	**Duration:** 1-2 days, up to 5 days **Signs: SHARP** **S**welling, **H**eat, **A** Loss of function, **R**edness, **P**ain Vasodilation, leukocyte infiltration	**Duration:** ~48 hours to 6+ weeks **Activity:** Fibroblast activation = Collagen synthesis (poor quality collagen initially), macrophages clear debris, angiogenesis	**Duration:** ~3 wks-12+ months **Activity:** Collagen remodeling ↑ tissue strength. Scar tissue gains ~80% original strength, residual fibrosis
Key Points: Superficial wounds may benefit from topical antimicrobials (Polysporin). Avoid agents that affect clotting and prolong bleeding	**Clinical Objectives:** Relieve pain, Prevent further injury ↑ circulation, maintain muscle tone & ROM Reduce ischemia effects Address psychosocial influences	**Clinical Objectives:** Prevent early adhesions Align repair tissue along tension lines Improve ROM & normal muscle tone Reduce edema Address psychosocial influences	**Clinical Objectives:** Maintain nutrition Ensure proper collagen alignment Reduce fibrotic adhesions Increase strength and elasticity Address chronicity risks

METH (movement, exercise, traction, heat)

Parameter	METH
Blood flow	↑ **Increased**
Collagen formation	↑ **Encouraged**
Healing time	↓ **Shortened**
Range of motion	↑ **Increased**

Food is Medicine!

Generally, treatments that increase local blood flow, neural stimulation & provide nutrient building blocks improve healing. Biopsychosocial support, nutrition, sleep and movement are critical to healing. Short term use of natural analgesics are of benefit - **SUPPORT natural inflammatory reactions that lead to healing**

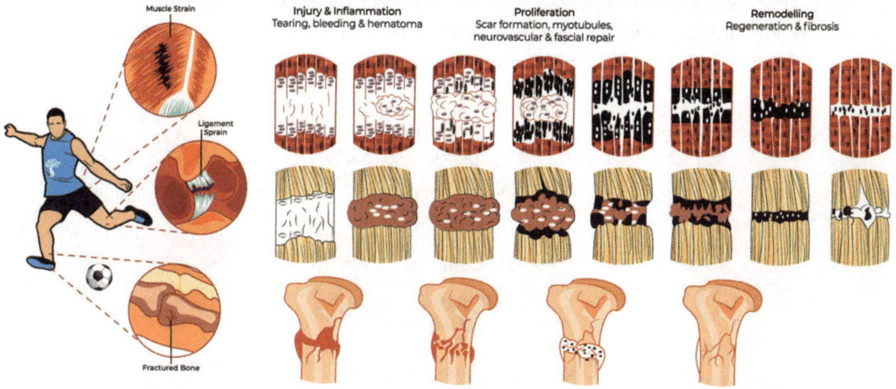

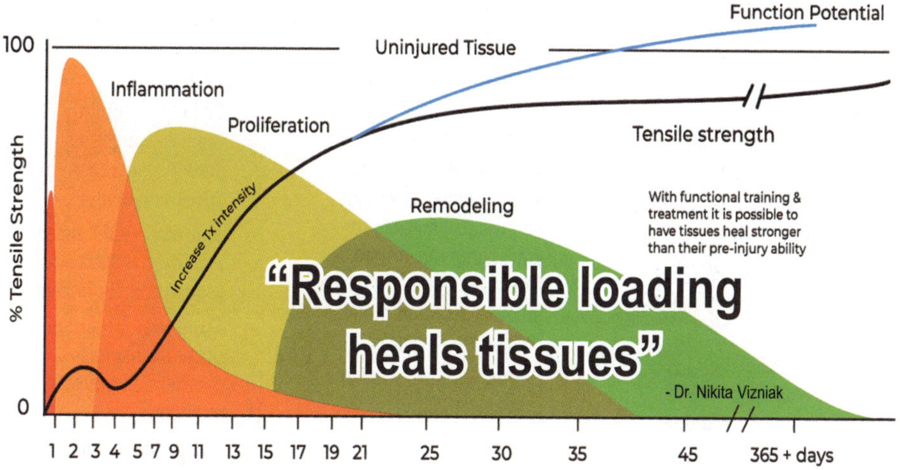

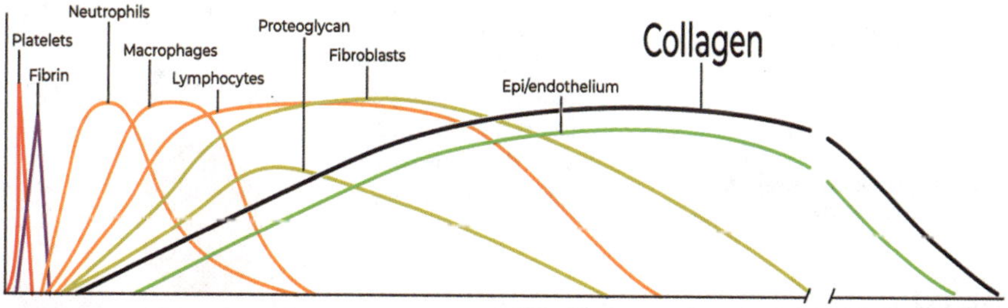

Bleeding	Inflammation	Proliferation	Remodeling
Coagulation to start hemostasis **Weak bandage tissue**	Immune infiltration Debris reabsorption Pathogen killing **Temporary thin tissue**	Fibroblast proliferation (collagen synthesis) Scar formation (contracture) Angiogenesis & neurogenesis **Stronger tighter tissue**	Scar maturation Extracellular Matrix Remodeling Apoptosis **Restored final tissue**

Realize the graphic representations above are influenced by a number of factors including severity of injury, tissue type, pre-existing cofactors, nutrition, age, genetics, activity level, treatment options given & patient compliance.

PMID: 31529731, 32589450, 28436583, 34906681, 30386805

Treatment plans should be personalized, goal-focused, and progress from least to most invasive using the **minimal effective dose (MED)**. Recovery depends on injury severity, age, health, mindset, & activity levels. Phases may overlap or relapse. Avoid chronic injury by not returning to activity too hard, too soon!

Acute Phase (1–5 days)

Goals: Reduce pain, prevent muscle loss, restore ROM, and support healing

- **Key Approach: METH** (Move, Exercise, Traction, Heat). Avoid re-injury.
- **Rest:** Max 1–2 days; avoid overuse to prevent delays
- **Therapy:** Light ROM, relaxation massage, and breathing exercises
- **Caution:** METH contraindicated for compartment syndrome
- SHARP = inflammation

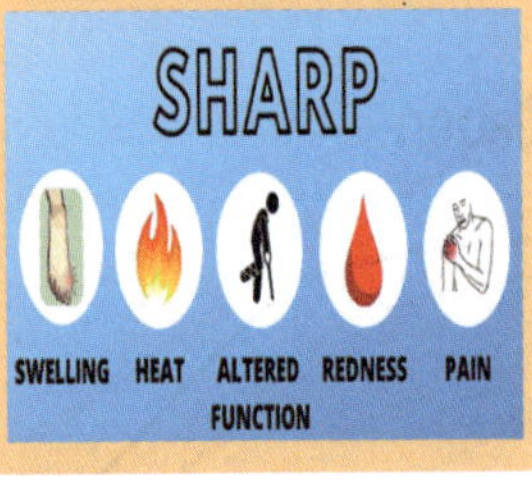

Post-Acute (2 days –6 wks)

Goals: ↑ strength, restore ROM & ADLs, ↓ pain

- **Progression:** Warm up → isometrics → concentric → eccentric exercises
- **Therapy:** AROM, light strengthening, massage, and aquatic therapy for low-impact movement. Generally earlier pain free or low discomfort motion helps (0-4/10 pain)
- **Focus:** Gradual load to prevent re-injury

Good vs Bad Pain

Good pain challenges tissue safely and you can breath through it ('joyful discomfort'). **Bad pain** is sharp or stops your breath. **Respect pain, but challenge it safely.**

Remodeling (3-52+ wks)

Goals: Maintain function, prevent contractures, and improve strength

- **Strength Training:** Start with low weight/high reps, gradually increase (max 10% per week)
- **Therapy:** ROM, massage, IASTM to reduce scar tissue/promote healing
- **Supervision:** Introduce eccentric exercises carefully, and build strength
- **Return to Activity:** When affected side matches 90–100% of unaffected side

METH (movement, exercise, traction, heat)

Parameter	METH
Blood flow	↑ Increased
Collagen formation	↑ Encouraged
Healing time	↓ Shortened
Range of motion	↑ Increased

ACTIVITY DISCOMFORT SCALE

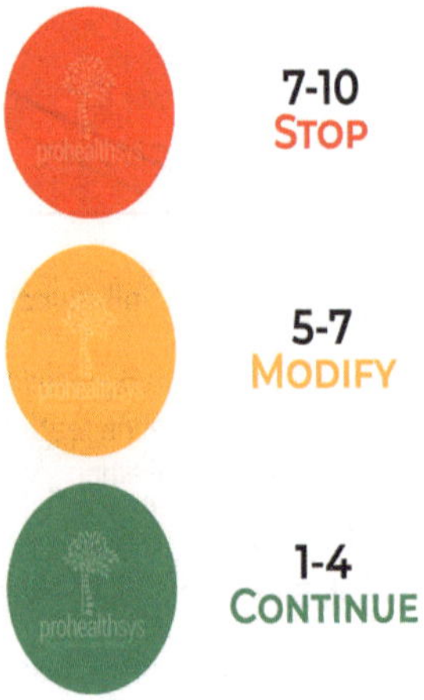

DOI: HTTPS://DOI.ORG/10.1101/2024.08.19.608601

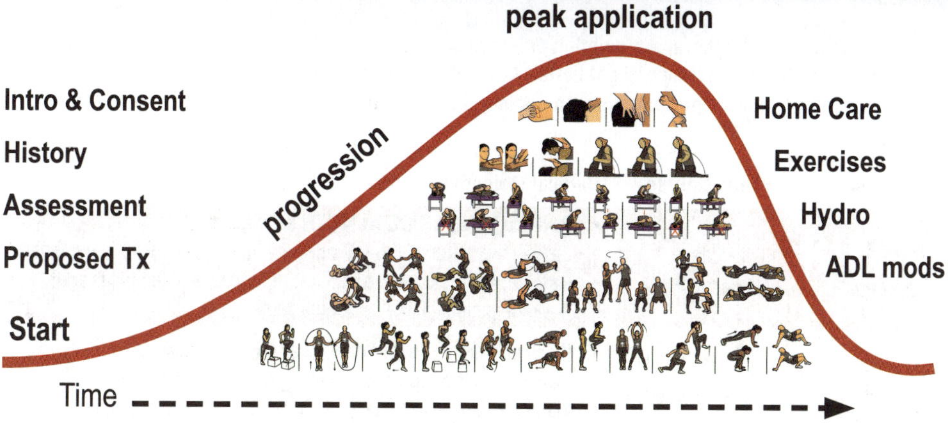

Most Invasive

- **Surgery** – Minor & Major
- **Injection** – Medications, Stem Cell
- **Ingestion** – **FOOD**, Meds, Herbs, Botanicals
- **Insertion** – Dry Needling, Acupuncture
- **Electrotherapy** – Ultrasound, laser, TENS, IFC
- **Osseous Mobilizations** – Joint mobilizations & manipulation
- **Therapeutic Exercise** – Walking, Strength, Aerobics, Balance, Yoga, Pilates, Tai Chi, Sports
- **Soft Tissue Mobilization** – Stretching, Massage, PNF, CR, IASTM, Acupressure, Heat, Cold, Hydro
- **Meditation** – Breath work, Sitting, **Visualization**, Art therapy, Garden therapy
- **Talk** – Counseling (breath & boundary work), Help groups, Prayer, Music therapy

Least Invasive

Diet, activity, sleep and social support are the foundations of health

This is not a complete list & individual practitioners may offer a variety of therapeutic interventions depending upon the local scope of practice & practitioner educational level, experience and preference.

US = ultrasound (therapeutic), TENS = transcutaneous electrical neuromuscular stimulation, MENS = microcurrent, IFC = interferrential current, CR = contract-relax, PNF = proprioceptive neuromuscular facilitation, IASTM = instrument-assisted soft tissue mobilization

The most powerful therapeutic option any clinician has is the ability to give their patients the confidence to realize they can get better. A positive mind set & the belief of future wellness is the single most important factor in healing for most out-patient health care encounters.

Phase	~Time Course	Clinical Objective
1 Acute*	2-3 days (up to ~7 days)	• **Reduce pain; PRICE or METH as indicated** • Emergency referral if required, prevent excess swelling/ischemia • Basic PFROM, activity as tolerated, and relaxation massage • Address psychosocial concerns (anxiety)
2 Post Acute	2 days - 6 weeks	• Pain reduction, prevent early scar tissue adhesions • Begin orienting repair tissue along line of tension • Maintain normal muscle tone, ROM & functional capacity • Basic stretch, strength, functional & proprioceptive retraining
3 Chronic*	3 wks - 12 months or more	• Proper loading of repair collagen & myofascial tissue • Increase elasticity of scar tissue (increase ROM & strength) • Reduce fibrotic adhesions, relieve muscle spasms • Advanced stretch, strength, functional & proprioceptive retraining • Address psychosocial concerns (somatization, depression, etc.)

*Chronic recurrent episodes have acute flare-ups; PFROM = Pain Free Range of Motion, METH = Movement, Exercise, Traction, Heat

Modality	Phase	~Duration
Cold therapy		
Cryotherapy	1, 2	5-15 min
Ice Massage	1, 2	2-5 min
Heat Superficial		
Infrared heat light	2, 3	10-20 min
Hot packs	2, 3	10-20 min
Paraffin	2, 3	7-10 dips (10 min)
Hydrotherapy	2, 3	10-30 min
Laser	1, 2, 3	sec - minutes
Heat Deep		
Continuous US	2, 3	5-10 min
Pulsed US	2, 3	2-8 min
Diathermy	2, 3	5-30 min
Electrical		
MENS (subsensory)	1, 2, 3	none established
IFC (sensory)	1, 2, 3	10-30 min
TENS	1, 2, 3	10-30 min
Muscle stimulator	2, 3	10-30 min
Motor stimulation	2, 3	2-10 min

Modality	Phase	~Duration
Mechanical		
Bed Rest	1	0-2 days
Massage & IASTM	1, 2, 3	5-45 min
Mobilization/manip.	1, 2, 3	1-20 min
Traction (in-office)	1, 2, 3	1-20 min
Flexion-distraction	1, 2, 3	1-15 min
Ext. compression	1, 2, 3	1-15 min
Exercise (in-office)		
Passive	1, 2, 3	5-30 min
Active (gym, yoga)	1, 2, 3	15-90 min
ADLs	1, 2, 3	10-30 min
PNF/CR	2, 3	5-10 min
Bracing	1, 2	short duration
Graded work return	3	2-8 hours
Acupuncture **Dry needling/IMS**	1, 2, 3	by technique
Nutrition/Herbal	1, 2, 3	entire treatment
Medications/Prolo	1	short duration
Surgery	1, 3	emergency or last resort

Specific treatment regimes must be tailored to the individual patient presentation.
In most cases, medication use should be short-term (long-term use can result in chemical dependency & mask important signs & symptoms). Surgical intervention should be offered only in emergency injuries or as a last resort when conservative treatments have failed (surgery is not a guaranteed cure).

Sleep is when you recover physically and mentally. Healthy sleep habits can make a huge difference in your quality of life. Sleep benefits include:

1. Improved mood and function
2. Better maintenance of body weight (yes you can burn fat in your sleep)
3. Improved immune function
4. Look more attractive & lower injury risk

Practice a relaxing bedtime ritual away from bright lights. A relaxing routine helps separate your sleep time from activities that can cause excitement, stress or anxiety which can make it more difficult to fall asleep. Spend the last hour before bed doing a calming activity such as reading. **Avoid electronics before bed or in the middle of the night.**

"Remove electrons from your room"

Exercise daily. Vigorous exercise is best, but even light exercise is better than no activity. Exercise at any time of day, but not at the expense of your sleep.

Bedroom Setup

- Temperature cool ~18°C (60°F)
- **Quiet and dark** (consider using blackout curtains, eye shades, ear plugs, "white noise" machines, fans etc.)
- Comfortable mattress and pillows (mattress life expectancy ~10 years)
- **No work materials, computers, phones and TVs** in sleeping environment. Use your bed only for sleep and sex to strengthen the association between bed and sleep.

See the Morning Light. Your body's internal clock is sensitive to light and darkness, so getting a dose of the sun first thing in the morning will help you wake up. **Avoid bright light in the evening, especially blue light.**

It's not just what you eat—it's when you eat. **Avoid alcohol, cigarettes, and heavy meals in the evening**. Avoid eating large meals for two to three hours before bedtime. Try a light snack 45 minutes before bed if you're still hungry.

PMID: 36841492, 38837997, 34607184, 32593135, 35777076

You Cannot Out Train a Bad Diet

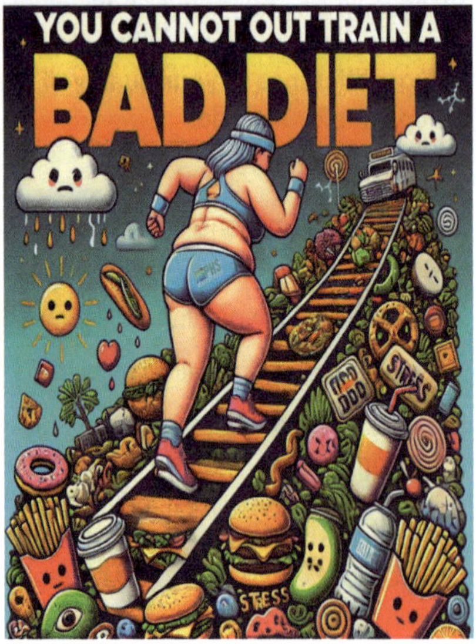

No amount of exercise can undo the effects of poor nutrition. Imagine climbing an endless hill of unhealthy choices—burgers, fries, and sugary drinks. Every step feels heavier, progress slower. This is the struggle of relying on workouts alone to fix a bad diet.

True progress starts with fueling your body right. **Food is more than fuel—it's the foundation of energy, performance, and recovery.** A nutrient-rich diet turns that insurmountable hill into a clear, achievable path.

Focus on whole, unprocessed foods that empower your body. Prioritize protein, healthy fats, and vibrant produce. Small, positive choices add up and build momentum.

Your potential is limitless when your nutrition supports your effort. This is your reminder: **lasting transformation isn't about training harder—it's about fueling smarter.** Start now. You've got this!

8 CALORIE-DENSE FOOD/DRINKS AND THEIR ACTIVITY EQUIVALENCE

FOOD TYPE	CALORIES APROX.	WALK OFF KCAL (MEDIUM WALK 3-5MPH)	RUN OFF KCAL (SLOW RUNNING 5MPH)
Sugary Soft Drink (330ml Can)	138	26 min	13 min
Cereal (1 Bowl)	172	31 min	16 min
Standard Chocolate Bar	229	42 min	22 min
Blueberry Muffin	265	48 min	25 min
Medium Mocha Coffee	290	53 min	28 min
Sandwich (Chicken & Bacon)	445	1 hr 22 min	42 min
Large Pizza (1/4 Pizza)	449	1 hr 23 min	43 min

PMID: 36231976, 33672920, 30217210

Respected food writer Michael Pollan says everything he's learned about food and health can be summed up in seven words: **"Eat food, not too much, mostly plants."** Eat real food -- vegetables, fruits, whole grains, and, yes, fish and natural organic meats and **avoid "edible food-like substances."** There is no need to over complicate the science, the hard part is sticking to the regime and finding good food sources. Here are some words of advice:

1. **Don't eat anything your great grand parents wouldn't recognize as food.** "When you eat something with 15 ingredients you can't pronounce, ask yourself, "What are those things doing there?"
2. **Don't eat anything with more than 5 ingredients, or ingredients you can't pronounce.**
3. Bacteria eat real food, so should you. **Don't eat anything that won't eventually rot.** "There are exceptions -- honey -- but as a rule, things like Twinkies that never go bad aren't food."
4. **Always leave the table a little hungry**," Pollan says. "Many cultures have rules that you stop eating before you are full. In Japan, they say eat until you are four-fifths full. Islamic culture has a similar rule, and in German culture they say, 'Tie the sack before it's full.'"
5. **Families traditionally ate together, around a table and not a TV, at regular meal times.** It's a good tradition. **Enjoy meals with the people you love.**

Eat less CRAP:

- C - carbonated drinks
- R - refined sugar
- A - artificial sweeteners
- P - processed foods

Eat more FOOD:

- F - fruits & veggies
- O - organic lean proteins
- O - omega 3 fatty acids
- D - drink water

WHOEVER PUT THE S IN FASTFOOD IS A MARKETING GENIUS.

PMID: 30215930, 31683759, 32483625, 36079848, 34664675

Exercise prescription is the foundation of effective exercise therapy. It involves designing individualized programs to improve health, restore function, and optimize performance. Programs are guided by evidence-informed principles to ensure safety, progression, and long-term adherence.

FITT-VP model = Frequency, Intensity, Time, Type, Volume, Progression

Part	Definition	General Guidelines/Examples
Frequency (F)	How often exercise is performed	- **Cardio:** 3–5 times per week - **Strength:** 2–3 times per week - **Flexibility/Mobility:** 2–3 times per week, or daily for optimal results
Intensity (I)	How hard the individual works	- **Heart Rate Zones:** 50–85% of HRmax aerobic fitness - **RPE:** 1–10 scale, with 7–8 for strength & endurance - **Weight-lifting:** 70–90% of 1RM for strength
Time (T)	Duration of each session	- **Cardio:** 20–60 minutes - **Strength:** 30–45 minutes - **Flexibility:** 15–30 seconds per stretch, multiple sets
Type (T)	Mode of exercise	- **Cardio:** Running, swimming, cycling, jujitsu, wrestling - **Strength:** Free weights, machines, resistance bands - **Flexibility:** Yoga, static stretching, PNF
Volume (V)	Total workload per session	- **Formula:** Sets × Reps × Load - **Example:** 3 sets × 10 reps × 50 lbs = 1500 lbs of volume - **Strength: Higher loads, fewer reps** - **Endurance: Lower loads, higher reps**
Progression (P)	Gradual increases in workload	- **Increase weights, reps, frequency, or intensity by ~5% weekly to avoid plateaus**

PRESCRIBING EXERCISE WITHOUT INTENSITY

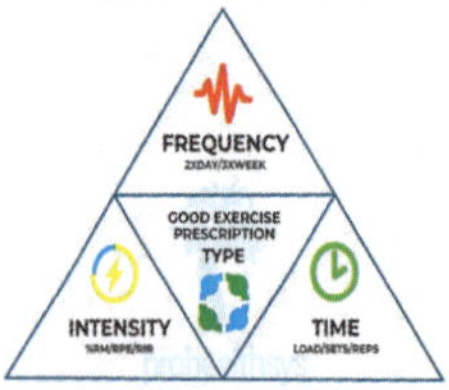

IS LIKE A DOCTOR PRESCRIBING MEDICATION WITHOUT A DOSAGE!

MEN WHO EXERCISE REGULARLY CAN GAIN ~2 HRS OF LIFE EXPECTANCY FOR EVERY 1 HR OF EXERCISE (ADDS ~2 YRS OR LIFESPAN ON AVERAGE)

HARVARD LONGEVITY STUDY (N=17,321)

PMID 7707624

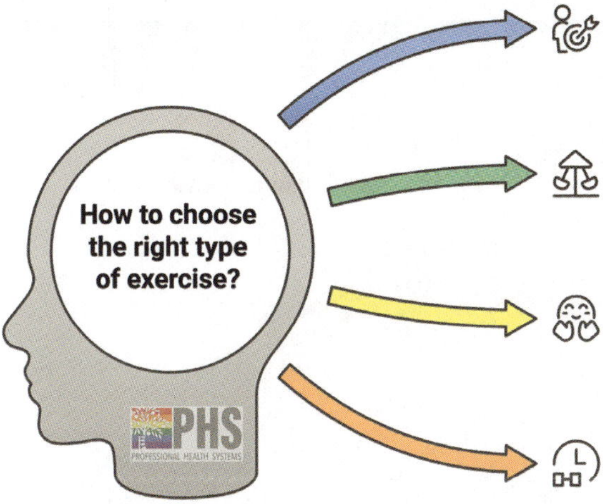

Personal Goals
Align exercises with specific fitness objectives like weight loss or muscle gain

Fitness Level
Select exercises that match current fitness capabilities, from beginner to advanced

Enjoyment
Choose activities that are enjoyable to maintain motivation and consistency

Time and Resources
Consider available time and equipment for workouts

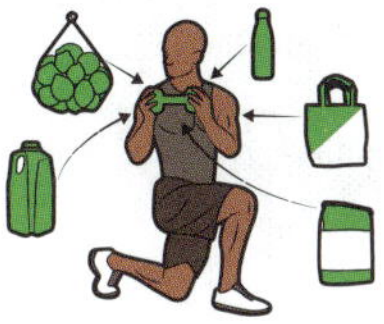

- Warm-up
- Push
- Pull
- Core
- Cardio

Rule out red flags
↓ informed consent

Choose an Exercise
↓ Yes ↑ No

Can the person do it?
↓ Yes ↑ No

Does the person enjoy doing it or want to do it?

- **Too hard or painful?** reduce intensity, time, ROM or load → This is a good exercise
- **Just right?** → This is a good exercise
- **Too easy?** increase intensity, time, ROM or load → This is a good exercise

This is a good exercise

PMID: 32896055, 31401727, 35477256, 37142892

THE COGNITIVE TRIANGLE

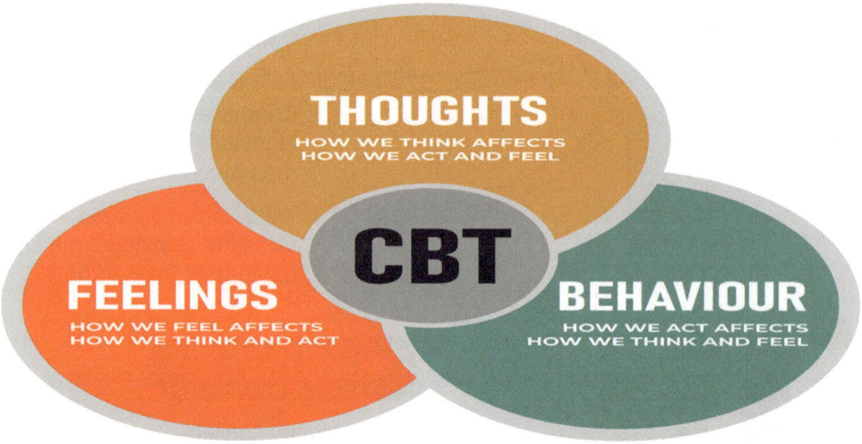

DIALECTICAL THINKING

- WHERE TWO OPPOSITES CAN CO-EXIST

- I AM TRYING MY BEST → I STILL WANT TO DO BETTER
- I MISS SEEING YOU → I NEED MY SPACE
- I CARE ABOUT OTHERS → I AM FOCUSING ON MYSELF
- I AM FEELING ANXIOUS → I CAN OVERCOME THESE FEELINGS
- I ACCEPT THINGS → I AM GOING TO MAKE CHANGES
- THEY ARE UPSET WITH ME → THEY STILL LOVE ME
- I WANT TO SPEND TIME WITH YOU → I STILL NEED TIME ALONE

THE FOUR 'F'S OF TRAUMA RESPONSE

FIGHT

How do you act?
- Bullying
- Impulse to control
- Defensiveness
- Raging
- Pursuing power
- Narcissistic tendencies
- Demanding perfection from others
- Criticizing

What are you feeling?
- Angry
- Upset
- Irritated
- Offended
- Stressed out
- Provoked
- Clenched jaw
- Tensed muscles
- Racing heart

What can you do about it?
- Physical movement
- Use grounding techniques
- Accept support
- Practice self-care

FLIGHT

How do you act?
- Difficulty staying still
- Workaholic tendencies
- Perfectionist
- Worrying
- Adrenaline-junkie
- Hyperactive
- Performance anxiety
- Panic and constant fear

What are you feeling?
- Anxious
- Panicked
- Worried
- Hard to focus
- Scared
- Spacing out
- Distracted
- Wanting to escape

What can you do about it?
- Learn to pace yourself
- Practice setting boundaries
- Incorporate contemplation time

FREEZE

How do you act?
- Social anxiety
- Isolated
- Difficulty making decisions
- Dissociated
- Couch potato
- Daydreaming
- Depression

What are you feeling?
- Numbness
- Zoned out
- Shame
- Brain fog
- Bored
- Constant fear
- Emptiness
- Stiff body

What can you do about it?
- Expand your comfort zone
- Realize you are not alone
- Do random acts of kindness
- Start saying 'Yes'

FAWN

How do you act?
- People pleasing
- Trying to fit-in at all costs
- Lack of identity
- Always saying 'Yes'
- No boundaries
- Codependent
- Prioritising others needs

What are you feeling?
- Overwhelmed
- Fear of saying 'No'
- Can't be true to yourself
- Disconnected from own body and needs
- Emotional burnout
- Feeling responsible for others

What can you do about it?
- Build healthy relationships
- Learn to value yourself
- Accept that you can't please everyone
- Start saying 'No'

COPING SKILLS

- Listen to music
- Spend time in nature
- Do some exercise
- Get enough sleep
- Watch a funny movie
- Do some yoga
- Laugh
- Eat healthy food
- Practice positive affirmations
- Read
- Be grateful
- Ask for help
- Spend time with an animal
- Spend time with friends
- Do some deep breathing
- Do some journalling

PHS
PROFESSIONAL HEALTH SYSTEMS

12 SCIENTIFIC WAYS TO IMPROVE HAPPINESS

PMID: 37566759, 29702043, 30601719, 25080035, 18785370, 37626305

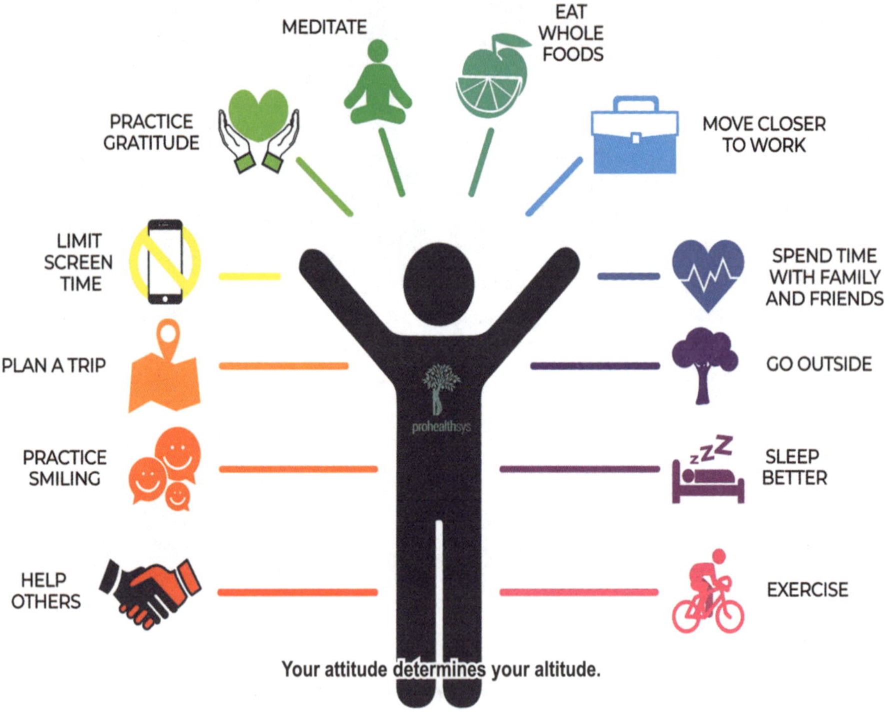

Relaxation Techniques

PMID: 17044345, 23685993, 24043951 21818724, 30020610

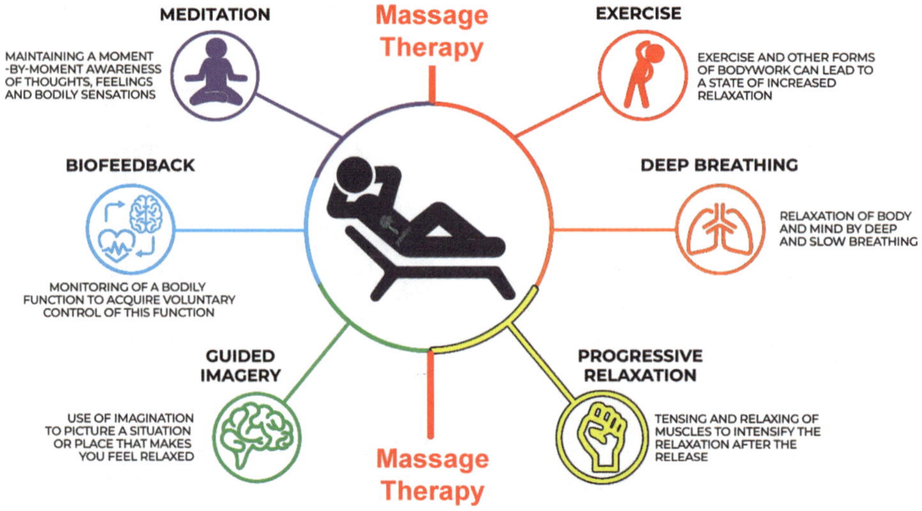

Exercise Handouts

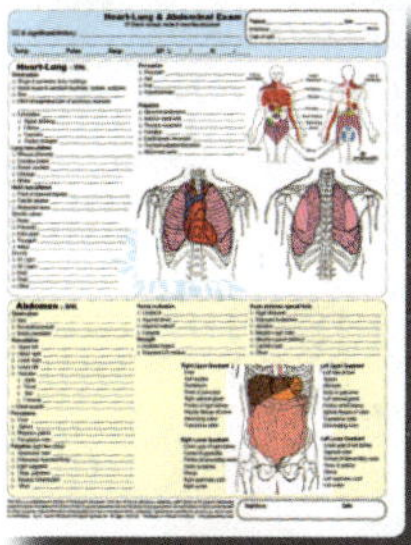

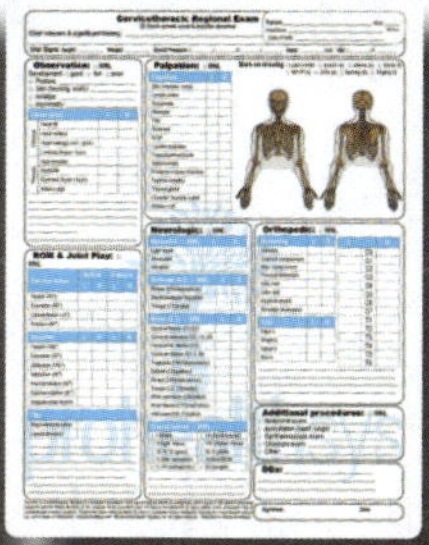

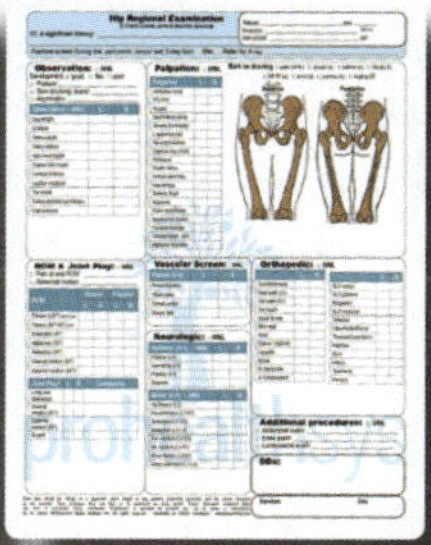

Forms

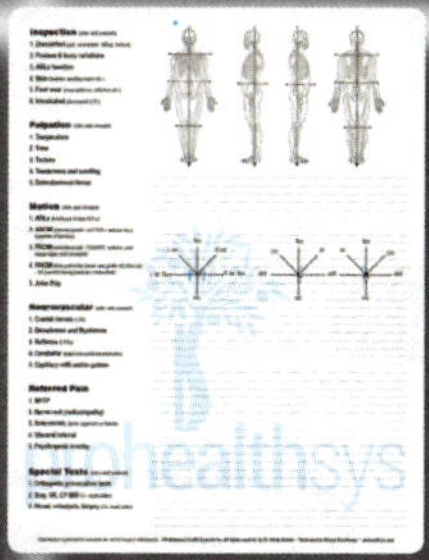

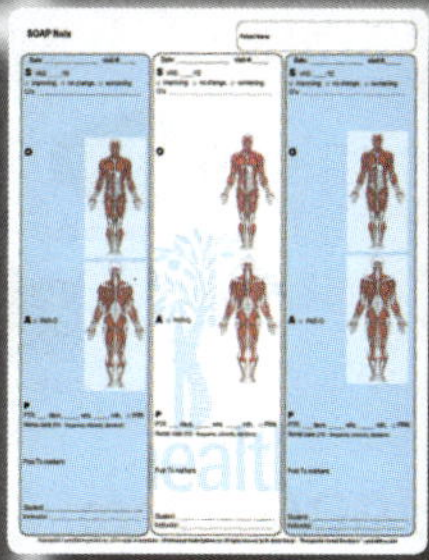

Physical Exam Forms

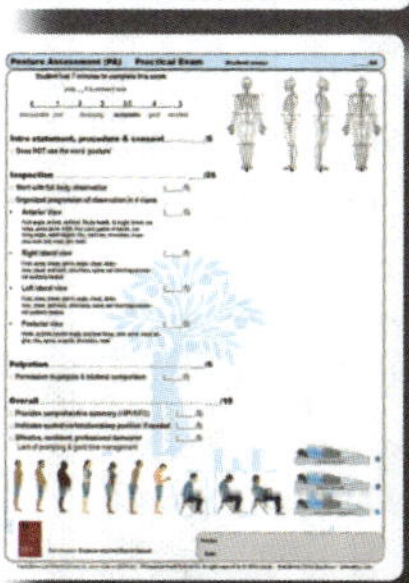

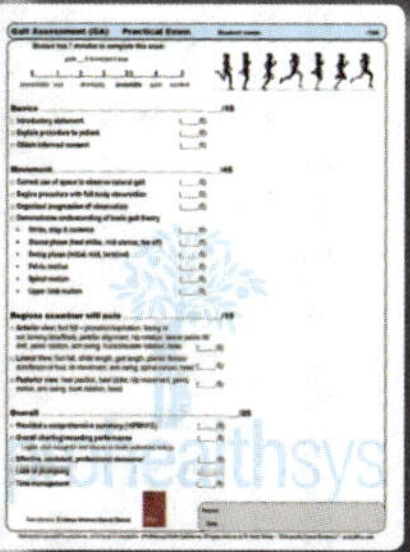

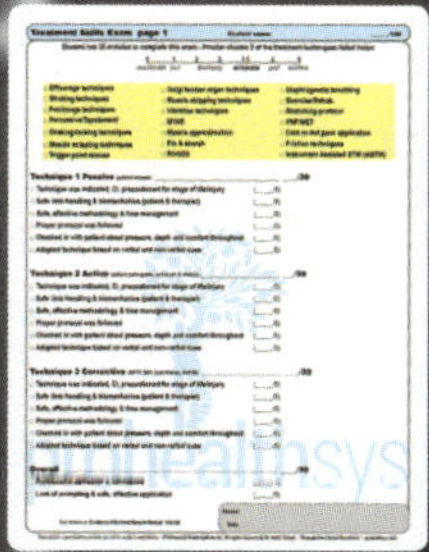

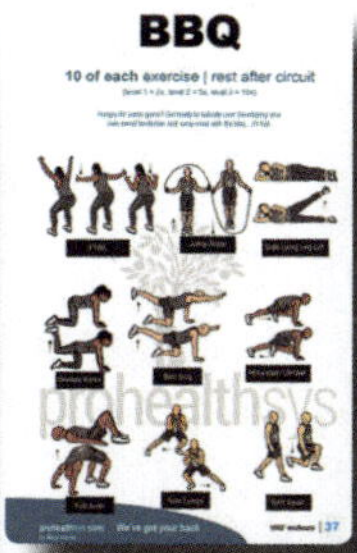

Hithera

Write YOUR top 3 GOALs here:

1.

2.

3.

PHS
PROFESSIONAL HEALTH SYSTEMS

hithera

Trusted evidence-informed best-practices

Join Your Friends - we've got your back